at Durham University and then pur-
protecting the environment by working for Friends
Earth, latterly as Administrative Director. Following graduation
as an MBA from the London Business School, he worked for an international firm of consultants helping multi-national firms in the UK and
the USA resolve strategic management problems.

He has provided consultancy services to not-for-profit organizations
for twelve years, working with aid agencies including Oxfam, Save
the Children and Christian Aid; health and disability organizations
including the Royal National Institute for the Blind, Tadworth Court
Hospital, Mencap and the Health Education Authority; social-welfare
organizations such as RELATE and the Samaritans; housing associations including Housing 21 and the Guinness Trust; education bodies
including Thames Valley University and Outward Bound; campaigning
organizations such as Greenpeace and Amnesty International; and arts
organizations including the Royal National Theatre and the Scottish
Chamber Orchestra. He has also worked for funding bodies such as the
Home Office, the Department of Health, the Arts Council and the
Charities Aid Foundation. His overseas work has included assignments
in Uganda, Nepal and Bangladesh.

Mike Hudson has four children and lives in Marlow. He is a Fellow of
the Royal Society of Arts.

MIKE HUDSON

# MANAGING WITHOUT PROFIT

## THE ART OF MANAGING
## THIRD-SECTOR ORGANIZATIONS

PENGUIN BOOKS

Published in association with Directory of Social Change

PENGUIN BOOKS

Published by the Penguin Group
Penguin Books Ltd, 27 Wrights Lane, London W8 5TZ, England
Penguin Books USA Inc., 375 Hudson Street, New York, New York 10014, USA
Penguin Books Australia Ltd, Ringwood, Victoria, Australia
Penguin Books Canada Ltd, 10 Alcorn Avenue, Toronto, Ontario, Canada M4V 3B2
Penguin Books (NZ) Ltd, 182–190 Wairau Road, Auckland 10, New Zealand

Penguin Books Ltd, Registered Offices: Harmondsworth, Middlesex, England

First published 1995
1 3 5 7 9 10 8 6 4 2

Printed in England by Clays Ltd, St Ives plc

# Contents

# Acknowledgements

This book could not have been written without the immense support and guidance I have received from a large number of people.

I would particularly like to thank all the clients of Compass Partnership who have invited me into their organizations and given me opportunities to learn about management from practical experience. You have taught me more than I have learned from any course or textbook. I would also like to give special thanks to Charles Handy for being a mentor, giving me wise advice over many years, encouraging me to embark on this venture and introducing me to Penguin.

A book such as this which attempts to draw together many different strands of thinking inevitably relies on many academics and authors who have written on the subject. I therefore want to express particular thanks to the leading academics in the UK whose work has informed my writing, including Rob Paton, Julian Batslear and Chris Cornforth at the Open University, David Billis and Margaret Harris at the Centre for Voluntary Organizations, London School of Economics, Jeremy Kendall at the University of Kent, David Wilson at the University of Warwick, Diana Leat and Ian Bruce at VOLPROF, City Business School and Susan Saxon-Harold at the Charities Aid Foundation.

I have also drawn heavily on the work of American academics because they have a larger base of experience to inform their research. Particular thanks are therefore due to Dennis Young of the Mandel Center for Non-profit Organizations at Case Western Reserve University, Lester Salamon at Johns Hopkins University, John Bryson at the University of Minnesota, Richard Chait at the University of Maryland, Thomas Holland at the University of Georgia and Cyril O. Houle at the University of Chicago.

The book has been substantially improved as a direct result of the insightful and constructive thoughts I received from many people who willingly gave their time to read the drafts and comment in detail. Thank you:

| Ian Bruce | Director General of the Royal National Institute for the Blind |
| Mike Dempsey | Assistant General Secretary of UNISON |
| David French | Director of RELATE |
| Sandra Greaves | Editor, *Third Sector* |
| Dave Harker | Deputy Chief Executive of SENSE |
| Robert Hazell | Director of the Nuffield Foundation |
| Lew Hodges | Director of Finance and Resources of the Arts Council |
| Rob Paton | Director of the Voluntary Sector Management Programme at the Open University |
| Su Sayer | Chair of the Association of Chief Executives of National Voluntary Organizations and Director of United Response |
| Ian Wallis | Director of Ealing Tertiary College |

I am also grateful for the many helpful comments I received on the management of organizations that fund the third sector from Steven Burkeman of the Joseph Rowntree Charitable Trust, Richard Worsley of the Carnegie Third Age Programme, Paul Curno of the Calouste Gulbekian Foundation and Joel Joffe and Des Palmer of Allied Dunbar. Kate Kirkland of the National Council of Voluntary Organizations greatly improved the two chapters on governance.

Very special thanks need to be given to Michael Norton of the Directory of Social Change and Sandy Adirondack, who both went through manuscripts in meticulous detail and made huge improvements to the work, and to Robert Hazell of the Nuffield Foundation, who provided encouragement from the germ of the idea to its final completion.

The book could not have been written without the generous support I received from current and past colleagues at Compass Partnership, most of whom commented on many separate drafts of the book. Thank you Allison Aldred, Valerie Calvert, Sarah Legg, Joy MacKeith, Lesley Moreland, Roger Parry, Clare Redfarn and Judy Weleminsky for all your hard work on the drafts and for your kind support and assistance. Chris Bemrose has to be singled out for particular thanks, not only for his comments on the book, but also for managing Compass Partnership while I hid in my bunker.

I also must acknowledge the assistance I received from Francis

Henson, Head of Godstowe School, and Val Martin, Chief Executive of Lewisham Hospital NHS Trust, who gave me valuable insights into the management of schools and hospitals. I am particularly grateful to Henley Management College for use of their facilities, my mother Jean Hudson for lending me her holiday house on numerous occasions and Tony Lacey at Penguin for his wise counsel and support.

Debbie Emerson deserves particular thanks for her heroic effort in turning many untidy and virtually indecipherable drafts into a perfect typescript. I am truly appreciative of the way she cheerfully managed to meet all the deadlines.

Finally, I must give most thanks to my wife Di who backed and encouraged me throughout, knowing that every time I disappeared she would be responsible both for her own work and for the exhausting task of bringing up our four young children. I will always be deeply grateful to her and to our children Jennifer, Timothy, Jessica and Katherine for providing loving support from the start to the finish of this project.


Mike Hudson
Seaview, Isle of Wight
October 1994

# Introduction

Not-for-profit organizations exist throughout the world.

They prosper in industrialized economies, and they are also a central part of the social fabric in developing economies. They thrive in free democratic societies and they play an important role in less democratic regimes. They flourish in urban areas and are equally important in rural areas. Not-for-profit organizations exist everywhere because of a human quality that brings people together to provide services for themselves and others and to campaign against abuse of people and the environment. People want health, welfare, educational, humanitarian, environmental and cultural services to improve the world we live in. They expect the organizations that provide them to be 'not-for-profit' and also 'not-in-the-public-sector'.

This book is about managing not-for-profit organizations. It describes how to improve the performance of organizations that are part of the expanding 'third sector'.

## DEFINING THE THIRD SECTOR

This sector consists of organizations whose primary objectives are social rather than economic. The core of the sector includes charities, religious organizations, arts organizations, community organizations, campaigning organizations, trade unions, professional associations and other voluntary organizations.

The term 'third sector' distinguishes these organizations from the 'private sector' and the 'public sector'. The ethos that unites all these organizations is that they are value-led. They are established and managed by people who believe that changes are needed, and they want to do something about it themselves. To stress this point I have often called them value-led organizations in this book. These organizations share two characteristics. Unlike private-sector organizations they do not distribute profits to their owners, and unlike public-sector organizations they are not subject to direct political control. These organizations have the independence to determine their own futures.

Around the periphery of these core third-sector organizations are a growing number of bodies that are semi-independent from the public sector. Examples include housing associations, education colleges, grant-maintained schools, quasi-non-governmental organizations and, perhaps in the future, hospital trusts. There is also a group of organizations such as independent schools, friendly societies and provident societies which sits on a periphery that overlaps with the private sector. These organizations are also value-led and can use management practices from the third sector.

## SCOPE OF THE SECTOR

Until relatively recently it was not thought that this diverse range of organizations had much in common. All were seen as separate strands of social life, each with its unique history and role in society. Increasingly, these organizations are seen as part of one sector because they share a common heritage and set of beliefs about improving the world in which we live.

They are coalescing because they recognize that many have more in common with each other than with organizations in the public or private sectors. The process began in the USA some twenty years ago. In America the sector is much larger because many hospitals, colleges and universities have always been independent, not-for-profit organizations. There, the state has tended to contract out the provision of a wider range of services. In the UK this process is happening now as these organizations, many of which were independent until the early part of the twentieth century, are moving back from the public sector into the third sector.

The third sector is enormously influential. Many of the greatest social changes and innovations have been brought to fruition through the creation of a third-sector organization. Hospital services, education, services for disadvantaged groups and people with disabilities, research into disease, spiritual development, benevolent funds for industry employees, social welfare services, international aid and, more recently, environmental protection and women's rights campaigns have all emanated from third-sector organizations.

This sector is currently growing in confidence. At a time when many public-sector organizations are perceived to be inadequate at dealing efficiently with the social problems of today, the third sector sees itself as having the potential to play an expanded role. It has the unique ability to combine entrepreneurialism with a social conscience – the very characteristics that are needed to address some of the most deep-rooted social problems facing both industrialized and non-industrialized countries.

## THE MARRIAGE OF MISSION AND MANAGEMENT

Third-sector organizations are driven by a desire to improve the world in which we live. People who manage, work and volunteer for them believe in the creation of a fairer, more caring, better-educated and healthier world.

The mission often pervades all aspects of these organizations. Board members volunteer their time because they support the mission; staff often work long hours because they believe in the mission and funders give money to demonstrate their solidarity with the mission.

However, management is equally important to the success of these organizations. Until the middle of the 1970s management was not a word many people used when talking about third-sector organizations. Management was seen to be part of the culture of business and was not felt to be appropriate in value-led organizations.

The dramatic growth and the increasingly professional and skilled approach of these organizations has completely changed that view. Nowadays management is being colonized for value-led organizations and its language and concepts are beginning to trip off people's tongues as easily as eloquent speeches about the cause.

But management cannot be imported unchanged and imposed on value-led organizations. Subtle and critical differences that are rooted in the different ethos that underlies these organizations have to be understood. All too often people from both the private and the public sector believe, or make the implicit assumption, that their management theories should be applied to third-sector organizations to make them more effective. 'If only this charity were more business-like' is a common sentiment. However, while these theories can bring benefits, they are often of limited value because they fail to recognize that the critical issues are different in third-sector organizations.

In order to understand how to manage these organizations effectively, theories which are currently implicit need to be made explicit. Approaches by managers that are currently based on experience need to be understood and documented to provide a body of knowledge that can be taught and shared amongst people with less experience. The third sector needs its own management theories adopted and adapted to suit its own needs.

## THIS BOOK

This book draws together an overview of the management of value-led organizations. It sets out the essential elements of management that are needed to make organizations more successful. It is based on a series of propositions about management, which in summary are that:

- boards need to take responsibility for 'governing organizations'. They need to delegate 'management' to chief executives and their paid staff
- the process of strategic management is a powerful way of focusing the diverse constituencies of these organizations on their purpose
- making management processes work effectively is more important than getting the structure right. Processes for planning, managing people, enabling them to participate and monitoring performance are critical ingredients of effective management
- management, board and committee structures need to become increasingly flexible, responding with frequent small adjustments rather than once-in-a-lifetime reviews
- chief executives have to both manage their organizations and provide them with leadership – creating a sense of mission, inspiring people and focusing the organization on the achievement of ambitious objectives
- managers have to take responsibility, work as part of a team, and learn the subtle arts of planning and delegating work and holding individuals accountable.

In schematic form the chapters have been grouped together as follows:

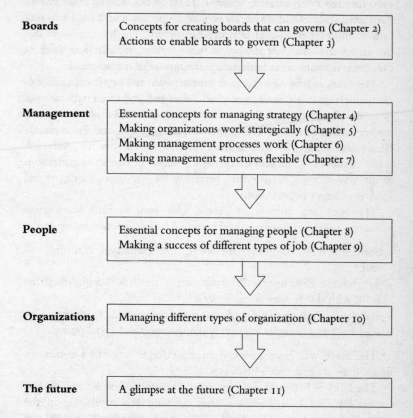

**Boards**

Concepts for creating boards that can govern (Chapter 2)
Actions to enable boards to govern (Chapter 3)

**Management**

Essential concepts for managing strategy (Chapter 4)
Making organizations work strategically (Chapter 5)
Making management processes work (Chapter 6)
Making management structures flexible (Chapter 7)

**People**

Essential concepts for managing people (Chapter 8)
Making a success of different types of job (Chapter 9)

**Organizations**

Managing different types of organization (Chapter 10)

**The future**

A glimpse at the future (Chapter 11)

The book is prescriptive. It demonstrates ways to improve the management of organizations. It is, however, based on the premise that third-sector organizations are full of contradictions and ambiguities. There are no right or wrong solutions for many situations. These organizations are complex and messy. They have many stakeholders with different values, and they attract an extraordinarily diverse range of people as volunteers, managers and board members. Consequently, advice that is appropriate in one set of circumstances may be totally inappropriate in another. The book should therefore be seen as offering guidance and experience, not a set of blueprints.

The aim of the book is to explain best management practices. However, these organizations do not survive on management alone. They need flair and imagination to succeed. They do not exist to make profits, but they do need to be driven by prophets – people who have a vision of how to improve the world in which we all live. The book assumes that the values and beliefs of the people who govern, manage and work in these organizations are as important as the quality of management.

The book is aimed primarily at medium-size and larger organizations including those with more than a handful of staff and those with national or international scope. It is relevant to single-site and multi-site organizations, those with local branches and those without, and those undertaking one activity as well as those offering many services. Although many of the ideas are relevant to the thousands of smaller organizations in this sector, it has been written primarily for governors, managers and funders of larger organizations.

The book was written for people who want succinct briefing on managing value-led organizations. It should be of particular interest to:

- board members, committee members, chief executives, managers and staff
- government departments, local authorities and health authorities that work with third-sector organizations
- foundations, governments and companies that provide funding
- academics and students who study management and social policy.

The book will have achieved its objective if dog-eared copies are found in all these people's briefcases.

The book is based on the experience that my colleagues at Compass Partnership and I have gained from working and consulting in the sector. Since starting to undertake consulting assignments in 1982 we have worked for over 350 organizations of almost every type and size. We have helped with the establishment of new strategies, the development of management processes, the restructuring of management, the development of boards and committees and many other challenges.

I could have written many books with the mountain of material I have collected from my consultancy work and the literature I have gathered from the UK and the USA in my research for this book. However, my aim was to distil it all into a practical overview for busy managers who need to learn a lot in a short space of time. People who want more detail should therefore refer to the further reading section.

Finally, this is the first edition. In the spirit of cooperation and striving to do better that pervades the sector, comments, feedback and examples of good practice would be most welcome. They should be sent to me at: Compass Partnership, 10 Barley Mow Passage, London W4 4PH. Tel. 0181-994-6477.

---

## OVERCOMING LANGUAGE PROBLEMS

The diverse histories of third-sector organizations mean that they all use very different language to describe the same idea. To maintain clarity and avoid repetition the following terms are used consistently throughout the book.

**Organization** The body that is providing services or organizing campaigns, whether it is a voluntary body, a charity, a trust, a trade union, a professional institution, a school, a college, etc.

**Stakeholders** People or other organizations who have a stake in the organization including members, funders, service users, board and committee members, managers, staff, volunteers and branches.

**Service users** The people who benefit from a service provided by a third-sector organization whether students, trade union members, patients, clients, people with disabilities, church-goers, members of an audience, or society as a whole in the case of campaigning organizations. Although somewhat prosaic, this term is better than beneficiary, which is condescending, or customer, which implies people pay for the service.

**The Board** The body that is legally responsible and accountable for governing and controlling the organization, sometimes called Council, Management Committee, Board of Directors, Board of Trustees, Executive or Governing Body. Although this term has a corporate feel, it is succinct and clear.

**Board Members** People, usually unpaid, who sit on the Board and are legally accountable for all the organization's work. Sometimes called Council Members, Management Committee Members, Trustees, Directors, or Members of a Governing Board.

**Officers** The Chair, Vice-chair, Treasurer and Secretary to the Board.

**Committees** Small groups, consisting either exclusively or predominantly of Board members, who are delegated responsibilities by the Board, sometimes called sub-committees, advisory panels or working groups.

**Chief Executive** The senior paid member of staff who reports to the Board. Sometimes called the Director, the Head, the Principal, the General Secretary, the Director General and other similar terms. This term is increasingly being used in the sector, despite its bossy overtones.

**Divisional Directors** The paid managers (usually in large organizations) who report to the Chief Executive and who have managers reporting to them.

**Senior Management Team** The chief executive and the divisional directors or senior managers who together have overall responsibility for the day-to-day management of the organization.

**Department** The level of organization below the senior management team. In smaller organizations it may be called a team or a project. In larger organizations it may be called a division.

**Service** What the service user receives, irrespective of whether it is a conventional service, a campaign, a performance, an education, spiritual development, some information or another desired benefit.

**Service Delivery Unit** The lowest level of the organization at which human and financial resources are brought together by a manager to deliver a service with specific objectives, a budget and performance measures.

**Branches** Field outposts of the organization including national branches of international organizations, local groups and church dioceses, and autonomous branches of federal organizations that have come together as part of a movement.

# CHAPTER ONE

# The Undiscovered Sector

## 1.1 A HISTORICAL PERSPECTIVE

The central philosophy that permeates virtually every part of the third sector is the human desire to assist other people without requiring personal benefit. Most people think of it in terms of charity and assume that it is a modern phenomenon. Some suggest it goes back to Elizabethan times or at most to Roman times. After all, the word 'charity' has a Latin origin, *caritas*, meaning either love of other people or beneficence and liberality to those in need or distress. And the word 'philanthropy' has a Greek origin – meaning love of people. In fact the philosophy goes back much further. People say, 'Charity begins at home' – and so it did. From earliest times it was the extended family that looked after its young, sick, disabled, elderly, widowed and orphaned members.

However, the growth of the first towns and cities and the movement of people away from their families meant that new forms of social provision were needed. Early Egyptian civilizations developed a strong moral code founded on social justice. This code encouraged people to help others in relation to their need – for example, by ferrying a poor person across the river without charging. The Pharaoh himself contributed by giving shelter, bread and clothing to the poor almost 5,000 years ago.

In ancient India the Buddhist Emperor Asoka (*c.* 274–232 BC) provided medical facilities, ordered wells to be dug and, in an early environmental initiative, planted trees for people's enjoyment. In early Greek society wayfarers were either given food and shelter in the houses of wealthy people or they would share the hospitality of peasants. The Jewish prophets were the forerunners of the modern campaigning organization. They worked tirelessly for social, economic and political justice and put pressure on their governments to change both policies and administrative practices. The idea of alms-giving was also widely recognized. In Roman times the right to free or cheap corn was dependent on citizenship and was hereditary, passing from father to son. Trusts also date back to Roman times as people established schemes to maintain control over the fate of an economic asset after their death.

Throughout history, charity has also been closely interwoven with the growth of religious organizations. Jewish teaching promoted the view `that the poor had rights and the rich had duties. Early Christian Churches established funds to support widows, orphans, the sick, the infirm, the poor, the disabled and prisoners. Church-goers were expected to bring gifts which were laid on the Lord's table so the recipients obtained them from the hands of God. The first legacies were authorized by Emperor Constantine I in AD 231, enabling endowments to be established for charity.

In the Islamic world philanthropy was used to establish many great hospitals. Early examples of 'hardship funds' also come from Islam when indigent patients were given five pieces of gold on their discharge. In short, the charitable sector has been around for a long time, always playing a significant role.

## Management problems have a long history

The issues facing these organizations also have a long history. Many of the dilemmas which perplex organizations today also confounded their predecessors. British medieval monasteries tended to be indiscriminate in their alms-giving. They consequently fostered a class of professional beggars which in time contributed to the breakdown of this system of relief. Similar problems occurred when hospitals designed for use by the poor were placed at the service of rich people. The issue of means testing clearly concerned these organizations as much as it troubles modern charities.

Arguments about the conflicting roles of the public and charitable sectors raged during the sixteenth century, when Henry VIII and Edward VI confiscated hospital and guild property. During this time, the Reformation undermined the church-centred welfare system and the gap was filled by greater state intervention funded by increased taxes. This included money given to almshouses, hospitals, university colleges, loan schemes to help people start businesses and for capital works such as building bridges and repairing roads. Indeed, the boundary with the state was just as much an issue then as it is today. For example, in 1572 Elizabeth I passed a law that allowed parishes to levy a poor rate to pay for the upkeep of almshouses and workhouses, effectively subsidizing charitable provision with state money.

Abuse by charities is also an old phenomenon. In 1601 Elizabeth I passed the Charitable Uses Act, which gave the Chancellor power to investigate the misuse of charitable funds. The Act provides an interesting perspective on the history of the third sector. Charitable endowments could only be given for:

> relief of aged, impotent and poor people, maintenance of sick and maimed soldiers and mariners, schools of learning, free schools and scholars in universities, repair of bridges, ports, havens, causeways, churches, sea banks and highways, education and preferment of orphans, relief, stock or maintenance of houses for correction, marriages of poor maids, supportation, aid and help of young tradesmen, handicraftsmen and persons decayed, relief or redemption of prisoners or captives and aid or ease of poor inhabitants concerning payment of taxes.

## The beginning of a more strategic approach

One of the first examples of proposals to take a more strategic approach to the delivery of social support was made by the Spaniard Juan Luis Vives in 1526. He proposed a census of the indigent population, detailed inquiries into individual cases, the application of measures aimed at permanent rehabilitation and improved coordination of charitable activities. This theme was taken up across sixteenth-century Europe, and enormously detailed censuses were carried out, for example in London and Norwich.

Nevertheless, for much of the period up to the middle of the nineteenth century charity in Britain was characterized by a large number of often jealous organizations pursuing activities with a poor understanding of the extent of the underlying causes of poverty. Organizations often worked with little knowledge of what others were doing and with little examination of the circumstances of individual beneficiaries.

However, during the second half of the nineteenth century charities began adopting a more coherent approach. The Poor Law Amendment Act of 1834 had drastically reduced relief for the poor. Paralleling government action, charities wanted to clarify the distinction between the poorest people with no resources and less deserving people who could rely on workhouses.

The emerging sector took a great leap forward with the formation of the Charity Organization Society in 1869. It is an example of how many of the great innovations in human welfare subsequently became third-sector organizations and part of an accepted way of working. It was founded after Henry Solly read a paper to the Society of Arts and aimed to encourage responsible spending on the poor and avoid welfare dependency. Henry Solly became its first General Secretary and remained in that position for forty years.

This organization, today called the Family Welfare Association, was among the first to put into place what would now be called a strategic approach to meeting people's needs. It strove to:

- prevent indiscriminate giving of relief
- promote careful inquiries into individual cases
- discover the causes of an individual's distress
- remove the causes of distress
- coordinate charitable activities to prevent excessive help being given to particular people.

In addition to taking a more strategic approach, which is now a central part of managing third-sector organizations, it also combined service delivery with a sharp and effective campaigning role, both against the state and against voluntary organizations, which, it believed, encouraged dependency.

---

## WHEN WERE THEY ESTABLISHED?

Providing housing, hospital care, services for disabled people, protecting the environment and campaigning for social change all have a venerable history, illustrated by the establishment of the following organizations:

| | |
|---|---|
| 1123 | St Bartholomew's Hospital |
| 1215 | St Thomas's Hospital |
| 1697 | Oxford Hospital, Ampthill |
| 1698 | Society for Promoting Christian Knowledge |
| 1702 | Hospital for Fisherman, Yarmouth |
| 1707 | Almshouses at Abingdon |
| 1823 | Anti-Slavery Society |
| 1824 | Royal National Lifeboat Institution |
| 1824 | Royal Society for the Prevention of Cruelty to Animals |
| 1830 | Society for the Improvement of the Condition of Labouring Classes |
| 1854 | Oxford Economic and Sanitary Association |

| | |
|---|---|
| 1862 | Peabody Trust |
| 1865 | Salvation Army |
| 1866 | Barnardos |
| 1868 | Royal National Institute for the Blind |
| 1870 | British Red Cross |
| 1881 | The Children's Society |
| 1884 | National Society for the Prevention of Cruelty to Children |
| 1886 | Octavia Hill and Rowe Housing Trust |
| 1889 | Guinness Trust |
| 1895 | The National Trust |
| 1902 | Imperial Cancer Research Fund |
| 1908 | Scout Association |
| 1910 | Girl Guides Association |
| 1918 | National Council for One Parent Families |
| 1919 | Save the Children |
| 1921 | Royal British Legion |
| 1923 | Cancer Research Campaign |
| 1924 | Wellcome Trust |
| 1930 | Youth Hostels Association |
| 1937 | Nuffield College Oxford |
| 1938 | RELATE – National Marriage Guidance |
| 1939 | Glyndebourne Arts Trust |
| 1942 | Age Concern |
| 1942 | Oxfam |
| 1946 | MENCAP – Royal Society for Mentally Handicapped Children and Adults |
| 1946 | Outward Bound Trust |
| 1948 | Leonard Cheshire Foundation |
| 1950 | Queen Elizabeth's Hospital, Bristol |
| 1952 | War on Want |
| 1953 | Samaritans |
| 1956 | Abbeyfield Society |
| 1956 | Fitzwilliam College Cambridge |
| 1958 | Voluntary Service Overseas |
| 1961 | National Institute for Social Work |
| 1966 | SHELTER (National Campaign for Homeless People) |
| 1967 | St Christopher's Hospice |
| 1971 | Greenpeace |
| 1976 | Stonham Housing Association |
| 1979 | Child Accident Prevention Trust |

Organizations are referred to by their latest name.

## State intervention increases

The trend towards a more strategic approach took place simultaneously with increased state intervention in social affairs. As a result, many of the innovative schemes for meeting people's needs that were established by the third sector over the last 150 years have gradually been adopted by government. It started when government began playing a greater role in education in the 1840s. As a result, one of the basic principles of state provision, that of ensuring minimum standards, was established and it was extended to many services including pensions, school meals, unemployment and health insurance.

Nevertheless, until 1948 the voluntary and charitable organizations remained major providers of direct services. Voluntary hospitals were part of the sector, and services for children and people with disabilities relied heavily on voluntary organizations. However, voluntary provisions, such as hospitals, were increasingly criticized for rivalry among themselves and for their inability to provide universal services available to everyone without payment at the point of delivery. As state provision expanded, the role of the voluntary sector was seen as supplementary to state provision and not as the parallel system that had been envisaged earlier.

In the period immediately after the Second World War, the role of the voluntary sector was therefore reduced as the state took over hospitals and other services and offered more comprehensive provision through local social services departments. For a period the third sector played second fiddle.

## Revival of the sector

However, from the beginning of the 1960s the voluntary sector began to exert its influence again as new needs were identified and new means of raising income were established. It has not looked back since that date. In particular:

- large service-providing organizations have focused on services not provided by the state
- specialist organizations have been established for almost every conceivable cause (the National Council for Voluntary Organizations directory alone lists over 2,000 national voluntary organizations)
- government and local authority funding has grown dramatically.

More significantly, in the last few years the move by government to separate purchasers from providers of services has presented many new opportunities for value-led organizations. Some are now returning to their previous role as mainstream providers of services. They are competing for the growing number of contracts that government, local and health authorities are putting out to tender, often with considerable success.

These new opportunities, combined with the break-up of monolithic health, education and welfare providers into smaller, more independent organizations, are fuelling the growth of the sector. Many institutions that were until a few years ago undisputably part of the public sector are becoming indistinguishable from state-funded voluntary organizations. Colleges of education, grant-maintained schools and hospital trusts are beginning to see themselves as semi-independent third-sector organizations rather than part of the public sector. There is consequently a need to define and explain the boundaries between the public, private and third sector in a little more detail.

## 1.2 BOUNDARIES OF THE SECTOR

The sector consists of an extraordinarily diverse range of organizations: some are charitable (Oxfam), some are not (the Automobile Association), some are based on vast membership (the National Trust), some are not (the Royal Opera), some are primarily government funded (Victim Support), some eschew government funding (Amnesty International), some are politically left of centre (the Transport and General Workers' Union), some right (the Adam Smith Institute), some are large (Nuffield Nursing Homes Trust) and many are small (the British Hedgehog Preservation Society).

There are many names which broadly cover the notion of this sector. Each establishes different boundaries, but they all overlap:

- the **charitable sector** consists mainly of all organizations which meet the strict conditions required for charity registration
- the **voluntary sector** includes charities and many other organizations with social and political aims that have not registered as charities or do not meet the criteria
- the **NGO sector** (an acronym for Non-governmental Organization that is widely used in the international aid field) refers to voluntary or charitable organizations

- the **not-for-profit sector** is a wider term which emanates from the USA and includes independent not-for-profit universities and hospitals, trade unions, professional associations and other organizations which can make profits but do not distribute them
- *économie sociale* is a term increasingly used in the European Union which includes not-for-profit organizations and many business-type organizations such as mutual insurance companies, savings banks, cooperatives and agricultural marketing organizations whose profits are used to benefit their members or customers.

None of these definitions suits the purposes of this book. The charitable and voluntary sectors are too narrow; many of the propositions about management have much wider application. The non-profit sector is a negative definition which emphasizes the intention not to make profits – when in practice many of these organizations need to make a financial surplus to replace their capital and to fund new activities.

The *économie sociale* is a little too wide. Many of the additional organizations captured in this definition have a better fit with private-sector management theories.

This book therefore adopts the term the third sector and includes within it all organizations that:

- exist primarily for a **social purpose** rather than having a profit-making objective
- are **independent from the state** because they are governed by an independent group of people and are not part of a government department or a local or health authority
- **reinvest all their financial surpluses** in the services they offer or the organization itself.

## The boundaries are fuzzy

The boundaries are not clear-cut. Some organizations are widely agreed to be at the heart of the sector. Other organizations sit on the periphery of the sector. Many share the values of the sector but also have characteristics in common with either the public or the private sector.

A useful way, therefore, to think of the sector is as a core of pure organizations and peripheries which overlap with both the private and public sectors. Many of these, such as museums, quangos and TECs, can use third-sector management skills but are ultimately controlled by the government.

BOUNDARIES BETWEEN THE THIRD, PUBLIC AND
PRIVATE SECTORS

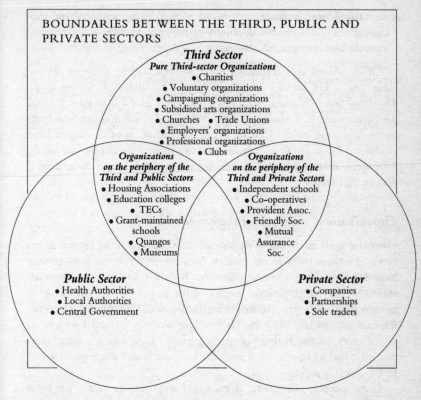

*Third Sector*
*Pure Third-sector Organizations*
- Charities
- Voluntary organizations
- Campaigning organizations
- Subsidised arts organizations
- Churches   • Trade Unions
- Employers' organizations
- Professional organizations
- Clubs

*Organizations*
*on the periphery of the*
*Third and Public Sectors*
- Housing Associations
- Education colleges
- TECs
- Grant-maintained schools
- Quangos
- Museums

*Organizations*
*on the periphery of the*
*Third and Private Sectors*
- Independent schools
- Co-operatives
- Provident Assoc.
- Friendly Soc.
- Mutual Assurance Soc.

*Public Sector*
- Health Authorities
- Local Authorities
- Central Government

*Private Sector*
- Companies
- Partnerships
- Sole traders

Examples of pure third-sector organizations include voluntary
organizations, campaigning organizations and clubs. Other types of
organization, such as trade unions, churches, professional associations
and employers' organizations, are less commonly seen as part of the
third sector but are equally part of the core.

While the core accounts for the majority of the sector, many organizations sit on the peripheries. These include organizations on the
periphery of:

- the **third and public** sectors, such as further and higher education
  colleges, which have been given greater independence and are currently migrating into the third sector. It also includes Training and
  Enterprise Councils and other quasi-non-governmental organizations
  such as the Arts Council, which are heavily government funded but
  operate with a degree of managerial independence

- the **third and private** sectors, such as friendly societies and co-operatives which do not distribute profits, but in most other respects operate like commercial companies.

Other writers and academics have adopted slightly different definitions (for a UK model see, for example, D. Billis, *A Theory of the Voluntary Sector*, Working Paper 5, LSE, 1989, and for an international perspective see L. Salamon and H. Anheier, *In Search of the Non-Profit Sector*, Voluntas, 1992). Debates about the definition of the sector have continued for many years and are unlikely to be resolved by one book. The spirit of the sector is driven by its diversity – and long may it remain that way!

## *Organizations move across the boundaries*

Over the years there has been considerable movement of organizations across the boundaries of the sectors. Movement across the third:private boundary has been mainly one-way. Building societies and mutual societies now see themselves as part of the private sector, operating in competition with profit-distributing businesses. The Abbey National, for example, began when twelve building workers formed a society to save money for purchasing houses. It gradually grew into a huge institution that had to operate in a competitive market and consequently lost its third-sector roots.

Until recently movement across the third:public boundary has been dominated by the state taking responsibility for services that are needed by the majority of people. Starting with the maintenance of bridges (a common charitable purpose of monastic foundations), through the care of prisoners (originally a charitable activity) to the more recent case of hospitals taken over to create the NHS, the movement has been towards the public sector.

That trend is now being reversed. The perceived limitations of the public sector as an efficient supplier of services are persuading governments around the world to delegate responsibility for the management of services. Schools, hospitals, colleges, youth and other services are increasingly being required to operate more like independent non-profit-distributing organizations than under the rules of public service. These organizations are finding that they have to compete against each other for funds and service users and have to diversify their funding sources to top up their government grants. When this happens they begin to behave like independent not-for-profit organizations and consequently move into the third sector.

This flood of organizations moving from the public to the periphery of the third sector is being driven by:

- a political philosophy that believes state-run organizations are neither efficient nor responsive to people's changing needs
- the consequent separation of the functions of the *purchaser* (to specify standards, and desired outcomes) and the *provider* (to deliver services efficiently and effectively, responding quickly to changes in the external environment)
- a desire to give local managers greater control over the management of their organizations
- tighter control over public expenditure coinciding with increased social need
- a belief that competition between suppliers can lead to efficiency gains, even though the notion of competition in the provision of basic services is deeply uncomfortable, particularly to professionals in these services.

In my view this trend will continue because the political philosophy that favours independence from the state has become well established. Indeed, as providers are given greater independence, they are becoming managerially more sophisticated, require less support from centralized bureaucracies and place increasing value on their independence.

In summary, even before these new organizations joined the third sector, it was a significant part of the social fabric in the UK and many other countries. Today it is becoming increasingly responsible for the provision of a huge range of essential services.

## 1.3 THE SECTOR IS SIGNIFICANT AND GROWING

The scope and scale of the third sector is now so huge that it affects virtually everyone. They may be members of professional associations, attending a college or university, attending an artistic event, worshipping, joining a trade union, supporting a campaign, donating to charity or joining a club or society.

Many of our lives are touched by the third sector more than once a week, and some more than once a day, as we:

- call a motoring organization (the AA and RAC are both non-profit-distributing)
- attend a trade union meeting
- seek advice from a Citizens Advice Bureau (nearly 8 million people do every year)
- volunteer (13 million people do every month)
- visit a sports club (there are 150,000 in the UK)
- call a charity help line (35,000 people do every day)
- read the *Guardian* or the *Observer* (they are both owned by the not-for-profit Scott Trust).

The sector is not only diverse, it is also very influential. In 1948 William Beveridge wrote, 'the strength of voluntary action is the distinguishing mark of a free society.' More recently, Professor Ken Young

## ESTIMATED SIZE OF THE THIRD SECTOR

| | Number of organizations[1] | Income £million[2] |
|---|---|---|
| Registered charities | 170,000 | 16,000 |
| Hospital trusts | 320 | 10,000 |
| Universities | 88 | 7,100 |
| Further-education colleges | 550 | 3,700 |
| Subsidized arts organizations[3] | 1,500 | 2,250 |
| Housing associations | 2,200 | 2,000 |
| Grant-maintained schools | 830 | 1,200 |
| Trade unions | 300 | 620 |
| Employers' organizations | 200 | 165 |

[1] Excludes churches, clubs, sports organizations and unregistered bodies. If these are included, the sector is thought to include over 500,000 organizations (*Facts and Figures on the Voluntary Sector*, NCVO, 1993).

[2] Figures from various sources, not necessarily for the same accounting period. Some are estimates.

[3] An estimate. Many are also registered charities.

## GROWING MEMBERSHIP OF THIRD-SECTOR ORGANIZATIONS

Growth of membership of most organizations is indicative of the massive increase in activity.

|  | 1971 | 1991 |
| --- | --- | --- |
| National Trust | 278 | 2,136 |
| Royal Society for the Protection of Birds | 98 | 847 |
| World-Wide Fund for Nature | 12 | 365 |
| League of Hospital Friends | 250 | 350 |
| National Society for the Prevention of Cruelty to Children | 20 | 500 |
| Friends of the Earth | 1 | 230 |

*Social Trends,* 22, HMSO, 1992.

has argued in his essay entitled 'Meeting the Needs of Strangers' (Gresham College, 1991) that the voluntary sector makes three crucial contributions to society:

**Representation**   Voluntary action in today's changed circumstances has a wider role – and is of greater social and political significance – than that of an adjunct provider of social services alongside mainstream state provision. It contributes to the representative process, to the development of public policy and to the processes of social integration and cohesion.

**Innovation**   The representations of voluntary bodies are a source of innovation. Governments today address issues that are often formulated and shaped by those outside the central departments. The history of social policy in Britain is largely one in which the agenda for action has been set by voluntary bodies turning hitherto tolerated conditions into problems and claims to action.

## THE THIRD SECTOR AFFECTS EVERY STAGE OF OUR LIVES

Most of the 500,000 third-sector organizations in Britain are small. This is how some of the medium-sized and larger ones affect our lives.

**Before conception**
Sex Education Forum
Family Planning
    Association
Birth Control
    Campaign

**During pregnancy and birth**
National Childbirth Trust
Baby Life Support Systems
Active Birth Centre

**Early childhood**
Pre-school Play Groups
    Association
National Toy Libraries
    Association
Child Accident Prevention
    Trust

**During education**
Nuffield Foundation
Barnardos
Save the Children

**In adolescence**
Childline
National Children's Home
YWCA

**In further education**
London Business School
Workers' Educational
    Association

**In employment**
Confederation of
    British Industry
UNISON

**In leisure**
National Trust
Royal Opera

**In sport**
British Olympic
    Association
British Blind Sport

**In housing**
Anchor Housing
Abbeyfield Society
Guinness Trust

**In campaigning**
Amnesty
    International
Greenpeace
Shelter

**In sickness**
Stroke Association
Great Ormond
    Street Hospital
MIND

**In health**
Royal Society for
    the Promotion
    of Health

**In relationships**
RELATE
Childline

**In disability**
Royal National
    Institute for Deaf
    People
Leonard Cheshire
    Foundation
MENCAP

**In emergencies**
Royal National Lifeboat
    Institution
Women's Royal Voluntary
    Service
British Red Cross
Victim Support

**In research**
Cancer Research
    Campaign
Cambridge University
British Heart Foundation

**In poverty**
Family Welfare
    Association
Salvation Army

**In retirement**
REACH
Pensioners Link
University of the
    Third Age

**In old age**
Age Concern
Help the Aged

**At death**
Exit – Voluntary
    Euthanasia
Natural Death
    Centre
St Christopher's
    Hospice

**After death**
Cruse – bereavement care
Compassionate Friends
Stillbirth Society

**Citizenship**        The effectiveness of voluntary bodies as advocates of change owes much to their informal nature. Whether or not people are excluded from effective citizenship rests in no small measure upon the strength of the local voluntary sector.

In short, no significant governmental decision is usually taken in a sophisticated democracy without many third-sector interest groups being consulted or making their case.

## 1.4 MANAGING VALUE-LED ORGANIZATIONS

There are many similarities in managing organizations in all sectors of the economy. All rely on skilled managers who need to have objectives, control resources, work in teams and have professional development and need to be praised and criticized. The third sector has particular parallels with the private sector, because organizations which sell services, sometimes at subsidized prices, need some of the theories of the market place. Likewise, many are providing public services with the attendant problems of limitless demand and little connection between service users and payment for the service.

Indeed, it is fair to say that the similarities between all sectors are growing. Greater use of contracts, which link funding to levels of service and outcomes, requires skills that have been well understood in the private sector for many years. Equally, private- and public-sector organizations are increasing their effectiveness by building staff commitment to missions and core values, skills that are widely understood in the third sector.

### The crucial differences between the sectors

Nevertheless, a central theme of this book is the proposition that managing value-led organizations is subtly different from managing in the private or public sectors. Managers who have transferred from either the public or the private sector to the third sector quickly discover that there is something intrinsically different about making things happen in a not-for-profit context. It is difficult to spot the relevant differences and distinguish them from the superficial ones. The symbols of informal dress, cramped offices and seemingly endless meetings hide more deep-seated differences in people's values and beliefs. Yet it is these values and beliefs that are at the root of the differences.

Many senior managers in the third sector are recruited from the public and private sectors and not from the third sector itself. Those from the private sector usually bring the economic logic of the market place and the values of shareholders, customers and profits. Those from the public sector bring the political perspective and the public-service values which influence that sector.

Most third-sector organizations can recount experiences of recruiting talented people from the private and public sectors who come to grief in the third sector. Examples abound of the talented military commander who decides to continue in public service by directing a charity, or the high-flying business executive who takes responsibility in a church or a hospital trust.. Those who come to grief have usually failed to make the necessary changes in their implicit assumptions about the differences between the sectors.

In the private sector there is a relatively straightforward relationship between suppliers and customers. Suppliers offer customers goods and services and in return customers pay a market price. In the public sector, government and local authorities supply public services and in return the voters choose the government which they believe offers the most appropriate programme of taxation and public services.

In the third sector a different model of transactions applies. In most cases donors give money which the organization uses to fund projects, supply services, or carry out research. Oxfam, the Royal National Lifeboat Institution and the Cancer Research Campaign are typical examples. A variation of this is where money comes from grants or contracts. This source is growing rapidly at present. Although it is widely believed to be a new source of funds, contracts were in fact used extensively in the early part of this century when the liberal government of 1905 funded Friendly Societies and Councils for Voluntary Service to deliver its reforms.

Another variation is where services are part funded by the service user and part funded by grants, contracts and donations. This happens in housing associations, disability organizations, arts organizations and education colleges. Nevertheless, in all these cases the key difference between the third and the other two sectors is that there is only a weak link between the service users and the funders of the service. The feed-

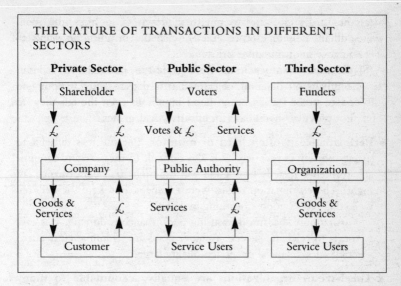

## THE NATURE OF TRANSACTIONS IN DIFFERENT SECTORS

| Private Sector | Public Sector | Third Sector |
|---|---|---|
| Shareholder | Voters | Funders |
| Company | Public Authority | Organization |
| Customer | Service Users | Service Users |

back which companies get from customers (or lack of them) and which the public sector gets from the ballot box is very weak in the third sector. This crucial difference in the nature of transactions means organizations have to manage the problems of:

- demand for their service being limitless or contained only by minimizing the marketing and promotion of the service
- being caught between the different expectations of funders and users
- not being directly accountable for the quality of service provided.

In addition to the different nature of the transactions there are seven other characteristics of third-sector organizations which, although not exclusive to the sector, combine together to make management a challenging occupation:

- **It is easy to have vague objectives**. Social, health, educational, environmental and spiritual objectives are difficult to specify precisely. Think, for a moment, about what the objectives of an orchestra, a political party or a church should be. It is extremely difficult to define exactly what these organizations should aim to have achieved in, say, three years' time. Third-sector organizations do have to specify strategic objectives, as we shall see in later chapters, but when they do it quickly becomes clear that:

(a) the harder one tries to pin them down to specifics, the more difficult it is to capture exactly what the organization wants to achieve in quantitative terms

(b) different constituencies in the organization place greater or lesser emphasis on different objectives; it is consequently tempting to adopt broad statements of good intentions even though they do not provide a good basis for effective management.

- **Performance is often hard to monitor**. Because it is difficult to specify objectives precisely, it is also difficult to measure and monitor achievements. Exactly how good was the orchestra's performance last night? The examination results were excellent, but were the children well educated or good at learning by heart?

  Furthermore, because measuring performance is difficult, it is easy to forget to celebrate success. Achievements are seldom as clear-cut as meeting sales, financial or service-quality targets.

- **Third-sector organizations are equally accountable to many stakeholders.** Members, funding bodies, individual donors, staff, volunteers and service users all have a different stake in a third-sector organization. They are often in a position to have a powerful influence on the organization, yet they invariably have different views of priorities and sometimes on the style and culture of the organization as well.

- **Management structures are intricate.** The need to balance delicately the interests of different stakeholders and to involve different specialisms in management results in complex structures of governing bodies, committees and sub-committees, each of which has a legitimate position in the structure. Taken together this requirement creates a complex machine which has to be consulted, coordinated and managed in order to get things done. Even organizations that have streamlined their structures often have more intricate arrangements than equivalent-sized organizations in the private sector.

- **Voluntarism is an essential ingredient**. The majority of third-sector organizations have unpaid voluntary governing boards whose members may not have management experience. Many rely on voluntary labour and the 'voluntary' commitment of employees, giving extra time for no financial reward. In return for this voluntary commitment people often expect to have their views listened to and to be actively involved in decision-making.

- **Values have to be cherished.** Third-sector organizations are at their most effective when the people involved share common values and assumptions about the organization's purpose and its style of operation. Insensitive trampling on cherished values quickly results in demotivation and lengthy argument. The point is not that organizations in other sectors do not have values, but that they have to be treated with much greater sensitivity in third-sector organizations.

- **Lack of a financial 'bottom line' to determine priorities.** Third-sector managers can seldom use a financial bottom line of profit or a discounted cash-flow projection to guide their choice of future priorities and investments. These organizations have to rely more heavily on internal negotiation to agree priorities. Unfortunately there is no standard methodology or template for this. Every organization has to develop its own criteria for allocating resources that suit its circumstances at a particular time.

## People have multiple motives

Beyond these explicit characteristics, there is a human perspective that needs to be understood to gain a complete picture of the challenges of managing these organizations. This issue is seldom discussed openly but nevertheless is central to an understanding of their management.

Virtually everyone who contributes time and effort to these organizations has well-founded altruistic and philanthropic motives. Indeed, without these values, the sector could not exist. However, people often have other private motives for contributing to these organizations:

- They join governing boards, particularly of larger and more prestigious organizations, because of the recognition, esteem and status that is attached to board membership. Such membership frequently leads to contacts with other people in powerful positions, to increased influence and a greater sense of self-worth.
- Some donors give money to acquire national recognition, for public-relations benefits, to salve their consciences and, sometimes, to gain greater influence over the organization's affairs.
- Volunteers give their time because of their need for friendship and social activity, to gain useful skills, to enhance their employment prospects and to give them a role in the broader community.

- People seek employment in third-sector organizations because they would not find it comfortable working with the ideology of the private sector or the constraints of the public sector.

This is not to argue that altruism does not exist. It does, and it is present in most value-led organizations. But people have multiple motives and the hidden ones have a significant impact on management. At their most extreme, these motives can combine to make the survival of the organization a greater priority than the services it gives to users.

Fortunately, not all these explicit and implicit characteristics apply to all organizations simultaneously. However, they do create a special set of circumstances that explains why managing these organizations needs to be based on an understanding of their special characteristics. They illustrate why the management tools and styles that work in the other sectors are only partially applicable to this sector. Finally they explain why theories about management need to start from a set of propositions that are derived specifically to help managers of third-sector organizations.

---

## SUMMARY OF KEY POINTS

### Historical perspective

- The history of the third sector goes back to the earliest civilizations.
- The special problems of managing these organizations have an equally long history.
- Following rapid growth in the nineteenth and early twentieth century, the sector was eclipsed by the welfare state.
- It has re-emerged with the entrepreneurial skills and social conscience needed to address today's problems.

### Boundaries of the sector

- The third sector includes organizations that:
  - exist primarily for a social purpose
  - are independent of the state
  - reinvest financial surpluses in their services.
- The boundaries with the public and private sectors are not clear-cut.
- Over time, organizations move across the boundaries.

### Growth of the sector

- The number and size of organizations are both growing.
- The crucial contributions of the sector are its ability to represent people's views, to innovate and to provide people with a sense of citizenship.

### Managing value-led organizations

- The central difference between the third and the other sectors is that there is only a weak link between providers of funds and service users.
- Seven other distinguishing factors are that:
  - it is easy to have vague objectives
  - performance is hard to monitor
  - organizations are accountable to many stakeholders
  - management structures are intricate
  - voluntarism is an essential ingredient
  - values have to be cherished
  - there is no financial 'bottom line' to determine priorities.
- Management is complicated by the fact that people who contribute to third-sector organizations have a pot-pourri of motives which are both philanthropic and also very private.

# CHAPTER TWO

# Concepts for Creating Boards that Govern

## 2.1 BOARDS HAVE SPECIAL FUNCTIONS

In the conventional view of third-sector organizations, the board is the all-powerful group that establishes the mission, sets the objectives, appoints the staff and monitors their performance. The board is the top of the hierarchy, accountable for all the organization's actions. It sets the overall strategy and the staff implement the decisions.

In practice the reverse is sometimes nearer the truth. The board meets infrequently and has agendas that are predominantly concerned with short-term issues and crises. The board is highly dependent on the staff not only for information and advice but for preparing strategies and plans for the board to approve. In the worst cases, the board's deliberations merely repeat decisions that have effectively been made by the staff.

Not only does the staff control the board, it frequently plays a significant role in determining its membership. Boards often rely on staff for proposing names of potential new members and for making preliminary contact with them. The implicit message to potential members is that power lies with the staff.

So, the perception of the board as the centre of power is frequently far removed from the reality. In practice many boards are more dependent on their staff than staff are on their board. But this need not be the case. Some boards perform a leadership function. They add value to the organization by steering, anticipating and providing wisdom and good judgement. They are concerned with the vision of the organization, its values and culture and its achievements. They pay close attention to the systematic development of a strong board that not only plans succession but strives to increase the calibre of people it attracts. These boards recognize the essential contribution that boards make in the very limited time members give to the organization. They compare favourably with those that try to control details and usually end up being unable to see the wood for the trees.

Effective board members recognize that the task of running a board is a complex and subtle activity. Boards have to fulfil the very different functions of:

- governing the organization
- providing accountability for the organization
- resolving tensions between different stakeholder groups
- giving advice to management.

Consequently, the simple view that the board has a totally clear-cut function, that of setting policy, and the staff's function is purely to implement policy is not entirely applicable in practice.

This chapter sets out some fundamental concepts about the roles and structures of boards. It:

- makes the distinction between governance and management
- introduces the idea of the life cycle of boards
- identifies the critical roles of boards that govern effectively
- investigates different institutional structures
- describes different board and committee structures.

It avoids the many legal and constitutional issues relating to boards (for example, company and charitable status), since these are more a matter for legal books. It also assumes that there is no one solution to the structure and role of boards. Every organization has to define both according to its needs. There is, nevertheless, a set of ground rules which can be applied to create more effective boards. This chapter describes those rules.

The next chapter describes application of the concepts and the actions needed to create strong and effective boards.

## 2.2 DISTINGUISHING GOVERNANCE FROM MANAGEMENT

Boards have many functions. First they have overall responsibility for the **governance** of the organization. They are responsible for agreeing the mission and the objectives, approving the strategy and monitoring the organization's performance against the agreed plans. They have to be aware of the changing external environment and ensure the organization is geared up to respond to new circumstances.

Second, the board is ultimately **accountable** for the organization. It is responsible for all the organization's work, for appointing high-calibre staff, in particular the chief executive, and setting up the necessary reporting procedures to ensure it can discharge those responsibilities. Depending on the nature of the organization, it is accountable to members, funders, regulatory bodies and often the general public who, because of the high profile of these organizations, take a great interest in their work.

Third, the board has the function of **resolving tensions** within the organization. Since these organizations are coalitions of people with different interests, such as service users, funders, staff and volunteers, the board has to arbitrate between competing demands placed on the organization.

In the limited time board members devote to the organization they have to focus their efforts sharply on those critical functions that no one else can discharge. The most common mistake boards make is to spend time on activities that should be delegated to paid staff. To separate the roles of the board and staff it is useful to think in terms of the distinctive functions of governance and management. This concept has been strongly promoted by the National Center for Non-profit Boards in the USA and is rapidly taking hold in the UK.

There is no clear-cut distinction between governance and management. Unfortunately, the roles of the board and paid management cannot be neatly separated. But neither do they need to overlap entirely. The critical functions of the board are different from the tasks of paid staff.

Governance is the board's responsibility. It is about ensuring that the organization has a clear mission and strategy, but not necessarily about developing it. It is about ensuring that the organization is well managed but not about managing it. It is about giving guidance on the overall allocation of resources but is less concerned with the precise numbers. Governance is about taking responsibility for the organization's performance, but not about meddling with the detail of the performance measurement system. Governance is ultimately concerned with providing insight, wisdom and good judgement. Boards have to find ways of providing this which move beyond setting abstract policies that are full of good intentions but of little practical use.

Management is a staff responsibility. Staff are responsible for implementation of strategy agreed by the board. They are responsible for turning the board's intentions into action and for administering the systems and procedures needed to get results. In practice staff also do much of the work required to prepare and flesh out the detail of strategies and policies agreed by the board. They also help to ensure that the mechanics of the board process run smoothly.

The balance of responsibility depends on circumstances. Organizations where the staff are effective and share a common set of values require less intervention from the board. In this situation, it is easier for the board to stick closely to its governance role. Organizations with a strong board but a weak or divided staff will find the board intervening in detail more often and crossing the boundary between governance and management. This is common in smaller organizations that have few staff but have board members willing to work voluntarily. Indeed, even larger organizations have to acknowledge that for many people it is the actual work of the organization that motivates board members to give their time voluntarily to the organization. Few people join an organization's board because they are motivated by an interest in governance!

Organizations with a strong staff and a weak board often find that staff interests begin to predominate. In these circumstances it becomes increasingly difficult to maintain an appropriate balance between the interests of different stakeholder groups.

Organizations with a weak board and weak staff are in serious difficulty. They need the power of a highly competent chief executive or an outside intervention to avoid a spiral which starts with a declining reputation, leads to difficulty in attracting effective staff and board members and results in deteriorating services and a further fall in reputation. The dedication of a few people over an extended period will be required to start the process of building a new board, carving out a governance role and creating a stronger team of staff.

## 2.3 THE LIFE CYCLE OF BOARDS

One way of developing insights into the work of the board and its changing relationship with staff is to think in terms of a life cycle which many boards follow. The detail of the cycle varies from one organization to the next, but the pattern is so common that it helps boards to understand the way their work has to evolve in line with the develop-ment of the organization.

## The founding phase

Many organizations are established by a charismatic founder who has the vision and personality to define a social, cultural or environmental problem and create an organization to address it. The founder gathers together a group of people who share the same views, and an organiza-tion is created. The founder is sometimes the first chief executive and may hold on to that position when other staff are hired.

The appointment of staff frequently leads to the first crisis. Board members find that their role as both the doers and the deciders is usurped. The board goes through its first transformation and has to dis-tinguish its role more clearly from that of the staff. In well-established organizations this will have happened tens or even hundreds of years ago.

## The youthful phase

When new roles are agreed, often implicitly, the board settles down into the second stage of the cycle. The organization grows, staff are appoint-ed and soon the chief executive has a senior management team that assumes responsibility for most of the work of the organization. The board often takes a back seat, and meetings become routinized, attend-ance falls, discussions become less sharp and respect for the board declines. Suddenly a crisis jerks it out of its complacency. It may be the fact that the organization has outgrown the capabilities of its chief exec-utive, a dispute with staff or a difference of opinion on a policy issue. Whatever the trigger, the board is forced to reassess its role and usually its membership as well.

## The adult phase

A review will frequently conclude that the board needs people with more professional skills. Once found, these people generally bring a dif-ferent set of assumptions, and after a period of difficult relationships many of the founding members leave. The organization settles into the third stage of the cycle. The new board brings the rational mind-set of setting objectives, monitoring performance and managing the budget.

They risk, however, losing the original sense of mission that inspired the organization in the first place.

Because members are often new to the role, this new board feels the need to grasp the detail of the organization. It meets more often and establishes sub-committees. Board papers become thicker, and before long it is accused by staff of meddling in detail.

Eventually another crisis precipitates a review, which concludes that the board's role of establishing policy and the staff's role of implementation need to be adhered to more rigorously. Committees are streamlined, new operating procedures are written and the role of the board is again transformed. Members heave a great sigh of relief, start to meet less frequently and give the staff greater freedom within agreed boundaries.

## The mature phase

As the years pass the board adopts a more hands-off role. The well-established organization finds it easier to recruit new members who are often leading figures in their own fields and who will have less time to devote to the board. Some attract 'big names' who are willing to lend the respect that goes with their name but unwilling to get involved in the detail of the organization's work. Some boards become dominated by establishment figures and members who are unwilling to challenge accepted views about the organization and its work. Meetings become ritualized and membership stagnates. Eventually the board slips back into bad habits, a crisis erupts, some members leave and the board returns to a previous stage of development.

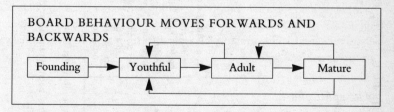

BOARD BEHAVIOUR MOVES FORWARDS AND BACKWARDS

Founding → Youthful → Adult → Mature

Although the life cycle varies from one organization to another, the pattern is sufficiently common to be helpful in describing dispassionately why a board is in the midst of a crisis that no one can really understand. Having a picture of the old stage and the new one is a powerful tool when helping people relate to the problem and find ways forward that are acceptable to the majority.

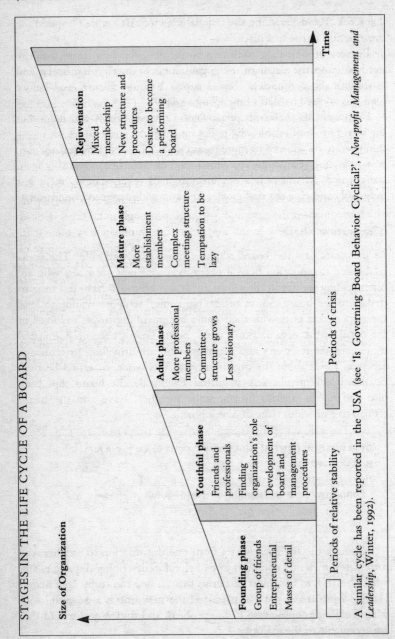

STAGES IN THE LIFE CYCLE OF A BOARD

**Size of Organization**

**Founding phase**
Group of friends
Entrepreneurial
Masses of detail

**Youthful phase**
Friends and
professionals
Finding
organization's role
Development of
board and
management
procedures

**Adult phase**
More professional
members
Committee
structure grows
Less visionary

**Mature phase**
More
establishment
members
Complex
meetings structure
Temptation to be
lazy

**Rejuvenation**
Mixed
membership
New structure and
procedures
Desire to become
a performing
board

**Time**

Periods of relative stability

Periods of crisis

A similar cycle has been reported in the USA (see 'Is Governing Board Behavior Cyclical?', *Non-profit Management and Leadership*, Winter, 1992).

## 2.4 KEY ROLES OF AN EFFECTIVE BOARD

Irrespective of their stage of development, the best boards strive to give high value to their organization, creating policy when needed and meddling with detail only when members have a significant contribution to make. These boards ask for information about achievements and for figures that enable members to make judgements about value for money. They work hard on developing the role of the board and regularly take time to assess their own performance and initiate actions to improve board procedures.

The effective governing board sees its role as a **partnership** with the chief executive and the senior management team. It is a partnership in which the board is the first among equals. Although some organizations are dominated by their boards and others are dominated by their staff, neither type works as well as those in which both have distinctive roles to play in achieving common objectives. Both the staff and the board need to work at carving out distinctive functions for each other. Each needs assiduously to avoid duplicating the work of the other.

In defining its role, the board needs to **add value** to the organization. The key question to ask is: what is different as a result of the board's work? In many cases it is not clear that the board has added value to the organization. It can be a significant drain on the staff who

---

THE ROLE OF THE BOARD IS SUBTLE

'What exactly is the role of the board in this organization?' asked the recently appointed Chief Executive.

'We have a simple rule,' replied the Chair. 'The board agrees the overall strategy and the staff implements it.'

'But how does the board distinguish between strategy and implementation?' asked the Chief Executive.

'It's simple,' replied the Chair, 'whatever the board wants to discuss is strategy and everything else is implementation.'

**Work seldom divides neatly into strategy and implementation.**

Adapted from *Govern More and Manage Less*, R. Chait, National Center for Non-profit Boards, USA.

have to prepare for and attend meetings, and it can cost substantial amounts in travel and accommodation expenses. In the worst cases the board and its sub-groups can be a net drain on the organization's resources, costing more than it is worth. In others the board is a critical ingredient of the organization's success and effectiveness.

Effective boards usually take few decisions. They have a much more sophisticated role. The critical ingredient of an effective board is to **anticipate decisions**. Boards that anticipate are in command of the organization's affairs. Boards that fail to anticipate find that events run out of control, and they are driven by circumstances into crisis management. All too soon the board finds itself dragged into the detail and unable to raise itself into a more strategic role.

When a board has a commanding view of what it is trying to do and how it is going about the task, the following require active anticipation:

- establishing processes for determining the organization's strategy and monitoring its overall performance
- significant changes in the funding environment
- significant changes in the size and needs of the beneficiary group or campaign priorities
- the need to change the overall structure of the organization or the senior management structure
- succession of the chair
- review of the chief executive's contract and personal performance and, when necessary, replacement of an under-performing chief executive.

With good anticipation the effective board finds that **shaping decisions** is just as important as taking them. It creates the context within which the organization functions. It influences the organization by asking the right questions at the right time. It guides with wisdom and good judgement rather than by making decisions on matters of detail.

A key role of the board is to **balance** different stakeholders' interests in the organization. Members, staff, funders, service users and the general public have an interest in the organization. These interests are seldom synonymous. Each group therefore attempts to influence the organization in favour of its own priorities. Funders may place unnecessarily burdensome conditions on their grants; members can make unreasonable demands on staff; service users can develop expectations beyond the organization's resources; and staff may put their own interests before those of the organization. The board is **morally accountable** to all

## DILEMMAS OF THE BOARD'S ROLE

'This board shouldn't be involved in setting the prices of our services,' said the recently recruited board member who was also a company chief executive. 'Pricing decisions are an operational matter for our talented team of staff.'

'But they do have critical impact on our overall success,' replied a long-standing board member and respected member of the local community. 'If we increase our prices fewer people will be able to afford our service – and our aim is to reach as many people as possible.'

'I know that,' replied the company chief, 'but if we meddle with the prices, we will get drawn into a discussion about the type of service we offer, the quality of the service and even how it is promoted. Before long we will be doing management's job.'

'I'm not suggesting we should get into that detail, but I do think that as representatives of the community we have a responsibility to ensure that we keep our prices as low as possible,' retorted the slightly angry community leader. 'We can't do that if we just let staff put the prices up without discussion by this board.'

**Boards need to discuss and agree their roles and, periodically, review them.**

these groups and **legally accountable** to some. It has to act as **mediator** between their competing interests.

The practical roles which an effective board needs to discharge fall into two categories: one concerned with the organization's work and the second concerned with the work of the board.

## *Roles concerning the work of the organization*

Roles in which the effective board can legitimately involve itself include:

- shaping and periodically redefining the mission
- agreeing long-term objectives and strategic plans
- influencing the overall allocation of resources to different purposes or user groups (usually through the strategic planning and budget-setting processes)

- establishing performance measures for the organization as a whole and monitoring against these measures
- ensuring the financial security of the organization and establishing effective financial management systems
- appointing, supporting, supervising and monitoring the performance of the chief executive (sometimes by delegating this to a sub-group)
- establishing broad policies for the way the organization should work (e.g. financial policy, personnel policy and policies on ethical issues such as special support for people with disabilities and ethical investments)
- monitoring the overall performance of the organization against its plans.

## Roles concerning the work of the board

The key roles of the board in determining its own work programme include:

- defining the ideal size and composition of the board (if necessary, by proposing adjustments to the constitution)
- structuring committees and working groups to anticipate the future needs of the organization
- recruiting and inducting new members to meet present and future requirements of the organization
- ensuring board members are clear about the board's responsibilities and how they are discharged
- providing training and support to meet members' development needs
- determining its own agenda and priorities
- monitoring its own performance and that of its committees.

For many boards this will look good on paper and be difficult in practice. The most common reason for this is that the board is investing insufficient time in discussing and agreeing its own roles and the operational procedures needed to discharge those roles. As a result it steps on to the slippery slope that leads inexorably to excessive involvement in detailed operational matters.

An effective board can anticipate spending a significant proportion of its time discussing and agreeing its own role, structure and ways of working. This investment pays handsome dividends. When complex issues arise there is an agreement and a framework within which they can be discussed and resolved. It takes time to agree roles and procedures, but once it has been done meetings run more smoothly and decision-taking is easier.

Defining the board's role is a never-ending task. Over time external circumstances will change, new members will join the board and a new chief executive will bring different assumptions. These changes should all encourage the board once again to spend more time redefining its own role and the demands it makes of its staff to enable it to discharge its role.

---

## SIX BOARD COMPETENCIES

Research by Richard Chait, a well-known American guru on non-profit board performance, has correlated the competencies of boards with the effectiveness of the non-profit organizations they manage. These are described in six dimensions.

| Competency | Definition |
|---|---|
| 1. Contextual dimension | The board understands and takes into account the values and beliefs of the organization it governs |
| 2. Educational dimension | The board ensures that board members are well informed about the organization, the profession and the board's role, responsibilities and performance |
| 3. Inter-personal dimension | The board nurtures the development of members as a group and fosters a sense of cohesion |
| 4. Analytical dimension | The board recognizes complexities in the issues it faces and draws upon different perspectives to find appropriate solutions |
| 5. Political dimension | The board accepts the need to develop healthy relationships with key constituencies |
| 6. The strategic dimension | The board helps ensure a strategic approach to the organization's future |

His research concluded that organizations which had boards that exhibited all six competencies performed significantly better than those lacking one or more of these competencies.

---

## Different arrangements for choosing board members

The role of the board is also influenced by the constitutional arrangements for choosing members. These arrangements are usually one of four different types.

### 1. The Elected Board

Most federal and many linear organizations (see section 2.5) have this arrangement. The board is chosen by a large membership which elects from among itself individuals to serve on the board. Most membership organizations, such as trade unions, and some service delivery organizations, such as The National Trust and the Consumers' Association, have this model. The roles of these boards are influenced by members' views. Members vote their representatives on to the board. They also influence the board's agenda by passing at AGMs motions requiring action by the board.

### 2. The Selected Board

In this model a small membership, usually of much less than a hundred people, is responsible for selecting people (often without elections) to be members of the board. These 'guardians' may be past members of the board or individuals who have made a significant contribution to the organization. These people tend to have relatively little influence on the board. They act only when the board is divided or when serious problems occur. Arts organizations, some national charities (for example, Oxfam) and some housing associations have this type of board.

### 3. The Appointed Board

On these boards a third party, such as a government Minister or the organizations that established the body, appoint members. This model is most common among quasi-non-governmental organizations and coordinating bodies that represent the interests of other organizations. These organizations appoint their representative to the board. They may require their representative to take action on an issue or vote in a particular way.

### 4. The Self-perpetuating Board

In this type, board members themselves are responsible for choosing their successors. This model is common among trusts, some charities and some campaigning organizations.

In addition to these methods, many boards have the power to co-opt members. This is a particularly useful way of filling gaps in competencies and skills. A review of skills after an election can point to specific requirements that the board can use to guide its search for people who will bring with them the necessary experience.

Difficulties sometimes arise when boards have a mixture of these electoral arrangements. A common example is where some members are elected and others are appointed by nominating organizations. On these boards different members may expect the board to play different roles. This is a further argument for discussing the role of the board openly and encouraging members to understand that their different but equally legitimate perspectives arise from the different roles they are expected to perform.

## Size of the board

The size of the board also influences its role. There are three fundamentally different models, each of which can accommodate a different number of members. In all three cases they are the governing body of the organization, accountable in law for its work and decisions. The sizes shown below are broad guidelines, since precise numbers depend on circumstances. In practice the number of people who attend meetings is often more important than agreed limits.

The **hands-on board** usually has between seven and twelve members. It generally meets regularly, and members can all participate equally in the governance of the organization. Boards of less than seven members can seldom represent all the constituencies (e.g., geographical regions) of the organization. They also risk having insufficient breadth of specialist skills and expertise to discharge their responsibilities. Hands-on boards of more than twelve members become increasingly cumbersome to manage; members have less 'air-time' in meetings, and each feels less personally responsible for the decisions that the board takes. These boards do not necessarily have to delegate much to committees.

The **representative board** has between twelve and thirty-five members. It ensures that a wide range of views are presented. Its meetings have to concentrate on fewer critical issues because it is less efficient at taking decisions. Boards at the larger end of this spectrum may need to appoint an executive committee to perform some of the hands-on functions of governance. This type of board is suitable in situations where representation of different constituencies is paramount.

The **policy-making board** has more than thirty-five members. It functions as the organization's parliament, debating broad policy issues but remaining distanced from month-by-month decisions. These boards meet less frequently so delegating decision-making and most of the practical functions of governance to an executive committee is essential. It is most useful where many disparate viewpoints need to be taken into account in decision-making and where representation of many constituencies is necessary.

Every so often, the size of the board becomes a hot topic in an organization. The advantages and disadvantages of larger or smaller boards are fiercely debated because everyone has strongly held views on this issue. However, these debates frequently fail to recognize that the appropriate size depends on the need for representation of different constituencies and on the role that the board is designed to perform. There

---

## BOARDS TO SUIT DIFFERENT CIRCUMSTANCES

The board of LEWISHAM HOSPITAL TRUST has ten members and meets twelve times a year. It has separate Remuneration and Audit sub-committees. Its roles include shaping issues with a time horizon of more than one year, taking capital-expenditure decisions, managing the interface with the local community and resolving major strategic and organizational issues. It is a **hands-on board**.

The board of MENCAP, called the National Council, consists of thirty-four people, twenty-four of whom come from local MENCAP societies. They are chosen to represent all parts of the country. They meet three times a year and appoint a management committee to govern the organization in between their meetings. It is a **representative board**.

The governing body of the SAMARITANS, called the Council of Management, consists of 200 people, each representing a branch or a region of the organization. It formulates policy for the movement, approves the annual budget and elects an Executive to govern the organization. The Executive meets five times a year and the Council once a year. It is a **policy-making board**.

is consequently no right or wrong size. Currently many organizations with large boards are reducing their size and creating non-executive forums to provide mechanisms for representation and consultation. The Cancer Research Campaign, Save the Children and the Royal National Institute for Deaf People have reduced large boards to groups of approximately twenty people. Sometimes this can be done within the existing constitution; in other circumstances changes to the constitution may need to be proposed and agreed.

Another trend is the separation of legal accountability for the organization from the body at the top of the institutional structure. This is done by creating an 'advisory board', sometimes consisting of the organization's elder statesmen, who advise and may even elect the main board but are not legally directors or trustees of the organization.

Such arrangements provide for a degree of accountability to the board and, consequently, to management without creating a group of people that is so large that no one feels personally responsible for the organization.

## 2.5 THE IMPACT OF INSTITUTIONAL STRUCTURES ON THE BOARD'S ROLE

The term 'institutional structure' refers to the constitutional arrangements that organizations adopt to enable the various parts of the enterprise to relate to each other. This section describes the different institutional structures of medium- and larger-size organizations and how they affect the work of the board. It is not concerned with the organization's legal structure (i.e., whether it is a company, a charity or both). It is concerned with the arrangements that enable local, national and international parts of an organization to work together.

These are best seen as existing on a continuum between what could be called 'linear' and 'federal' structures.

Organizations at the **linear** end have a straight-line structure in which members (or the government or another external body) appoint a board to govern the organization. In some cases the board appoints its own members, so the membership and the board are just one group. They in turn appoint a staff that runs the organization on a day-to-day basis. Sometimes the organization also creates regional offices or local branches to support its work. The linear structure is 'top-down'.

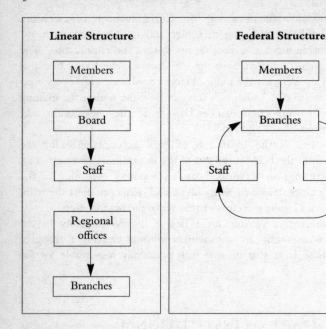

Organizations at the **federal** end of the continuum are circular in nature. The board is responsible for managing the organization, but it is appointed by the branches and is accountable to them. This situation usually arises from historic circumstances when independent branches of an organization have seen the need for national coordination. They establish the centre to provide branches with advice and support. In other circumstances a national organization may have encouraged the establishment of local branches and believed the organization would be most effective if they had some real power within the institutional structure. In both, the resulting structure is a federation in which the branches both appoint the board and recognize its authority. Many trade unions have federal structures. Well-known examples of voluntary organizations with federal structures include the Red Cross, the Samaritans and Citizens Advice Bureaux.

The critical determinant of these two institutional structures is the role of branches. In the linear structure the centre ultimately controls the branches and retains the power to open and close them and to control their behaviour. In the federal structure the branches control the centre.

## CANCER RESEARCH CAMPAIGN
### A linear structure

The Cancer Research Campaign has over 1,000 local committees that raise money in the Campaign's name but have no direct input into its management. It has a linear structure consisting of approximately 120 members, who elect a council of sixteen people to govern the organization. In summary its institutional structure is:

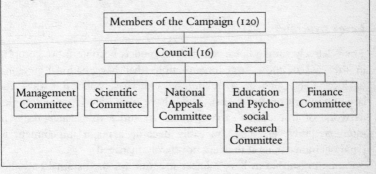

## THE SAMARITANS
### A federal structure

The Samaritans organization is ultimately controlled by its local branches, which have a total membership of 23,000 people. They elect members onto the Council of Management who in turn appoint an Executive Committee which oversees the work of the General Office.

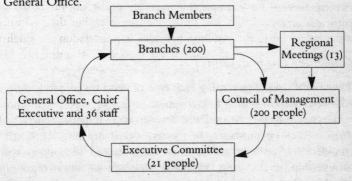

Between these two ends of the spectrum many organizations have institutional structures that are either more linear or more federal in orientation. Some organizations with linear structures reserve a number of board places for people elected from the branches. Some establish consultative councils to provide branches with a constitutionally agreed way to put their views to the board. Some have places on the board for regional representatives. All these mechanisms are designed to create an appropriate balance of power between the centre and the field.

## Large structures

The relatively simple linear and federal models become more complex in the case of those large organizations that have national, regional or local tiers (such as trade unions, churches, political parties and large voluntary organizations). These have often developed a complex network of institutional arrangements in order to balance different interests. However, they can easily become a major impediment to rapid decision-taking if they are not tightly managed.

Some organizations have a linear structure for the national body but are part of an international federation. Others, such as the Red Cross, have federal structures at both national and international level. These organizations have the added difficulty of creating institutional arrangements that balance both the interests of each level and the different cultural assumptions about organization design in different parts of the world.

Organizations seldom change from one type of structure to the other. They do, however, make small adjustments to reflect changing circumstances – for example, by reserving places on the board for a particular group.

## Governing linear structures

The critical tasks of governing each type of structure are subtly different. Although the tasks listed below appear at first sight to be common to both types of board, the critical difference is the importance attached to them in each circumstance. In a conventional structure the board has considerable freedom, and in those organizations without a separate membership it has great freedom. Members of linear-organization boards need to pay particular attention to:

- **surveying the external environment** and bringing a range of perspectives into the organization from their experiences as members of the organization, or of branches, or as individuals with particular skills and specialisms
- **setting policy, strategy and objectives** so the organization is given a clear sense of direction by people who have authority to drive the organization 'from the top'
- **monitoring performance,** since the board is ultimately accountable for the achievements of the organization
- **proposing entrepreneurial initiatives** because the board is responsible for the renewal and development of the organization.

Although boards of organizations with linear structures are not directly accountable to their branches (where they have them), their views cannot be ignored. The organization is dependent on their support and goodwill. Managers who are tempted to push through changes that are not supported by the field will face loss of morale, lack of commitment and opposition by stealth. They do need to listen to the field, respond to its concerns and keep it informed of plans and decisions.

## Governing federal structures

In federal structures power ultimately lies with the branches or the field units of the organization. The governing board is elected by them and has to respond to their demands and needs. This is not to argue that the board should not survey the external environment, set policy and strategy or monitor performance. But these are secondary to the critical functions of:

- **setting standards** that all members of the federation will agree to adhere to (for example, over the quality of professional work, and accreditation of workers)
- **establishing policies** that can be agreed throughout the federation (for example, on forestry in an environmental organization)
- **coordinating decision-making** because many parts of the organization need to be involved
- **controlling the name and logo**, since independent local branches create many variations if their use is not controlled

- **establishing and implementing a branch agreement** that sets out the terms and conditions for being a branch and the services and support the central office will provide (for example, providing training or campaign materials)
- **promoting the cause** through public speaking and publishing materials on behalf of the federation when a national voice is required to promote common interests
- **strategic planning** to give the whole federation a sense of direction and national purpose.

The board has to do all of this with the consent of the field. Branch representatives ultimately have the authority to agree or veto proposals. This means that change can be slow. In particular, those organizations that lack external pressures to force through changes (for example, from funders) find it difficult to keep themselves up to date because no one part of the organization has the authority to drive through difficult changes.

The boards of federal organizations can be a source of considerable conflict. Representatives of the members of the federation have two separate interests to balance. As board members they have legally prescribed duties and are responsible for the overall management and development of the institution – for example, meeting funders' requirements or collaborating with other agencies. These objectives may conflict with their roles as representatives of the local branches who may have mandated them to vote in particular ways on contentious issues.

Board members of federal organizations face many knotty problems. Members often wish to be consulted on more issues than is consistent with quick, decisive action. Both the freedom and the boundaries of the centre need to be very clear to avoid unnecessary arguments. Another common issue is poor performance of one part of the federation. Since branches are often predominantly voluntary, achieving improvements requires skill to encourage recognition of the problem and action to overcome it. This problem is often exacerbated by the different perspectives of the centre (often London-based, cosmopolitan, influenced by the media, Parliament and the civil service) and the field (usually urban or rural and influenced by local people and community values).

Boards have three main mechanisms by which to bring about change in federations:

- they can bring about change through leadership. By charismatic appeal and the logic of their proposals, the centre can command the authority needed to make things happen

- they can bargain with the branches by offering additional support in return for changes in branch priorities. For example, by offering additional services or agreeing to consult more frequently, managers can encourage branches to accept new national standards for the quality of services or the income to be remitted to the head office
- they can use the agreed rules and procedures to enforce change. All federations need an agreement that sets out the rights and obligations of the branches and the centre. In the final analysis this can be used to force changes through.

The key is to choose the most appropriate combination of mechanisms for the circumstances. Leadership is a powerful influence but may be insufficient to achieve the required changes. Bargaining may be required to ensure a fair arrangement between all parties. If changes still cannot be agreed, application of the rules and procedures may be unavoidable.

In successful federations, managers work hard to establish realistic expectations. They establish many communication channels (e.g., meetings, newsletters, induction workshops) between different levels of the organization and continuously clarify what each can expect of the others. They make certain that the relationship is well documented and, more important, they ensure that there is consistency in the behaviour of the centre. In this way the field becomes clear about what it can reasonably expect from the centre, and the centre becomes committed to providing them with the highest-quality services.

## 2.6 COMMITTEES DO BOARD WORK

When organizations grow beyond a certain size or degree of complexity, most boards find that they need to create groups such as sub-committees, advisory panels and task groups to take responsibility for some of the board's work. Organizations use different words to describe these sub-groups, so clarification of the language used in this book is required. The term **committee** is used as a generic word to cover sub-committees, advisory panels and task groups. The term **sub-committee** refers to a permanent committee of the board to which specific, on-going functions are delegated. Sub-committees take decisions and are accountable to the board for their actions.

The term **advisory panel** refers to a group established to advise the board on an on-going basis. This group has no decision-making power, though in some cases, such as medical research advisory panels, they can be very influential.

The term **task group** refers to a group established to carry out a specific job in a given timescale and to report back to the board. The task may either require actions (e.g., coordinate preparation of the strategic plan) or it may require investigation (e.g., report on the implications of a new piece of legislation).

As problems arise, boards create committees. In some organizations these groups in turn create another layer of sub-groups. They grow incrementally until the structure sometimes is of labyrinthine complexity. As their number grows, the work required to recruit people, service and support them increases proportionately. Before long, there is a risk that the annual cycle of meetings becomes the dominant management process in the organization.

Committees are important to the functioning of organizations. When working effectively they:

- increase the efficiency of the board by taking responsibility for defined areas of work
- allow representatives of different stakeholder groups (e.g., parents, musicians, special-interest groups, major donors) to present their views in a coherent way
- help the organization keep more closely in touch with service users. Members of the committee are the antennae of the organization, able to listen to the views at the front line and report back directly to the centre
- are an effective means of representing and consulting on people's views. They perform an important role in keeping people in different parts of the organization (for example, regions and branches) in touch with plans and current activities
- provide support, guidance and wisdom for staff responsible for delivering the services.

Despite their importance, committees can be problematic if they are not tightly managed:

- their precise role and purpose easily becomes confused
- they are sometimes given roles (for example, press relations, membership, or information) that are inappropriate and should be a staff responsibility

- the total number grows inexorably because there are always reasons to establish more of them. Nobody likes cutting them because it implies they are not doing a useful job
- the board may delegate responsibility but then proceed to discuss the issues all over again when the committee reports back
- committees expand their remits beyond their stated responsibilities and cause confusion about who is responsible for what
- over time, sub-committees in particular grow larger, their deliberations grow longer but each member feels less personal accountability for the performance of their sub-committee
- committees can blur the direct line of accountability of the staff to the chief executive and then the board
- the cost of committees can exceed the value of the contribution they make to the organization in terms of the demands they make on staff to prepare reports and attend meetings and the travel and accommodation costs of members.

The objective of committees should be to add value to the organization in the same way as the board should add value. They need to be able to define their unique contribution to the enterprise and convince themselves and the board that the benefits which come from their committee are significant and are worth the costs of servicing it.

## Functions of committees

There are many reasons for establishing committees. Boards have limited time and need to delegate some board work. They may need specialist advice from groups of people with expertise in a small area of work. They may have particular problems that require detailed investigation in preparation for a board decision. These are legitimate roles for committees.

While there are undoubted advantages of committees there are also many dangers:

- establishing a committee can delay decision-taking
- too many committees can dilute the board's overview of the organization
- boards can abrogate their responsibilities and accept committee recommendations without challenge.

## Structure of committees

The overall structure of committees is a critical board issue. It has to be considered at two levels; first, the need for a coordinating executive committee and, second, the structure and functions of specialist committees.

Large boards that meet relatively infrequently usually appoint an executive committee (sometimes known as the management committee or by the rather quaint term Finance and General Purposes Committee). The board delegates specified responsibilities to this group to govern the organization in between its meetings. The executive committee may, in turn, appoint committees to delegate some of its work.

In this common arrangement the board needs to clarify:

- whether both groups should have a common chair (two chairs can lead to confusion and misunderstanding, but doing both jobs is a time-consuming task for one person and limits the number of people who will stand for the job)
- whether all the members of the executive committee should be members of the board (common membership simplifies matters, but it limits the opportunity for the executive committee to co-opt people with skills it requires)
- whether the chief executive reports to the board or the executive committee (it is usually a mixture of both, but it is worth clarifying where the buck stops to avoid problems)
- whether committees report to the board or the executive committee (it is often a mixture with some reporting to the board and some to the executive committee).

The next issue to consider is the structure of sub-committees. The theoretical options include structuring:

In practice most organizations have a mixture of all three types illustrated on page 65, the most common arrangement being one that matches the staff structure.

| By function | By service | By geography | By task |
| --- | --- | --- | --- |
| finance | education | Latin America | capital appeals |
| fundraising | social services | Africa | audit committee |
| personnel | research | Asia | board recruitment |

## OPTIONS FOR STRUCTURES AROUND EXECUTIVE COMMITTEES

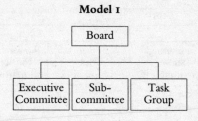

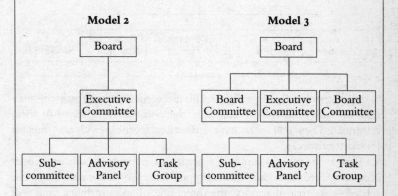

**Model 1** is suitable for a medium-sized organization that needs to delegate month-by-month work to an executive committee but also needs, for example, a specialist committee on professional standards or a working group on board member training.

**Model 2** would suit an organization with a large board that wishes to delegate most of its month-by-month work to an Executive Committee.

**Model 3** would be more appropriate for the largest and most complex organizations that have specialist problems at the board level (e.g., managing the election process) and need an executive committee which in turn finds it necessary to delegate part of its work to other committees.

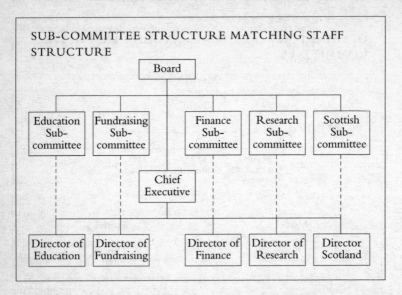

SUB-COMMITTEE STRUCTURE MATCHING STAFF STRUCTURE

In geographically dispersed organizations there may be sub-committees for each geographical area (e.g., the north-west, Scotland or Latin America). They will often have a direct relationship with the director for that territory.

This type of sub-committee structure presents a dilemma over accountability. Once there is a sub-committee which has a staff member related to its area of activity, the direct line of accountability from staff to the chief executive and then to the board is diluted. There is no straightforward solution to this dilemma. If the sub-committee is given a purely advisory role, and becomes an advisory panel, it can lose status. Members may feel it is less important to attend when they know that ultimately staff can ignore committee advice.

On the other hand if the sub-committee is given clear decision-making responsibility, the chief executive will inevitably become involved in its work to avoid his or her legitimate authority being challenged via the back door of the committee. Arrangements in which the sub-committee structure is a mirror of the staff structure are common but their roles need to be defined precisely and well understood. This needs to go beyond drawing lines on a chart which always over-simplifies a complex and subtle relationship. It needs a written description of the role and a thorough debate by members of the board and the sub-committee to ensure that all aspects of their roles are as clear as possible.

The best way to consider the committee structure is to work on the needs of the board for assistance with its governance role. Too often the committee structure is built on the 'wouldn't-it-be-a-good-idea-if – ?' approach, rather than pinpointing specific governance or representational roles that the board needs to delegate.

## Advisory panels

Advisory panels are essentially sub-committees without decision-making powers. They are useful when a board needs expert advice but does not wish to delegate responsibility for taking final decisions. Examples include medical research panels, which advise boards on spending research funds, and standards panels, which advise on professional or technical standards.

Recently some organizations, such as Save the Children, have reorganized some of their sub-committees into advisory panels to clarify the lines of accountability. Staff report to the chief executive who in turn reports to the council. Staff are advised by panels which bring wisdom, expertise and good judgement into the organization without allowing an alternative decision-making mechanism to emerge through the sub-committee structure.

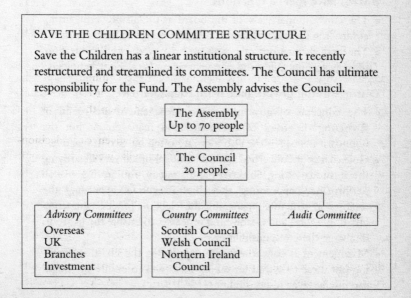

SAVE THE CHILDREN COMMITTEE STRUCTURE

Save the Children has a linear institutional structure. It recently restructured and streamlined its committees. The Council has ultimate responsibility for the Fund. The Assembly advises the Council.

The Assembly
Up to 70 people

The Council
20 people

| Advisory Committees | Country Committees | Audit Committee |
| --- | --- | --- |
| Overseas | Scottish Council | |
| UK | Welsh Council | |
| Branches | Northern Ireland | |
| Investment | Council | |

Advisory panels are appropriate when the board needs on-going advice over a period of years from a group that builds its experience over a long time horizon.

## Task groups

Task groups are groups established to resolve a well-defined problem within a given time frame. They are most effective at resolving very specific board-level problems. The board can set the group a brief, agree its membership and delegate the problem.

Task groups have the great advantage of flexibility. They can be created when required and disbanded when they have completed their work. Members are motivated by having a clearly articulated task to undertake within an agreed time frame. They have the satisfaction of completing specified tasks. Examples include purchasing new property, merging with another organization, recruiting a new chief executive, setting standards for work and overseeing a consultancy.

---

### SUMMARY OF KEY POINTS

**Boards have special functions**
- The conventional view of the board as the all-powerful group controlling the organization is often far removed from reality.
- The critical functions of boards are to govern the organization, provide accountability and resolve tensions between stakeholders.

**Distinguishing governance from management**
- The concepts of governance and management are useful in separating the roles of the board and management but the boundaries between the two ideas are often blurred in practice.
- Governance is concerned with the critical functions of clarifying the mission, setting objectives and strategy, monitoring overall performance, appointing the chief executive, approving the senior staff structure, managing the election process, inducting board members and establishing processes to enable the board to discharge these responsibilities.
- Management is concerned with supporting the board in carrying out these tasks and for taking initiatives to ensure the board can discharge its responsibilities.

## Life cycle of boards

- Boards go through phases of development, characterized as founding, youthful, adult, maturity and rejuvenation.
- They behave in different ways at each stage of their development.

## Key roles of an effective board

- An effective board is in partnership with the chief executive. It adds value to the organization, anticipates and shapes decisions and balances stakeholders' interests.
- Boards have roles concerning the work of the organization and roles concerning the board itself.
- Different constitutional arrangements for choosing board members lead to different types of board.
- The appropriate size of a board depends on the role it is required to perform.

## Impact of institutional structures on the board's role

- Institutional structures exist on a continuum between 'linear' and 'federal' structures.
- The critical tasks of governing each type of structure are different.
- Boards of federal organizations have to overcome lack of authority to introduce change by means of leadership, bargaining and the use of agreed rules.

## Committees do board work

- Boards establish committees to delegate board work, not to do management's tasks.
- Sub-committees, advisory panels and task groups each have different roles.
- Committee structures are best considered at different levels depending on:
  - the need for and functions of an executive committee
  - the functions and reporting lines of other committees.

# CHAPTER THREE

# Making Boards Govern

## 3.1 STRONG BOARDS ARE ESSENTIAL

Many chief executives will shudder at the notion of a strong board. Some believe that a strong board will only meddle with detail and create unnecessary work for staff. Some know that with a weak board they can manage the information it receives to achieve the outcome which they believe to be correct.

This is entirely logical in the context of a chief executive who has little knowledge about how strong boards work. But it is not appropriate for the demanding tasks organizations face today.

In the past, board membership was often treated as an honour or a duty. People saw it as something they did for the good of the organization and the wider community. Some viewed it as a hobby, others as light relief from the pressures of the office or an alternative to the chores of domestic life. Skills weren't seen as necessary – common sense and commitment were all that jobs required.

Nowadays, however, the task of managing value-led organizations is increasingly demanding. Over the last twenty years staff have become increasingly competent. Some managers have had a long career in the third sector and are highly talented. Sadly, many boards have not yet matched the dramatic rise in managers' capabilities. Some have neither strengthened their skills nor improved their performance.

Organizations need strong boards because:

1. They are legally responsible for the organization. Boards that understand their duties and responsibilities are better placed to carry them out efficiently.

2. They provide security and continuity to the organization, particularly at critical times such as the appointment of a new chief executive or the re-evaluation of strategy and direction.

3. A group of people is required to hold the chief executive accountable for his or her actions, to agree performance targets and, to conduct an annual performance review.

4. They need a group of people able to stand back from day-to-day operations and take a dispassionate view of the critical issues of:
   - the mission
   - the objectives
   - the allocation of resources to different purposes
   - the long-term financial security of the organization.

5. They need a body to monitor the organization's performance. In business, falling sales quickly tell managers that services are not meeting customers' requirements. Third-sector organizations either operate in the 'muted market' or have no paying customers at all. They need the board to keep staff alert to quality problems and to ensure that service-user interests are represented.

However, there is no one model of an ideal board. The way a board governs an organization depends on circumstances and the purpose of the organization. Organizations that have one purpose and work in one location or with one group of people are considerably more straightforward to govern than those that provide services and campaign, those with many outposts and those supporting different user groups.

The complexity of the board's work also depends on the diversity of its funding sources. Organizations funded by a mixture of donations, grants and contracts are more complicated to govern than those that are primarily dependent on one source.

This chapter:

- explains the many pressures that lure boards into ineffectiveness
- describes how to attract appropriate people to board membership
- suggests actions to improve the operational effectiveness of boards
- demonstrates actions to increase committee effectiveness.

## 3.2 FORCES DRIVING BOARDS INTO INEFFECTIVENESS

Despite the pressing need for strong boards, the reality is that most boards are surrounded by pressures that lure them away from their essential tasks:

- board members are volunteers and are not necessarily chosen for their skills and experience in governing organizations
- boards are required by their constitution or by law to take decisions on a wide range of essentially managerial issues such as agreeing contracts and leases, approving the annual report, setting staff terms and conditions, disciplinary actions and so on
- strong chairs have their own view of the board's role and dominate proceedings
- board members with specific interests raise issues of detail at board meetings when other fora would be more appropriate
- cliques form around a particular issue and incrementally take over board meetings
- chief executives need the security of knowing that they have the board's support on certain issues, even though they may not really be board issues
- staff avoid difficult decisions and produce compelling arguments to justify why an issue should go to the board
- the values and beliefs of the board and staff gradually move in different directions to the point where they interfere with practical management of the organization
- chief executives under-perform so the board is obliged to intervene in ever-increasing detail
- genuine lack of understanding exists about what the board's role ought to be.

Even if the board is strong enough to stand up to these pressures, there are other potential difficulties. Chief executives are seldom given training in the task of managing a board professionally. It is assumed that they will be able to master the intricacies of a complex relationship without any support. People in their first chief-executive position face particular difficulties, since their previous staff positions may not have included managing committee relationships.

In other circumstances the chief executive has the skills, but the people on the board do not fit the task in hand. Organizations that have grown rapidly or have diversified into a number of different activities frequently have board members who do not have the skills needed in the new circumstances. Boards that do not pay attention to developing their membership may slip incrementally into having too many people who need to be moved into other roles. These people may be able to make their contribution in other ways – for example, by joining a specialist advisory committee or a task group that can use their particular talents. This creates space on the board to bring in people who have the skills needed to take the organization forward.

Recently some boards have attempted to overcome skill shortages by bringing expertise from other sectors to their governing body. With the right calibre of people, this has many advantages. It is not, however, without its own pitfalls:

- some talented managers fear that the third sector is so different that their normally confident approach becomes weak and half-hearted
- others preach business or public-sector gospel only to discover that their approach and, more often, their underlying beliefs and assumptions are different from those of the third sector.

Another common problem is that boards, quite appropriately, bring together people from different professions such as medicine, the social services, accountancy and the law. However, they all bring with them their own assumptions about how a board should work and about the nature and purpose of the organization (see Appendix 2). These assumptions can be very diverse and consequently lead to tension and sometimes heated debates. Unable to resolve their different approaches, the board finds it has no alternative but to slip into detailed managerial issues upon which members can agree.

Faced with these compelling pressures, it is not surprising that many boards find it difficult to lift themselves above the purely managerial role and become boards that govern their organizations.

## 3.3 ATTRACTING TALENTED PEOPLE

Organizations need to attract to their boards people who can make a contribution to the future of the organization.

Talented people, particularly those with board skills, are a scarce resource. They are in a position to choose which organizations they are willing to help. This choice will depend on whether the organization can satisfy their motives for joining a board. Boards therefore need to present themselves as well organized. They need to understand the motives of the people they want to persuade to join the board and be able to meet their needs. At the end of the day, these people will join the board only if they respect the organization, and believe that the board is well managed and that their contribution will make a significant difference to the organization.

In searching for the most talented people that the board thinks it can attract, the potential relationship can be seen as a trade in which individuals give their time in return for rewards that meet their needs. These needs will be a balance of their desires to:

- see the organization succeed (often born of personal convictions or circumstances)
- find an additional role in their life
- make new contacts
- have the prestige that is attached to board membership
- develop skills and enhance their career prospects.

Board membership can be strengthened if the board takes a systematic and energetic approach to recruiting new members. Boards that put little effort into this issue can end up with weak members who are unable to contribute effectively to governance. The recruitment, selection and election of board members should be just as professional as the procedures that organizations use to appoint staff.

The first step is to develop a structure that allows people to join the board in stages. For example, they may be expected to join a committee to learn about the organization before they can stand for election to the board. They may be co-opted on to the board for a limited period before deciding whether to stand for election, or they may sit in on meetings to gain a better understanding of the organization.

Second, boards should make all appointments time-limited. This prevents the board from going stale and allows people to leave the organization with dignity. For most organizations three years should be a minimum time to serve. Six to nine years should be a maximum time to serve before members are required to have a break of one year and then, if it is appropriate, rejoin the board.

Then there is a series of actions concerning recruitment. The application of these depends on the type of board (i.e., elected, selected, appointed or self-perpetuating), but the principles are similar for all types. Effective boards:

- agree the balance of skill and representation required (e.g., financial, legal, educational, service users, donors, political)
- prepare job descriptions setting out what the board expects of members filling different 'posts' on the board. This ensures that potential candidates have clear expectations of board members' duties and the time commitment required. It deters inappropriate people from standing
- require staff and board members or nominating organizations to make a concentrated effort to seek people with the desired skills and motives. Current board members meet them informally to explain what is expected of board members and give them a briefing paper concerning the expectations of people standing for board positions
- expect people who stand for election to meet the criteria set out in the job description.

A final consideration is to create a group of people who can work effectively together as a team. A board can have all the skills required, and represent all constituencies, but be so diverse that members are unable to work together. Requiring people to attend a number of board meetings as observers and to meet board members informally helps to ensure that the board gets people who can both challenge the *status quo* and also work as part of a team.

For boards that are **elected** by a mass membership or **selected** by a smaller group, the democratic process has to be allowed to prevail. This does not, however, mean leaving the choice of board membership purely to an election. Quite the reverse – it means that the democratic process needs to be professionally managed to ensure that:

- the membership ultimately has the freedom to choose the board it wants
- nominees are advised about the organization's expectations of board members
- the board ensures that the organization is governed by a group of people who have an appropriate balance of skills, experience, values and knowledge.

Action can be taken to create a strong elected board. Details of the roles that board members are expected to discharge should be widely publicized. Current skill and experience gaps that the board wishes to fill should be announced. Existing members should positively seek out people with the necessary skills and time and persuade them to stand.

## THE DILEMMA OF SKILL AND REPRESENTATION

'People with disabilities should be better represented on this board,' argued a board member of an organization established 'for' people with disabilities many years ago. 'We need to empower disabled people to determine their own future; at present we only have token representation on this board.'

'But the organization is financially complex now we offer six different services and have contracts with twenty-two local authorities,' said the chair. 'We need people with marketing, strategic-planning, financial and legal skills if we are to have a chance of surviving in the competitive market.'

'We may succeed in getting more contracts, but if we lose our authority as the voice of disabled people, the contracts won't be worth the paper they are written on,' said the disabled board member. 'Already there is one organization challenging our authority to represent our service users. More of our members will join them unless we make a clear commitment to having a majority of people with disabilities on this board.'

'You know we tried before, but we just couldn't find enough people with disabilities who were willing to serve and who had the business skills,' retorted the chair.

'But we didn't organize a systematic initiative to define what we are looking for, actively seek out the people with the skills we require and sell membership of this board as an opportunity not to be missed,' said the member. 'We all know there are people with disabilities who have more skills than some of us. We just need to be more proactive in making the transition to an organization "of" people with disabilities.'

**Organizations need to balance representation and specialist skills when appointing board members.**

Similarly, on **appointed boards** the chair can give details of the skills and commitment required to the funding bodies or government departments that appoint members to ensure that the organization gets the people it needs and not people who happen to be available.

On **self-perpetuating boards** there is a tendency to appoint friends and contacts rather than engage in a systematic search-and-selection process. These boards need to be aware of the risk of becoming stagnant. They need to put extra energy into the search-and-selection process. They should look particularly for people who will challenge the *status quo*. This may be uncomfortable but will often provide a more robust board, better able to anticipate the future demands of the organization and to seek new opportunities that were not seen by existing members.

Boards can also take actions to strengthen people's skills once they have been appointed or elected. New members need:

- induction – they should receive a briefing on the organization's work, make visits to front-line operations and be given descriptions of how the board and its sub-groups work
- a mentor – they should be linked to an experienced member whom they can ask questions
- an opportunity to attend one of the growing number of training courses offered to board members
- to acclimatize themselves to the values and vision of the organization by reading past papers and, where applicable, sitting in on management meetings as an observer.

Boards that take actions to strengthen their own membership are in a much better position to discharge their governance role than those that leave membership to the luck of the electoral draw.

## 3.4 INCREASING BOARD EFFECTIVENESS

As well as strengthening membership, boards can increase their effectiveness by improving their working methods. Responsibility for improving board effectiveness lies ultimately with the chair. The chair is better placed than anyone in the organization to ensure that the board is governing. However, it is a time-consuming task, particularly if board practices have become sloppy. Since chairs seldom have time, increasing board effectiveness is often a joint effort between the chair and the chief executive. This joint effort is similar to the work that the chief executive and senior management team do to develop the skills of paid management.

In most organizations today, management development is beginning to receive more attention and larger budget allocations. Governance development is equally important and needs to be given similar attention.

## RESEARCH INTO BOARD EFFECTIVENESS

Researchers have striven for many years to discover correlations between different structures and roles of boards and the effectiveness of the organizations they govern. This is extremely difficult because of the need for criteria to measure that elusive quality called effectiveness. Results from America, which should be treated with some caution, suggest:

- the proportion of business people on boards was either not significantly related to organizational performance, or the relationship was negative, based on research in the YMCA (Siciliano, 1990)
- there is a positive relationship between board involvement in strategic planning and organization performance (Bradshaw *et al.*, 1992)
- ratings of organizational effectiveness are positively related to the extent to which board members feel informed about their responsibilities and duties (Herman and Tulipana, 1985)
- chief executives who emphasize working with and through their board are more likely to be seen as effective (Herman and Heimovics, 1987)
- board structure accounts only for a small proportion of the variations between the performance of different organizations (Bradshaw *et al.*, 1992)
- boards are largely risk-averse and play a limited role, mostly as trustees rather than entrepreneurs (Austin, 1991).

## *Involve the chief executive*

Since chief executives play a significant role in governance development, they need to be given a clear mandate by the board to assist with this task. The board needs to put the subject on its agenda, establish the priorities for action and agree an annual programme of work setting out what has to be achieved and by when. This encourages and legitimizes the role of the chief executive when he or she may be reticent to become involved in governance development.

When the board is unaware that its performance is an impediment to the success of the organization, the chief executive will have to take the initiative in close cooperation with the chair. The conventional notion that the chief executive merely follows the board's instructions needs to be thrown out in these circumstances. Chief executives cannot give their best performance when the board is weak. Sometimes they have to challenge the board about its own behaviour in order to strengthen the organization's governance.

## Establish the right agenda

One of the quickest ways of increasing effectiveness is to gain control over the agenda. All too often items arrive on the agenda from many different sources and no one scrutinizes the resulting agenda before it is distributed. This usually leads to a managerially driven agenda rather than one set by the priorities of governance.

The agenda and preparation for meetings should not be driven by regular reports from each department. It needs to start with governance issues. These might include:

- specific achievements for the service-user group in the last period
- the overall allocation of resources to different service-user groups
- new policies that the organization needs to adopt
- political and campaigning initiatives required to raise the profile of the service-user group
- review of the chief executive's contract
- succession of the chair
- improvement of board procedures and board information systems.

Gaining a grip on the agenda means that every item that is a contender for board attention needs to pass through a fine sieve. The chair and chief executive must ask:

- Is this a fundamental issue for the organization?
- Does it have policy implications?
- Is it a priority for board time?

Another action that will improve board effectiveness is to focus each meeting on an in-depth resolution of a small number of critical issues rather than attempting to consider briefly a wide range of issues. All too often board meetings touch briefly on many aspects of the work because members enjoy hearing about details. Some detail is essential, but it should not squeeze out thorough discussion, debate and resolution of the few critical issues that need board attention.

This course of action may evolve into an annual cycle in which specific items are a particular priority at the appropriate time of the year. Such timetabled items might include:

- review of achievements
- review of the strategic plan
- budget-setting guidelines
- approval of the budget
- debriefing of departing members
- induction of new members.

Small actions can stop the board embroiling itself unintentionally in detail. Items for information only can be distributed separately from board-meeting papers. Many matters that legally require approval from the board can be grouped together. These may sound trivial matters but they are critical. They prevent well-intentioned board members from raising unimportant issues and taking up valuable board time. Every minute spent discussing a minor item is a minute not spent on the crucial activities of governance.

## Clarify the staff's role

Staff play an important role in the working of an effective board. They inform, guide and make recommendations to the board. But they need to be careful not to step over the boundary and infringe upon the board's legitimate role. This is common when the staff are themselves the inspiration and, sometimes, the founders of the organization. In these circumstances the staff may have found and 'appointed' board members (because they are a legal necessity). In these situations the board is likely to be comparatively weak. It needs to put extra care into defining and clarifying its role with the staff.

One of the best ways to keep a clear distinction between board and staff is to control staff attendance at board meetings. In many circumstances it is a mistake to have all senior managers in attendance throughout all board meetings. Their presence can inhibit the board; it is not particularly good use of their time; and it encourages confusion between board and staff roles. In the worst cases staff can end up dominating board meetings both by their numbers and by the extent of their interventions. When this happens a thorough appraisal of staff attendance at board meetings is needed.

Generally, the chief executive should attend all meetings. Staff should attend board meetings when requested by the chief executive. This may be because they have detailed information to report to the board, because an item that directly affects their area of work is to be discussed or because the chief executive wants the member of staff to learn about the board's work. Staff should assume that they will attend board meetings only when requested and that often this may be only for the item that affects their work.

One good practice, particularly where there is a high degree of trust between board and staff members, is to have an agenda item called 'private matters'. This gives the board regular opportunities to discuss confidential issues without any staff being present. It also provides an opportunity to discuss the chief executive's performance and for board members to raise issues in private. Often, when the meeting gets to the 'private matters' item, people relax a little, and important reflections and opinions are shared among members.

---

### THE ROLE-SWAP GAME

This is a powerful exercise that board members and senior staff can undertake together to clarify roles. It takes less than an hour and can be both illuminating and entertaining.

The board and the senior management team meet together in one room. The board gathers at one end of the room and imagines that it is the staff. It has twenty minutes to address the question 'What do we expect of an effective board?'

The staff meet at the other end of the room and imagine that they are the board. They address the question 'What do we expect of an effective senior management team?'

The two groups then meet together and report on their deliberations for twenty minutes. The final twenty minutes should be spent agreeing the changes that need to happen for each to meet the expectations of the other.

It is remarkable what high expectations can be established when one group stands in the shoes of the other.

If boards adopt this practice, there should always be a commitment that the chair will brief the chief executive on the discussion immediately after the meeting, to ensure that mutual trust is maintained.

One problem with weak boards is that they can end up in conflict with the staff. The combination of misunderstandings about roles, differences of opinion on issues and poorly communicated decisions can lead to a break-down of trust. This needs swift and concerted attention. Both staff and board will need to put significant time into joint activities, including getting agreement on the mission and strategy, clarifying roles and building relationships.

## Making the chair–chief executive relationship work

A constructive working relationship between the chair and the chief executive is another essential ingredient of an effective board. It is the critical link between the work of the staff and governance by the board. A weak link leads to growing confusion over the distinctive roles of the staff and the board. A strong link ensures that both the board and the staff can be provided with effective leadership.

Among the many roles that chairs play in organizations, there are four activities for which they should see themselves accountable:

1. **The chair is the figurehead.** The chair has to represent the organization on key public occasions.
2. **The chair is responsible for the performance of the board.** Although this duty is discharged in conjunction with the chief executive, the chair is ultimately accountable for the quality of governance of the organization.
3. **The chair is usually the chief executive's line manager.** Although chief executives are appointed by the board, they need someone to act as a sounding board, to evaluate their work and to provide them with support. The chief executive has the most challenging role in the organization and requires a large amount of wise counsel and good advice. Chief executives need guidance about priorities and support in dealing with difficult management issues (e.g., under-performing managers). Good chairs will be the primary source of this support or will explicitly delegate the task to someone else.
4. **Chairs manage the boundary between staff and board.** The chair has a duty to protect staff from over-enthusiastic board members who become too involved in detailed managerial issues.

Experience demonstrates that there is no clear dividing line between the functions of the chair and the chief executive. Sometimes one will represent the organization and sometimes the other. Sometimes one will play a greater role in managing the board and sometimes the other. The best partnerships build upon the strengths of each individual. Both parties agree how the areas of overlap should be divided between them, whenever possible playing to each other's strengths.

Chairs and chief executives who want to work together well invest time in developing their relationship. They

- meet regularly
- talk openly
- agree expectations of each other
- plan work programmes together.

One common problem is when the chair has an office at the organization's headquarters or visits the office very frequently. The chair's efforts are often entirely well meant but being 'in the office' almost always blurs the roles of the chair and the chief executive. It can be very frustrating for the chief executive to have the chair too closely involved in the detail, and it can result in the chair not being able to retain a detached overview of the organization. It should almost always be avoided.

Another common problem arises when a new chief executive is appointed by a weak and ineffective board. The board may not have the resources to improve its own performance, but the chief executive will not have earned the authority to take the initiative on this issue. In these circumstances chief executives should bide their time, working in a series of calculated steps to strengthen the membership of the board and thus to develop a board that can govern the organization effectively. Catalysing the appointment of a strong chair is undoubtedly a good starting-point.

In circumstances where there is a weak board and a weak chief executive most organizations will sooner or later face a crisis. It may well be an unanticipated event that precipitates the crisis, such as the loss of a source of funding, the sacking of a member of staff or public criticism of the organization. In these circumstances external assistance is usually required because there is not a strong enough foundation on which to start building the future of the organization.

A SUCCESSFUL RELATIONSHIP

Watching the chair and chief executive of a national housing association work together I noticed:

- the chief executive went out of her way to ensure the chair was always kept informed of major developments by copying papers and talking regularly on the phone
- the chair always defended the chief executive in meetings and had a private discussion if problems needed to be resolved
- they met one month before the quarterly board meetings to agree the agenda and the papers needed at the meeting
- the annual performance review was a two-way discussion in which each reviewed the performance of the other
- they had dinner together at least twice a year to review progress and problems in an informal setting.

## Review the board's performance

At least once a year the board should review its own performance. Board members are often embarrassed about engaging in such discussion. There is sometimes an implicit assumption that the board's performance is something that shouldn't be discussed. However, it provides a structured setting for reviewing successes and problems and setting an agenda of actions to improve board performance in the future. An annual away-day provides an appropriate setting for such discussion. It should:

- review the performance of the board and its committees against agreed lists of governance responsibilities
  (a) for the work of the organization
  (b) for the work of the board
- confirm that members have attended the agreed minimum number of meetings to qualify for continued membership of the board
- identify areas for improvement
- agree a package of actions needed to implement improvements and the criteria for monitoring those improvements at the next annual review.

External assistance can be helpful when reviewing board performance. Research has shown that when groups review their performance without external input they are less harsh than others involved in the organization or independent external consultants believe they should be. An independent input from someone who is not a member of the board encourages consideration of difficult issues such as the performance of the chair or other officers. A third party is also invaluable when the board is split on a fundamental issue. When difficult matters are left to fester unresolved, the resulting tensions often spill over into other board discussions. The independent person can be used to see both sides in a dispassionate way and to develop new perspectives on the problems. Members can then either unite around a new solution or at least release tension through open discussion.

To get to a position where the board is in command but not involved in the detail takes time and effort. It requires that members are agreed both on the mission and objectives of the organization and on the way the board should work. This does not imply that board members are weak and compliant. On the most effective boards, members will challenge and question enthusiastically and persistently. Their questions will, however, come in appropriate ways, at appropriate times, and will be informed by a broad understanding of the way the board works.

## 3.5 INCREASING COMMITTEE EFFECTIVENESS

Actions needed to increase committee effectiveness are similar to those required to increase board effectiveness. However, committees are even more prone to falling into bad habits. Three common problems are lack of leadership by the committee chair, excessively large committees and poor-quality paperwork. This section shows how they can be overcome.

**Leadership** by committee chairs is an essential ingredient of effective committees. People respond to committee chairs who take the initiative to define the committee's work programme, prepare relevant agendas for meetings and ensure that staff write top-quality papers.

Good chairs involve everyone in the discussion but take the initiative when the time comes for decisions. They delegate work to members to free up their own time for the leadership function. They are clear about the committee's role and strive to ensure that it makes a significant contribution to the work of the organization and, in particular, of the board.

**Size** is the second determinant of committee effectiveness. If a committee is too small, it may have insufficient expertise to be effective. If it is too large, meetings become protracted and each member feels less personally responsible for the committee's effectiveness.

The correct size depends on the function of the committee. A committee that exists to advise the board on medical research may need to have ten or more members to reflect different disciplines. The audit committee, by comparison, may need just two or three members to check that proper financial management and audit procedures are in place.

There are many pressures that push boards into creating committees that are too large:

- many people would like to be involved
- some feel they will miss out on important decisions if they are not members
- there are always good justifications for bringing someone extra on the committee
- no one likes to say 'no' when members volunteer to give their time to a committee.

These pressures need to be resisted. When a committee grows too large, its effectiveness falls. Meetings take longer; more staff time is consumed; and members become frustrated with the lack of progress.

**Paperwork** is the third component of an effective committee. Effective committees have agendas that are short and prioritized and maintain the boundaries of committee and staff responsibilities. They plan their agendas ahead and do not allow their work to be hijacked by parochial concerns.

They also expect high-quality paperwork from staff. The chair can play an important role here by insisting that papers are short, focused, labelled 'for decision', 'for discussion' or 'for information' and include both a succinct summary and a clear articulation of options. Anticipation is once again essential, since a committee faced with a poor paper feels obliged to untangle the issues rather than send it back for improvement. The chair should generally agree the agenda before it is distributed and, when paperwork is a problem, should ask to see draft papers as well.

The outside world often sees third-sector committee meetings as cumbersome, inefficient, opportunities to reward time-serving members and expenses-paid trips for people who have nothing better to do with their time. While there is sometimes more than a grain of truth in this perception, there is no doubt that third-sector organizations need more committees than their private-sector counterparts. Committees do solve problems – they bring free expertise into the organization, they provide a training ground for potential board members, they represent user views, they provide funders with confidence and they can be a source of good judgement for the organization.

When they are not well managed they delay decisions, consume valuable staff time and make effective governance difficult. When they work well they embody the very essence of third-sector organizations – people working together voluntarily to achieve an important mission.

---

## SUMMARY OF KEY POINTS

### Strong boards are essential

- Board membership used to be an honour. Today it is a demanding task requiring specific competencies and skills.
- Strong boards are needed:
  - to provide the organization with security and continuity
  - to hold the chief executive accountable
  - to provide a long-term perspective
  - to monitor overall performance.

### Forces driving boards into ineffectiveness

- Boards are surrounded by forces that lure them into ineffectiveness and need to be resisted.
- Chief executives may need help to learn how to manage board matters professionally.

### Attracting talented people

- Talented board members are a scarce resource, so boards need to be energetic and systematic in searching for them.
- Procedures for recruiting and electing potential board members should be as rigorous as those for staff recruitment.
- The processes and priorities are different for elected, selected, appointed and self-perpetuating boards.

### Increasing board effectiveness

- Effectiveness is the chair's responsibility, often discharged jointly with the chief executive.
- Together they need to:
  - establish the right agendas
  - clarify the staff's role
  - work on their relationship with each other
  - ensure that the board reviews its own performance.

### Increasing committee effectiveness

- The essential ingredients of committee effectiveness are:
  - leadership by the chair
  - making the size of committee appropriate for the task
  - ensuring that staff produce top-quality paperwork.

CHAPTER FOUR

# Concepts for Managing the Strategy

## 4.1 THE STRATEGIC MANAGEMENT PROCESS

The next four chapters are all about the management of value-led organizations. They describe functions that are driven primarily by paid management, within boundaries and policies prescribed by the board. This chapter deals with the concepts required to manage strategy, and the next describes their implementation. The third of this group of chapters covers the essential processes required to manage organizations, and the fourth describes how to structure management.

In reality the boundaries between these topics are far less clear than they appear in the pages of a book. In particular the separation of over-all, or corporate, strategy (Chapters 4 and 5) from the process of creating strategies for individual services (Chapter 6) is far less distinct in practice than in the theory.

Strategy is particularly important in value-led organizations because they are always coalitions of people with different aspirations that need to be integrated for the organization to thrive. In recent years a bewildering number of ideas have been developed by management gurus to help people understand organizations and manage them more effectively. Management by objectives, critical success factors, zero-base budgeting, scenario planning, total quality management, corporate culture, business process re-engineering and even catastrophe theory are among almost 200 strategic management concepts recognized by the Strategic Planning Society. In practice, a coherent philosophy for managing strategy in value-led organizations can be derived from the three concepts of mission, objectives and strategy. These combine to form the notion of strategic management.

The essential components of strategic management are concerned with the creation of a clear view throughout the organization of its mission and objectives and the development of strategies and plans that lead to their achievement.

At first sight this sounds obvious. The ideas of mission, objectives and strategy have been used by the military for thousands of years, by business for almost a hundred years and, more recently, by the public sector as well.

However, many value-led organizations do not apply these three notions continuously at all levels of their organization. Some may have worked on them in the past, but since then staff may have left, new board members may have been elected and external circumstances may have changed. They may have forgotten the importance of strategic management or allowed parts of the organization to become sloppy in its application.

Sometimes the daily pressures on managers attempting to undertake complex tasks with limited resources can combine to put strategic management at the bottom of managers' agenda. The sheer volume and variety of tasks people are expected to undertake can be enormous: requests to meet funders, responding to press inquiries, politicians needing briefs, coordinating with other agencies, motivating volunteers, management meetings, regional conferences. Together these all divert managers' attention from the five critical questions:

- What specifically does our organization want to achieve in the next few years?
- How should we allocate resources between our different objectives?
- What quality standards should we aim to achieve?
- What have we learned from past experiences?
- What improvements are required to enable us to make better use of our resources?

This chapter unravels the essential components of strategic management:

- the mission – the fundamental purpose of the organization
- the objectives – statements about what the organization wishes to achieve in a given time frame
- the strategies – a description of how human and financial resources will be applied to achieve the stated objectives.

The notion of strategic management is completed with the concept of performance monitoring. This provides the feedback loop for reviewing corporate achievements against objectives. The performance-monitoring process is described in section 6.7 along with other management processes.

These concepts can be linked together into an overview of strategic management.

According to Johnson and Scholes (*Exploring Corporate Strategy*, Prentice Hall, 1993), the characteristic that distinguishes strategic management from other aspects of management is that it is complex in nature. Three facets contribute to this complexity.

Strategic management:

- usually involves **a high degree of uncertainty** – it requires people to make judgements about the future when information is only partial
- requires an **integrated** approach – thinking has to cross the functional boundaries (such as fundraising, service delivery, personnel)
- involves **major change** – it invariably challenges the values and power of particular groups in the organization.

## Strategic management links funders and service users

Strategic management is a powerful tool because it provides an **intellectual connection** between funders and service users. In the private sector the competitive pressures of the market place drive organizations to think strategically in order to survive. This pressure is weak in third-sector organizations because funders have only partial information about the service or the campaign. Strategic management provides the discipline to assess users' needs, orchestrate resources to meet those needs and monitor the outcomes.

Strategic management is also a **mechanism for building coalitions** around new priorities. The process of analysing needs, setting new objectives and agreeing new strategies can be both motivating and uni-fying. Strategic management provides a structure within which disparate views can be brought together into a shared vision of the future of the organization.

Some organizations are currently being given greater strategic free-dom than they had in the past. Schools have more control over their budgets and are seeing opportunities to use their buildings, facilities and staff in evenings and vacation time; universities are engaging in joint ventures with business to exploit new research findings; arts organiza-tions are seeking contracts with health authorities to exploit the thera-peutic effects of music and visual arts. Such diversification increases the need for organizations to **develop new conceptions** of themselves and to revise their view of their purpose.

Other organizations are losing strategic freedom as the proportion of their funds from contracts and other statutory sources continues to grow. Moreover, these funders are specifying the services they want in ever-increasing detail. These organizations need to grasp strategic man-agement to help find ways to maintain or **increase their independence**.

Strategic management is a powerful tool, but it cannot be separated from the values held by people in the organization. Consequently, developing an understanding of strategic management needs to begin by looking at the ideas of vision and mission.

## 4.2 THE MEANING OF MISSION

Before introducing the concept of mission, the distinction between **vision** and **mission** needs to be unravelled. The word 'vision' is used in many different ways. It is most usefully thought of as a desirable future situation. Visions are likely to be articulated with language such as 'We want a world in which . . .' They express a view of what the organiza-tion ultimately wants to achieve, knowing that it is unlikely to achieve it on its own.

Third-sector organizations need to have visions of the way they want the world to be. They are a powerful motivating influence on people. In terms of setting future direction a vision is often more effective than any number of environmental analyses or strategic plans.

Vision alone, however, is not an alternative to a strategy. Founders and leaders often bring vision, insight and enthusiasm to organizations. However, the vision always needs to be supported by sound analysis to confirm that it is realistic and achievable.

Missions are concerned more with an organization's **common beliefs** and the **reasons why it exists**. People who work in third-sector organizations are usually motivated by a deeply held desire to help change society. Consequently most third-sector organizations have a strong sense of mission. Christian Churches use the word 'mission' to describe their work; charity people often talk about 'our mission'; and people who work in hospitals know their mission is to make sick people healthy.

As a result, the missions of many organizations are implicit. They are part of the accepted beliefs which are often not discussed or written down. Most third-sector organizations begin with a missionary zeal that doesn't need to be made explicit. At the end of the first national meeting of parents who had children with cerebral palsy, the chairman slapped a £5 note on the table and said dramatically, 'I want this to be £5 million within five years.' The mission was clear: parents wanted a significant increase in services and were going to raise the money to establish new services. The Spastics Society, now called SCOPE, was created and this first mission was successfully achieved.

Third-sector organizations often have a much stronger sense of mission than their counterparts in the private and public sectors. Campaigning organizations and membership organizations that are championing a cause have a particularly strong sense of mission. Service-giving organizations that were set up by people with a disease or disability maintain a strong sense of mission for many years.

In contrast, intermediary bodies (such as the National Council for Voluntary Organizations), quasi-autonomous non-governmental organizations (such as the Health Education Authority) and government-inspired organizations (such as Training and Enterprise Councils) find it more difficult to develop a compelling mission. They still need one, but it may never be as powerful as the missionary zeal of organizations championing a cause.

In short, vision is concerned with the organization's ultimate objective, and mission is concerned with the reason why the organization exists. The concepts of vision and mission undoubtedly overlap, and the distinction between them is fine. Some organizations find the concept of mission sufficient: others make the distinction.

## VISION AND MISSION OF THE ROYAL NATIONAL INSTITUTE FOR THE BLIND

During 1993 the Royal National Institute for the Blind undertook a fundamental review of its achievements and went on to develop a new long-term strategy. This strategy was rooted in a vision of the place of visually impaired people in the world and a mission for the Institute.

### Vision

RNIB wants a world in which people with a visual impairment enjoy the same rights, freedoms, responsibilities and quality of life as people who are fully sighted.

### Mission

Our mission is to challenge blindness. We challenge the disabling effects of blindness by providing services to help people determine their own lives. We challenge society's actions, attitudes and assumptions. Many barriers are put in the path of people with a visual impairment – our task is to help dismantle them. And we challenge the underlying causes of blindness by helping to prevent, cure or alleviate it.

## *What is mission?*

The idea of mission has two essential components. The first element of mission is the **common values** held by people in the organization. People working in schools share many deeply held beliefs about the importance of education; people working in campaigning organizations share a passionate desire to achieve their campaign objectives. The first component of the mission is therefore a reflection of the values of the organization. (For a more detailed review of values and organization culture, see Appendix 2.)

Second, the mission is the organization's *raison d'être*. It explains why the organization exists and who benefits from it. From this perspective the mission is the intellectual rationale for the organization.

Mission is therefore concerned with both **hearts and minds**: the beliefs that come from the heart and the rationale that comes from the mind. All organizations have missions, even though they are often implicit and sometimes contradictory.

The concept of the mission should not be confused with the idea of a mission statement. The mission statement is a set of words that encapsulates some elements of the mission. It often states what some people want the organization to be and is sometimes a list of good intentions dreamed up by senior management.

Mission statements have an important role to play, particularly when it comes to reviewing future strategy. They need to be written and agreed, but their power as a management tool should not be over-emphasized. By contrast, working on the mission and taking actions to bring together the beliefs in the organization with its strategy can be a powerful lever for increasing the organization's effectiveness.

## THE ASHRIDGE MISSION MODEL

Research at Ashridge Strategic Management Centre led to the development of the idea that organizations need a 'sense of mission'. This notion of mission has four components.

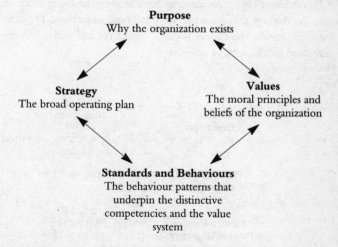

**Purpose**
Why the organization exists

**Strategy**
The broad operating plan

**Values**
The moral principles and
beliefs of the organization

**Standards and Behaviours**
The behaviour patterns that
underpin the distinctive
competencies and the value
system

Adapted from A. Campbell *et al.*, *A Sense of Mission*, Hutchinson Business Books, 1990.

## 4.3 THE HIERARCHY OF OBJECTIVES

> Alice: Which way should I go?
> Cat: That depends on where you're going.
> Alice: I don't know where I'm going!
> Cat: Then it doesn't matter which way you go!

*Through the Looking Glass*, Lewis Carroll, 1872.

The hierarchy of objectives is the second essential strategic management concept.

Objectives are statements of the aims and purposes of the organization. They can be both qualitative and quantified. They help to focus different parts of the organization on achieving the mission. They concentrate people's attention and guide their actions.

Organizations need objectives at every level of operation, from the board to front-line service providers. The notion of a hierarchy of objectives is therefore a useful way of organizing long-term strategic objectives, more specific medium-term objectives and very precise short-term objectives.

A hierarchy of objectives can also be related to the layers of an organization. At the top there are precise but broad objectives. Departments of the organization need more focused objectives and individual services require very specific objectives.

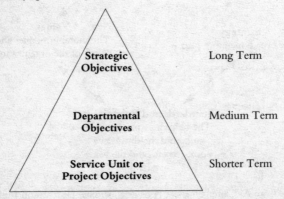

| | |
|---|---|
| **Strategic Objectives** | Long Term |
| **Departmental Objectives** | Medium Term |
| **Service Unit or Project Objectives** | Shorter Term |

Typically organizations will need a few strategic objectives, more departmental objectives and a larger number of service-unit objectives.

## Strategic objectives

Strategic objectives focus the organization on achieving those things that are most critical to its success. They should not be well-meant statements of good intentions that trip easily off the tongue. They should be words that focus and guide people's actions.

Strategic objectives are generally few in number. Between three and six provides a good discipline to force an organization to identify the most critical issues but allows for the diversity that is an essential ingredient of most third-sector organizations.

Even with this number an element of conflict between objectives is unavoidable. Most arts organizations want to present challenging works but also want large audiences. Aid agencies want to maximize their

---

NATIONAL ASTHMA CAMPAIGN STRATEGIC
OBJECTIVES 1992–1996

The National Asthma Campaign is a highly successful
organization that resulted from the merger of a medical research
charity and an organization of people with asthma. Following the
merger a five-year strategic plan was drawn up which included
the following strategic objectives:

1. to continue to fund a growing, purposeful and coordinated
   programme of research into the causes, treatments and effects
   of asthma
2. to act on the knowledge gained through research to reduce
   prevalence and mortality
3. to improve asthma diagnosis and the organization of care
4. to strengthen the education of health professionals, people with
   asthma and the lay public about the causes, treatment and
   effects of asthma so that treatment is more effective and the
   quality of life of people with asthma is improved
5. to expand National Asthma Campaign membership and the
   branch network and respond to the needs of the membership
6. to campaign within the UK for more government resources to
   improve asthma management.

## OBJECTIVES OF THE EDUCATION AND TRAINING DIVISION

The Royal National Institute for the Blind agreed a five-year corporate strategy (in line with the vision and mission described earlier) with four over-arching priorities:

- to challenge blindness by raising awareness and tackling discrimination
- to extend services to more blind and partially sighted people
- to increase the priority given to older blind and partially sighted people
- to improve the quality of service to users and supporters.

The Education and Training Division then reviewed its objectives so that its priorities could be adjusted to meet the new corporate objectives. It established aims under five headings:

- early identification and assessment
- information and support to parents
- education services
- staff development
- learning resources.

Within each heading it established between one and three specific aims – for example, to ensure that all visually impaired infants are identified at the earliest possible stage, their needs are effectively assessed and the services and support that they and their families need are provided.

Then within each of these broad aims it agreed a series of more specific objectives for the Division – for example:

- to develop a database of all visually impaired children and their families
- to develop an effective way of delivering materials to parents, including those from ethnic minorities.

income with dramatic appeals during emergencies, but do not want to devalue the pride of hard-working people who are struggling to survive in difficult circumstances.

Although strategic objectives have a long time horizon, they should not be seen as being entirely fixed. Circumstances do change. Some objectives are achieved. Others become a greater priority. Strategic objectives are therefore a tool to concentrate people's attention on specific goals that the organization as a whole wants to achieve at a particular point in time.

## *Departmental objectives*

Departmental objectives tend to be more specific and easier to quantify and to have a wide range of time horizons. Clearly they need to fit within the strategic objectives.

Ideally departmental objectives should be SMART – Specific, Measurable, Actionable, Realistic and Timetabled. This mnemonic is a useful quality check on proposed objectives.

## *Service-delivery unit, project and campaign objectives*

These are even more specific and will almost always be quantified. Service-delivery units are the lowest level of the organization at which people and money can be managed to produce a desired result. They are defined more fully in section 4.6. They can have long-, medium- and shorter-term objectives – their own hierarchy within the overall scheme. They ought to be very SMART.

## *Internal objectives*

Many organizations also find it useful to distinguish between external and internal objectives. External objectives relate very specifically to the organization's mission and the tasks it is trying to achieve. Internal objectives, on the other hand, are concerned primarily with building the capacity of the organization to achieve the external objectives. Internal objectives typically fall into five categories:

- **strengthening the governing board** – for example, implementing a new induction scheme, improving working relationships with staff

- **human resources** – for example, developing a staff-supervision process, creating management–development programmes
- **investing in management information systems** – for example, improving financial-management systems, developing performance indicators, investing in information technology
- **investing in plant and buildings** – for example, purchasing new equipment, renovating offices
- **fundraising** – for example, developing the public profile, marketing the cause and establishing the systems for raising money.

The value of clear objectives cannot be overstated. Once the objectives are clear, managers need to develop the strategies to achieve them.

---

## OBJECTIVES OF OUTWARD BOUND TRUST

Towards the end of the 1980s Outward Bound Trust agreed a strategic plan with six strategic objectives:

**External objectives**
- increase student numbers from 11,000 to 14,000 per annum within three years
- reverse the long-term decline in the open enrolment courses and add 1,000 new students per annum within three years
- improve the economics of the trust by producing a financial surplus of 12 per cent on income in three years' time.

**Internal objectives**
- upgrade the quality of physical facilities by investing £4 million in renovation and new buildings over the next five years
- introduce quality audits to monitor the quality of all courses
- introduce a research-and-development function to improve the content of wilderness courses and encourage new experimental initiatives.

## 4.4 STRATEGY EVOLVES

Strategies are broad categories of action that indicate how human, financial and other resources will be deployed to achieve agreed objectives. They draw people's attention to a limited number of ideas that enable them to fit the practical activities of the organization into a context. They also provide a rationale that explains how resources will be allocated to different objectives or activities.

In today's demanding environment managers have to work within a strategy. The days of just performing a functional or operational task have gone. Managers need to have a clear concept of how their work fits into the overall strategy of the organization. They need to anticipate relevant changes in the external environment and to develop appropriate responses.

The idea of creating explicit strategies has become popular in the third sector in recent years because organizations have had to respond to more rapid changes in their external environments. They have consequently needed more explicit means of setting new objectives and reallocating resources. They have also had to demonstrate to funders precisely what will be achieved with their money.

Strategy is not static. It changes with time, influenced by circumstances and people. Strategy evolves in three ways. First, it is an **incremental process**. It usually changes in a series of small steps. New ideas are tested. Experience is gained before major new strategies are agreed. Organizations reduce the risks inherent in any new idea by experimenting, learning from the results and modifying proposals as they are developed. Consequently, strategy should not be seen as something that happens only when the strategic plan is produced.

The evolution of strategy is also a **political process**. Strategy results from a process of bargaining, negotiation and trade-off between people with competing interests in the organization. Powerful individuals and groups therefore have a strong influence over an organization's strategy. How they view an issue may be more relevant than the factual accuracy of their arguments. Consequently, strategy is therefore not only the result of dispassionate analysis – it is more often a reflection of the power and influence of different stakeholders.

Finally, strategy is the result of an **analytical process**. From this perspective, strategy emerges from a systematic and logical analysis of the organization's environment and its current activities. This leads to

## POLITICS AND STRATEGY

The National Orchestra faced many competing demands when it began to think about future development:

- the musicians wanted good pay and opportunities to play new and challenging pieces of music
- the education department wanted more musicians to support their community music schemes in schools
- the fundraisers wanted a popular programme of events to attract corporate sponsors
- the board wanted high-profile public events to increase the status of the orchestra
- the conductor wanted more rehearsal time to increase the quality of performances.

Endless attempts at strategic planning failed to solve the problem. These competing demands on money and musicians' time had to be resolved through negotiation and agreement.

the establishment of new objectives and strategies, which usually take the form of a strategic plan. Although planning is an essential element of managing third-sector organizations, the analytical approach to the evolution of strategy needs to be seen as only one of the three processes that determine strategy.

## Strategy is required at many levels

Most organizations deliver more than one service. Some deliver many services to the same service-user group (for example, the professional association that sets standards for the profession and also promotes members' services). Others deliver different services to different groups (for example, the medical charity that funds research and provides patient care).

Just as there is a hierarchy of objectives, strategy is also required at a number of levels. In a smaller organization strategy may operate at two levels. There will be an overall strategy for the organization as a whole and separate strategies for each service or each service-user group.

Large organizations that are divided into different operational divisions may require strategy at three levels:

- overall strategy (explained below)
- divisional strategy (explained in Chapter 5)
- service-level strategy (explained in Chapter 6).

The overall strategy in both large and small organizations is concerned with the boundaries of the service-user group, the range of services to be offered and the allocation of resources between them. The divisional strategy is concerned with the strategy for a group of services and the service-level strategy is concerned with the objectives and performance of individual services.

## 4.5 STRATEGIC REVIEWS, POSITIONS AND CHOICES

The management of strategy can be divided into five basic elements:

These are shown as a diamond to emphasize that developing strategy is not a linear process. Although there is a logical sequence to reviewing the organization, considering alternative ways forward and developing an implementation plan, most of the time all the processes are going on simultaneously, each continuously informing the others. The concepts are explained here, and application is described in the next chapter.

### *Strategic review*

Reviewing strategy is a process of monitoring changes in the external environment and developments within the organization to gain a deeper understanding of the organization's strategic position. It may involve reviewing the mission, the objectives or the strategies the organization is pursuing or a combination of all three.

The process involves collecting data about the way the world around the organization is changing and assessing the impact of these changes. Although organizations are often swamped with data, key strategic information is frequently not collected or not available in an appropriate format to give clear insights into past achievements and key external trends. In the worst cases, people are so committed to the cause that they deliberately avoid collecting hard data.

The aim of reviewing strategy is to concentrate people's attention on the strategically significant trends – those few things that are '**driving change**'. From an improved understanding of the organization's strategic position managers can identify the key strategic issues that need to be given attention.

Reviewing strategy is best conceived as a continuous process that is supplemented by periodic in-depth research. It is not just an exercise that leads to a new review report once every few years. These formal reviews help people to learn about the underlying trends influencing an organization's strategy, but they are not a substitute for developing information systems that keep managers continuously abreast of changing circumstances.

The external part of the strategic review needs to provide data on:

- social and economic trends directly relevant to the organization and its objectives
- political trends (e.g., growth of higher education, European legislation)
- technological developments (e.g., for helping people with disabilities to communicate)

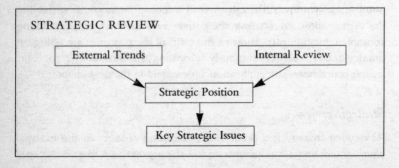

STRATEGIC REVIEW

External Trends → Strategic Position ← Internal Review

Strategic Position → Key Strategic Issues

- trends in funding sources and methods (e.g., contracting)
- demographics of the service-user group and its changing needs (e.g., demand for different types of services)
- cultural trends (e.g., user-centred service delivery, empowering people with disabilities, opportunities for women in management)
- strategic developments in other organizations that exist for similar purposes (e.g., new competition for funds or service users).

The internal part needs to provide information on:

- the overall portfolio of services and campaigns and their general nature (e.g., trends in the number of people assisted, campaign successes and why they were achieved, dependency of services on particular income sources)
- the subsidy each service is receiving from donations that have not been given to a particular service or campaign and that management can allocate as it wishes
- the human, physical and financial resource base
- intangible resources (e.g., reputation, contacts, goodwill).

Reviews invariably generate a great deal of information. The key is to distil the data and focus on the information that is most pertinent to the future development of the organization. These are the data that need to be monitored on an on-going basis.

## Developing insights into strategic position

Strategic position sets the organization or the service in its environmental context. It draws together the information from the internal and external reviews to produce a summary of the situation. There are a number of techniques that can be used to enhance understanding of the strategic position of an organization or a service. These may sound rather elaborate, but in practice their greatest use is as thinking tools that help people to look at the review from different perspectives.

**Gap analysis** is a method of focusing attention on service users' needs. It involves preparing an assessment of service users' needs and comparing these with services currently available. This can be done by means of a survey of users, by talking with other providers or by seeking views from knowledgeable people inside or outside the organization. The aim is to make judgements that help to identify the most pressing

## GAPS IN SERVICES FOR PEOPLE WITH AIDS

Provision of services for people with HIV and AIDS grew rapidly in the mid and late 1980s as central and local government provided funds for a wide range of entrepreneurial initiatives established by voluntary organizations.

By the early 1990s it was unclear what the greatest unmet needs of people with HIV and AIDS were and which services required additional funding. Interviews with providers and funders led to the conclusions that:

- in London the most pressing gaps for the 2,100 people with AIDS and 19,000 HIV-positive people were for:
  - residential care
  - home support
  - drop-in centres
  - transport to service providers
  - welfare rights and housing advice

- outside London gaps in services for the 500 people with AIDS and 4,600 HIV-positive people varied within the seven cities where the largest numbers of people with AIDS lived. The only common gap was for terminal care services.

unmet needs of service users and therefore to point to areas where new services are required or existing services need to be expanded.

**Competitor analysis** is a technique used to compare an organization or a service with similar providers. It is likely to become more useful as third-sector organizations are forced to compete for contracts, donations and service users. It is used to compare the services, funding and costs of different providers and to pinpoint areas for improvement and development. Data can be obtained from annual reports and people with knowledge of other providers such as funders and service users.

**Value-for-money-analysis** is a method of comparing the benefits of different services to service users with the cost and, more specifically, the subsidy that needs to be found from fundraising or other sources to provide the service. This involves calculating the subsidy required to provide each service and dividing this by the number of service users

## COMPARING COSTS AND BENEFITS

An organization of people with disabilities carried out a review of the cost of services that yielded the following figures:

|  | Income £'000 | Expenditure £'000 | Subsidy £'000 | Users | Unit subsidy |
|---|---|---|---|---|---|
| Helpline | 15 | 55 | 40 | 2,000 | £20 |
| Holiday service | – | 25 | 25 | 2,500 | £10 |
| Residential care | 100 | 120 | 20 | 10 | £2,000 |
| Employment advice | 50 | 60 | 10 | 400 | £25 |
| Equipment loan | 10 | 25 | 15 | 500 | £30 |

As a result of the review the board agreed a strategy of :

- expanding employment advice because it was providing excellent value for money
- reducing the holiday service because similar holidays were available from other charities at a lower cost
- negotiating increased fees from local authorities to reduce the unit subsidy of the residential care home.

to give unit subsidy figures. These can then be compared with people's judgements about the importance of each service. This does not mean that services with higher subsidies are less valuable, but it does help to pinpoint the cost of expanding each service and the savings to be made from reducing them.

**SWOT** is a well-known mnemonic that is used to compare the strengths, weaknesses, opportunities and threats of an organization or of particular services. The aim is to produce a one-page summary of the organization's strategic position. It can be a useful way of summarizing data obtained from a strategic review. It is often used as a group brainstorming technique. This is more problematic, particularly when it is based primarily on the opinions of group members. There is a real danger of producing a series of platitudes that masquerade as a piece of rigorous work.

KEY ISSUES FOR HOUSING 21

Housing 21, formerly the Royal British Legion Housing Association, provides rented accommodation for 13,000 people. Following a strategic review, the organization concluded that it faced five critical strategic questions.

- Should it continue to focus on housing for active elderly people, or should it provide for other groups as well?
- Should it maintain its focus on sheltered housing, or should it provide a care and repair service to enable people to stay in their own homes?
- Should it offer housing for rent only, or should it offer shared ownership as well?
- Should it maintain its current stock or adapt some properties for frail elderly people?
- Should it develop profit-seeking housing ventures to finance subsidized housing?

## Identification of key strategic issues

Having gained an understanding of an organization's strategic position, the final step of a review is to distil all the learning into a set of key issues that need to be addressed. These are the limited number of critical factors that it is thought will determine the long-term success of the organization. This is one of the most important stages in the process. It provides the foundation upon which to build the strategic plan.

## Strategic choice

The process of strategic review identifies key issues. It may highlight new needs among service users, new or better ways of meeting needs, new threats such as changing funding arrangements or competition from other suppliers. The priorities may initially seem daunting. There is too much to do, and there are too few resources to do it. So governing boards and managers need to make choices.

Most organizations do not make explicit choices most of the time. Some, quite rightly, thrive on opportunism. The third sector is known for its ability to produce social innovations. New ideas and new funding

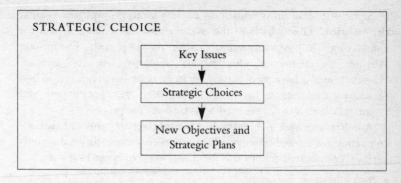

STRATEGIC CHOICE

Key Issues

Strategic Choices

New Objectives and
Strategic Plans

sources drive the organizations' strategy in a series of unplanned and incremental steps. In these organizations opportunism is a critical ingredient of a successful strategy. Nevertheless, the organization that is driven exclusively by opportunism risks becoming a hostage to external funders. Forced to pursue only those things for which it can raise money, an organization exposes its future to the whim of its funders. By comparison, organizations which gain control over their strategy begin to determine their own future.

Lacking the discipline of the bottom line, third-sector organizations frequently compromise when it comes to strategic choice. In part this is necessary – the diverse constituencies are often held together by giving a little to all the contributors. But too much compromise is dangerous. The organization that steps incrementally from focusing on a few key objectives to a brief so wide that it ends up doing a little of everything risks not doing anything particularly well.

A common mistake is to rewrite the strategy in such general terms that everyone can agree to it. This avoids imposing difficult choices, but it greatly reduces the value of the strategic management process.

## Concepts for making strategic choice more rigorous

Making choices about priorities will always involve making judgements based on experience and evidence. Every option will have benefits for the people whom the organization serves or the campaign objectives it wishes to achieve. The problem is one of weighing the benefits against the costs and the risks of pursuing different strategies. The process needs to be structured to encourage rigorous debate and sound decisions. A number of techniques can be used to assist organizations to make strategic choices.

Some organizations systematically **review strategic options against the mission**. Going back to the mission provides a rational basis for considering which of various priorities are most important. The mission provides the framework for rational discussion of the options. However, as we have seen already, strategy is an iterative process, and sometimes the mission has to be changed to incorporate new and important objectives. So the method is far from foolproof.

Another approach is to **attach a weighting** to proposals that are competing for limited resources. Line managers putting forward a number of proposals are asked to rate them according to criteria such as:

- critical strategic importance
- important but not essential
- pursue when funds available.

This exercise can be carried out twice, once for projects requiring capital funding and once for projects requiring revenue funding.

A similar approach involves identifying the different audiences that the organization is trying to influence and assessing the **potential impact** of different services and campaigns. To do this people are asked to give a 'more-stars-the-better' rating to the questions:

- What is our potential impact on this group?
- What is our current impact on this group?
- To what extent do the proposals increase our impact on the audience?

Another frequently used method is **scheduling**. This is similar to weighting methods in that those projects that have a higher priority are scheduled to take place before those with a lower priority. Scheduling is useful because it allows management to say that one project or initiative needs to happen before another. Furthermore it confronts people with the fact that financial and managerial resources are limited and choices have to be made.

Finally, as the market for funding becomes more competitive, some business techniques are becoming more appropriate. Organizations can compare themselves with other organizations receiving funds from the same sources. They can ask what their **distinctiveness** will be in future when compared with their competitors. They may be better placed to become a low-cost/high-volume supplier of the service or, alternatively, to become a niche provider servicing a carefully targeted service-user group. These considerations then influence the choice of projects and initiatives to pursue.

Before choices are finally made organizations can **test strategic choices**. One test is to consult relevant stakeholder groups and seek their reactions to the proposed choices. Another test is to analyse the sensitivity of particular projects to changing assumptions, looking, for example, at the implications of the loss of grant funding or the impact of new government regulations. The economic sensitivity of proposals to different assumptions can be tested by looking at the financial effects of growing or declining demand for a service.

In practice, making strategic choices will always be a highly judgemental process. Techniques help to structure the problem, but ultimately they cannot replace experience and wisdom.

## 4.6 THE DEFINITION OF SERVICES AND CAMPAIGNS

One further concept needs to be introduced in this first chapter on strategy. Most organizations deliver a range of interconnected services, often to the same user group. A prerequisite for developing strategies for these services is the definition of exactly what constitutes a service. Defining services requires careful thought. The very nature of services with social objectives is that the problems they attempt to address are multi-faceted:

- organizations for homeless people may provide a roof over people's heads, but they soon discover that the underlying problems many homeless people face may be medical or psychological, lack of skills or the need for a job
- disability organizations start providing services for people with disabilities but soon discover that the attitudes of able-bodied people are a greater obstacle to improving their lives.

Consequently the nature of the services offered tends to evolve. When a housing association uses existing staff to offer residents benefit advice or employment training and other 'foyer' services, these are initially inseparable from the housing service. But when they become significant activities, perhaps with their own staff and top-up funding, they may need to be considered as separate services. Similarly, when orchestral musicians do a few school workshops to drum up interest in a particular locality, they are inseparable from its main purpose. When the orchestra is selling its school education service to local authorities and using significant amounts of players' time, this eventually becomes a separate service.

The idea of distinct services is central to strategic management. Only when the services have been separated in people's minds can each develop a strategy to pursue specific objectives. Without this distinction it quickly becomes impossible to manage services efficiently, and everything becomes a tangle of activity without a clear logic to drive management and decision-taking.

Defining services is a matter of judgement. Individual managers cannot cope with the separate management of more than a limited number of services, so excessive subdivision is not helpful. Conversely, failing to distinguish between different activities that may be expanding or declining at different rates, or, more important, that may be consuming different amounts of subsidy, can be dangerous.

An approach I frequently use is to think about separate **service delivery units**. The concept is analogous with the idea of strategic business units in the private sector. Companies that produce a number of products for different customer groups in different parts of the world have strategic business units that cut across traditional, functional or geographical management structures to encourage managers to focus on customers and their needs. The concept also builds on the idea of a project centre or cost centre, but it is concerned with management of the strategy and services of the unit as well as its income and expenditure.

An activity can be considered as a service delivery unit only if it:

- has a clearly defined service-user group
- has specified objectives to be achieved for or with the service users
- can plan a strategy and deploy the resources needed to achieve the objectives
- can monitor achievements against plans
- has financial management information that sets out income and expenditure of the unit and the subsidy required to run the service
- has a manager who is responsible (either part- or full-time) for planning, delivering and monitoring the service.

To create a service delivery unit, managers have to define the service offered and to identify the staff who provide the service, the income it attracts and the expenditure it incurs. This is not always straightforward because staff sometimes work on many services, funding may be given for a variety of purposes and the accounts system may not be able to separate out the relevant costs. Staff time is a particular difficulty because people in third-sector organizations may feel uncomfortable about recording how they allocate their time.

A similar problem arises with campaigns. An environmental organization, for example, may be campaigning for the protection of wildlife, but it needs to clarify whether its marine ecosystems campaign and its habitat protection initiative are separate activities with their own budgets, managers and staff or both part of one strategic initiative.

---

### TROUBLE AT THE ENTREPRENEURIAL COLLEGE

For many years a college provided higher-education courses for students, paid for by student fees and grant funding. Over five years a number of entrepreneurial departments started providing contract courses for major local employers. Much of the course material was similar, and the contract courses often used facilities when students were away. As far as lecturers were concerned, they were providing 'more of the same'.

Using these new contacts with industry, some lecturers also developed a number of research contracts for local businesses, which, although time-consuming, were thought to engender good relations with local employers.

During the recession a fall in income led to a great debate about whether to cut expenditure, to seek more students, to offer more contract courses or to bid for more research contracts.

The debate raged for months and wasn't resolved until the college recognized that it had three entirely separate services:

- open enrolment courses for 16–25-year-olds
- contract courses for local employers
- research for industry.

Only when they began to separate out the three groups being served, the staff time and the income and expenditure attributable to each service could they begin to build a strategy for the future of each service.

Nevertheless, the concept of service delivery units is a powerful idea that helps to divide complex operations into manageable units. Each unit and each potential new unit becomes a building block in the development of the overall strategy.

## SUMMARY OF KEY POINTS

### The strategic management process

- The essential components of strategic management are concerned with clarifying the mission, the overall objectives and the strategies for achieving them.
- Systematically monitoring overall performance provides the feedback loop.
- Strategic management provides the intellectual connection between service users, campaigns and funders.

### The meaning of mission

- Visions express a view of what the organization ultimately wants to achieve.
- Missions are concerned with common beliefs and the reasons why the organization exists.
- Working to strengthen an organization's mission has more leverage than the preparation of a mission statement.

### The hierarchy of objectives

- Objectives exist in a hierarchy related to layers of the organization.
- Strategic objectives are few in number; departmental and service unit objectives are increasingly specific.
- Most organizations have external and internal objectives.

### Strategy evolves

- Strategies are broad categories of actions that indicate how human, financial and other resources will be deployed to achieve the agreed objectives.
- Strategy evolves in three ways – as an incremental process, as a political process and as an analytical process.

### Strategic reviews, positions and choices

- Strategic reviews gather data on internal and external trends, summarize the organization's strategic position and identify the key issues that the strategic plan needs to address.
- Different techniques can be used to develop insights into strategic position, to identify key issues and to make choices between alternative strategies.

### Definition of services and campaigns

- The notion of service delivery units helps to distinguish separate services.
- A service delivery unit has to have:
  - a defined user group
  - its own objectives and strategy
  - financial information to control income and expenditure
  - a manager to plan, deliver and monitor the service.

# CHAPTER FIVE

# Making Organizations Work Strategically

## 5.1 CHOOSING WHERE TO START

Strategic management is one of the most satisfying aspects of management. People find it motivating to be involved in setting the organization's long-term plans and priorities. They enjoy seeing more clearly how the organization fits into its environment. At the end of a long session on strategy people are often fired up to strive to achieve more ambitious targets or to work together in ways that are more effective.

The benefits of improved strategic management are immense:

- everyone becomes clearer about objectives and how they fit into the wider task of the organization as a whole
- it leads to more effective use of resources
- it is an ideal way of building commitment and motivation
- diverse constituencies can be brought together around a common purpose.

The role of the chief executive in strategic management is crucial. Choosing which issues to work on, why to work on them and how to approach them are central tasks for her or him.

This chapter demonstrates how to make organizations more strategic in their management and operation.

However, before starting to work on an organization's strategy, the board, the chief executive and senior management need to consider where their overall priorities lie. The essential components of the overall management of organizations include:

- strategic management (described here)
- the management processes (Chapter 6)
- the management structure (Chapter 7)
- the governing arrangements (Chapters 2 and 3).

Although all could no doubt be improved, choices have to be made about priorities. In many situations it can be counter-productive to attempt to make fundamental changes in more than one area at any one time. Major changes in the management structure can put work on the strategy seriously off-course because people become more interested in their position in the organization than in a dispassionate debate about strategy. Changing the governing structure at the same time as the management structure may open potentially difficult alliances among board and staff members threatened by changes. Improving management processes is problematic if a significant number of management posts remain unfilled.

The problem is an elaboration of the thorny old issue of whether the strategy should determine the structure or whether a new structure is needed to establish a new strategy. The answer always depends on circumstances and on board and senior-management judgements about the critical obstacles to the organization's development.

More often than not, organizations do not make explicit choices about these alternatives. Many slip into working on more than one without reviewing where their priorities should lie. However, if having reviewed the situation, the board and senior management decide that development of the organization's ability to work strategically is the most pressing problem, the first step is to decide which aspect of strategic management needs attention. Most books, including this one, present strategic management as a top-down process, starting with the mission and moving down through objectives to strategy, to action and, finally, closing the loop with performance monitoring. It is easy to think of it in this way, but in practice all the elements are changing simultaneously.

The first step in starting to work on strategic management is therefore to decide whether to focus time and effort on

- the mission
- the objectives
- the strategy
- the operational plans
- the performance-monitoring process.

The choice depends on which will produce the greatest benefits.

Sometimes the overall strategy is reasonably clear, but departments do not have detailed annual plans to encourage concise thinking about the specific activities that require time and attention. In other situations, the plans are well established, but there is no explicit process for reviewing achievements against the original intentions.

This chapter focuses on how to strengthen and clarify the mission, how to establish the objectives and how to determine the overall strategy. The next chapter looks at the corporate management processes that are needed to run an organization once the mission, objectives and overall strategy are agreed.

## 5.2 DEVELOPING THE MISSION

The idea of working on the organization's mission has recently come into vogue in the business world, and some of the enthusiasm has spilled over into the third sector. However, before rushing into following this business vogue it is worth remembering that many third-sector organizations understand mission far better than business precisely because most were created in order to achieve a mission. The charity created by a founder with vision and determination to improve services for people with disabilities, the trade union established by people who were being exploited and the foundation set up by the wealthy industrialist to respond to a particular human emergency are all organizations with mission in their very bones. Although the passage of time may have dulled that sense of mission, it is seldom difficult to rekindle the flame.

Organizations are more effective when they have a strong sense of mission. It is a powerful motivator that helps people to make sense of the organization. It ensures that people are clear in an abstract way about the overall direction of the organization and it encourages people to strive to achieve the organization's purpose. The mission integrates the organization's values with its strategy. In organizations with a clear mission there is a consistency between people's beliefs and the organization's strategy.

The mission therefore needs to be worked on:

- when the organization's purpose and *raison d'être* have become woolly and unfocused
- when the organization has become directionless and lacks a sense of its own distinctive competences
- when the motivation of the board, the staff and other supporters is low.

One essential prerequisite for creating a strong sense of mission is having a group of people on the board and among the staff who share similar aspirations and are willing to work together to make things happen.

---

## THE MISSION OF THE MEDICAL CHARITY

This organization existed to help people with a terminal neuromuscular disorder. It aimed both to raise funds for medical research and to provide care and support for people with the disease. The board included eminent medical researchers, senior social workers and people with the disorder.

One third of the board believed that the organization existed primarily to fund medical research and agreed grudgingly to fund care for people with the disorder. One third believed the organization should focus on helping social services departments to provide better care and felt that medical research was expensive and making little progress. One third felt that the organization should provide direct care itself because it knew best the particular problems that people with the disability and their families faced.

Not surprisingly, staff were very confused about the organization's purpose. Morale was low, and a great deal of time and effort was wasted on arguing about the allocation of resources to different activities.

To overcome the problem the board and senior staff held two special workshops to clarify the organization's mission at a neutral venue and with an outside consultant. They began to find common ground when it was agreed that, above everything else, they shared a common desire to help people with the disorder. They acknowledged to each other that the medical professionals, the social-work professionals and the volunteers all had distinctive contributions to make. They also agreed that close cooperation between these groups would yield more benefit for people with the disorder than working separately for the same cause. Finally they agreed a formula for allocating resources to different activities.

The mission was clarified, enthusiasm grew, arguments declined and the organization began to thrive again.

Another prerequisite to creating a sense of mission is continuity on the board, among members of the senior management team and in particular of the chief executive. It takes time to understand the fundamental beliefs of an organization and to see the varied ways in which the beliefs connect with the strategy. Particularly in larger organizations, it takes time for key individuals to become known and to be seen to be acting in ways that are consistent with the mission.

The board is ultimately responsible for managing the mission, but it needs to involve staff, members and sometimes service users as well in a joint effort to agree and strengthen the mission.

Management needs to construct a process, which can last for a few months in a small organization and for many months in a larger body. Relevant stakeholders need to know when and how they can make their contribution. The process may start with a board discussion, or it may start in lots of places and culminate with a board session that draws together the various strands needed to renew the organization's sense of mission.

Although it is tempting for the chief executive or senior management to draft a mission statement 'to give people something to chew on', this focuses the process on the wording of the mission statement rather than on creating a deeper understanding of the values and beliefs that underpin the organization's mission.

Debates about the future mission of the organization should aim to:

1. Define the purpose of the organization at the most fundamental and general level. This can involve asking seemingly simple questions about why the organization exists, who it exists for and what at the most basic level it aims to achieve.
2. Identify the core values and beliefs that the future of the organization can be built upon. Asking questions about what the organization stands for, what its philosophy is and what position it takes on the central issues of concern can help to clarify values and beliefs.
3. Clarify distinctive features and competencies. Identification of characteristics that distinguish the organization from others in the same field can help to develop a better understanding of an organization's special qualities. Similarly, looking at specific competencies can provide a useful perspective.

## THE MISSION OF VOLUNTARY SERVICE OVERSEAS

Following extensive debate, VSO defined its mission as follows:

### Purpose

VSO enables men and women to work alongside people in poorer countries in order to share skills, build capabilities and promote international understanding and action in the pursuit of a more equitable world.

### Values

- VSO values the individual and believes in the equal right of all to realize their potential
- VSO believes in countering disadvantage by practical action, person to person
- VSO values action motivated by and responding to the needs of others, both through their work abroad and through voluntary activity by supporters at home
- VSO values and respects diversity of culture
- VSO values two-way partnership that openly shares costs and benefits
- VSO values the learning and friendship which result from people living and working alongside each other in pursuit of shared goals.

### Features

VSO volunteers are men and women who easily relate to VSO's purpose. They share their skills and experience in ways that are sensitive to the cultural values of others. They receive a modest living allowance for their work. On their return, volunteers can help to inform attitudes that will support action in pursuit of a more equitable world.

Volunteers help individuals build greater independence and capabilities through teaching and training as well as by sharing ideas and different ways of working. Volunteers readily acknowledge how much they learn from the experience.

The two-way exchange of VSO work results in a strong, long-lasting relationship between people and cultures. It promotes international understanding – extending to the families, friends and colleagues of individual volunteers.

VSO is an independent charity. We rely heavily on the talents, commitment and generosity of supporters.

Developing the mission can be undertaken as part of a strategic planning process, or it can be a separate management initiative. It often results in statements that sound worthy and are easy to be cynical about. However, organizations that have ironed out common misunderstandings between people on the fundamental issues are undoubtedly more effective and more satisfying to work for than those that leave such issues unresolved.

Once broad agreement among key people has been achieved, continuous effort is needed to build commitment to the mission. The larger the organization, the greater is the effort required.

Once the mission has been clarified, effort is required to keep it alive and relevant to everyone's work. Annual general meetings can be turned into workshops that celebrate achievements and plan future developments. Regional meetings can be actively supported by senior headquarters staff. Branch chairs and directors can be encouraged to communicate regularly with the central office and can be brought together once a year to seek their views and discuss future developments. Managers can draw staff attention to the links between the mission and the daily grind of activities. They can remind people how their work is part of achieving the mission. Volunteers can be invited in to be thanked for their support and to be briefed and consulted on future plans. These are the actions that give an organization vibrancy, clarity of purpose and a sense of mission.

## Preparing mission statements

Mission statements are one way of documenting the outcome of an organization's effort to strengthen the mission. The preparation of a mission statement is a useful tool when a new board or management team needs to establish their beliefs and start understanding each other. However, the team should recognize that the greatest value of a statement accrues to those people who have been involved in its development. Management teams that have spent countless hours arguing about each word in the mission statement, in the belief that it will be a powerful tool for improving organization effectiveness, are usually disappointed. The carefully crafted copy sent down with a memorandum from the chief executive usually has the opposite to the desired effect. It promotes cynicism and a view that senior management doesn't know how to make good use of its time. People who have not been involved will see it as little more than well-intentioned advertising.

Nevertheless, mission statements are one way of communicating the organization's purpose to staff, volunteers, funders and the outside world. They need to evolve and be the object of widespread consultation. Senior management should coordinate the exercise and seek to involve as many people as possible in the process.

The content of a mission statement should ideally reflect both the organization's intent and its values. It needs to say something more than the strap-line on a logo or letterhead, while remaining simple and easy to communicate. Some organizations separate out their values statements. Others incorporate them into the mission.

Guy Kawasaki argues in *Selling the Dream* (HarperCollins, 1991) that good mission statements should have three qualities. They should be:

- **short** and easy to understand
- **flexible** so that they last for a long time
- **distinctive** in order to differentiate the organization from others.

---

### THE OUTWARD BOUND MISSION

Outward Bound impels people into adventurous personal-development experiences that are designed to meet the rapidly changing needs of our society.

We will pursue this mission, in the tradition of Outward Bound, by:

- offering challenge and enjoyment in supportive residential communities
- expecting tenacity in pursuit of the highest individual endeavour
- maintaining a commitment to the concept of service in the community
- encouraging team-working and the acceptance of responsibility for others
- using dramatic experiences to stimulate discussion, reflection and critical appraisal
- encouraging people to establish for themselves a renewed sense of value and purpose in life.

## THE AUTOMOBILE ASSOCIATION MISSION

**Our vision**
To make AA membership truly irresistible.

**Our mission**
To be the UK's leading and most successful motoring and personal assistance organization.

**Our values**
Courtesy and care for all our members and customers
Our people, and their skills
Our image of integrity and independence
Quality and value for money in all our services and products
Our business partners.

## THE GUIDE ASSOCIATION MISSION

Its purpose is to enable girls to mature into confident, capable and caring women determined, as individuals, to realize their potential in their career, home and personal life and willing, as citizens, to contribute to their community and the wider world.

## LONDON BUSINESS SCHOOL

To be a world leader in helping individuals and organizations enhance their managerial effectiveness.

To do so by pursuing a balanced excellence that links theory to practice in teaching and research that are innovative, rigorous and relevant to international, career-long learning.

## BARNARDOS

**Mission**
Working together to challenge disadvantage and create opportunity.

**Basis**
Barnardo's is an association whose inspiration and values derive from the Christian faith. These values, enriched and shared by many people of other faiths and philosophies, provide the basis of our work with children and young people, their families and communities.

**Values**
Respecting the unique worth of every person
Encouraging people to fulfil their potential
Working with hope
Exercising responsible stewardship.

## WORLD-WIDE FUND FOR NATURE

WWF's mission is to achieve the conservation of nature and ecological processes by:

- preserving genetic, species, and eco-system diversity
- ensuring that the use of renewable natural resources is sustainable now and in the longer term for the benefit of all life on Earth
- promoting actions to reduce to a minimum pollution and the wasteful exploitation and consumption of resources and energy.

WWF's ultimate goal is to stop, and eventually reverse, the accelerating degradation of our planet's natural environment and to help build a future in which humans live in harmony with nature.

THE PRINCE'S YOUTH BUSINESS TRUST

To help young people who would not otherwise have the
opportunity to develop their self-confidence, achieve economic
independence, fulfil their ambitions and contribute to the
community through the medium of self-employment.

## 5.3  CLARIFYING STRATEGIC OBJECTIVES

Clarifying strategic objectives is a management task that requires continuous attention. Managers need to ensure that:

- people affected are involved in agreeing them (usually the broader the
  objective, the more people need to be involved)
- they are as specific as possible, particularly in fields where it is easy to
  avoid being precise, such as arts organizations, aid agencies and
  Churches
- they are communicated to board, staff and volunteers
- they are regularly reviewed.

Most organizations are pursuing a number of strategic objectives
simultaneously, so there may be an element of contradiction between
different objectives. Organizations are coalitions of people with different
aspirations, so they need to reflect their range of interests without
producing objectives that are so general that they are of little practical
use.

THE FUNDRAISER'S DILEMMA

'Our objective is to increase fundraising income by 10 per cent
per annum above inflation,' said the Fundraising Director of the
aid agency. 'To achieve this ambitious target we need to highlight
the desperate plight of poor people. Pictures of starving children
will form the centrepiece of a new hard-hitting campaign to
change complacent attitudes,' she continued. 'My aim is to bring
in new money and give the field staff more resources for their
work.'

'My objective is to change the public attitudes and policies in developed countries because they are some of the causes of poverty,' replied the Director of Campaigns. 'People don't want us to portray them as poor and helpless. They are proud and honourable. Their problems are caused by exploitation by banks, local élites and middlemen. Hard-hitting campaigns might raise more money, but they will only increase the sense of dependency of poor people of the South on the rich people of the North. I think we should be tackling the root cause of poverty – not just addressing the symptoms.'

'But if I can't use the most effective fundraising method, you'll have to accept less money for your campaign,' retorted the Fundraising Director. 'I can't achieve the fundraising target if you tie my hands behind my back.'

## Setting strategic objectives

Strategic objectives are usually developed as part of the process of developing proposals for a strategic plan. The strategic review will have identified the key issues to address, so the proposals for addressing them will all need to begin with a statement of the strategic objectives.

The process of establishing any objective is iterative, starting with an individual or a group and evolving as different people help to refine the thinking. Strategic objectives usually go through many drafts before the most effective way of casting and communicating the ideas is discovered.

### STRATEGIC OBJECTIVES FOR RELATE – NATIONAL MARRIAGE GUIDANCE

After much discussion and debate, 'RELATE 2000', the organization's strategic plan, established six priority objectives for the agency, which together aimed to increase the number of clients the agency saw and the quality of the services that they received.

1. Implement a standard intake and assessment system to enable quick, appropriate and effective responses to clients' needs.

2. Develop career patterns for paid and voluntary counsellors, other practitioners and managers involving training, new work opportunities and clear contracts.

3. Create a network of payments for service at all levels for training, practising, supervising and managing to allow each activity to respond to changes in demand.

4. Establish a research and evaluation programme to monitor the effectiveness of the services and to speak with authority on family and social-policy issues.

5. Strengthen the supervisory networks to underpin quality and respond to varying needs.

6. Build an integrated and participative approach to management to ensure that the ambitious programme of change is well coordinated and sensitively implemented.

Each of these objectives was accompanied by a strategy and a timetable for implementation.

## Checking the quality of strategic objectives

Clear strategic objectives help to focus everyone on the task. Check that:

1. They are realistic – not wildly ambitious. Most organizations have limited resources and limited management capacity, yet the scope of the problems they are attempting to address is huge. It is always tempting to adopt objectives that far exceed the organization's resources. Having realistic objectives and achieving them is always more motivating than failing to achieve unrealistic objectives.

2. They are as specific as possible. It is easy to produce any number of generalized statements of good intentions but much more difficult to find the concepts and words that clearly fit with the mission and are seen as being practical by front-line staff.

3. They are not gratuitous. Strategic objectives are sometimes accepted because people are afraid to say no. A number of people may have hobby-horses or views that are not shared by everyone else. It is always tempting to add their objectives to the list. Managers should aim to gain agreement on the few objectives that are critical. Being disciplined will help focus people and avoid the 'all things to all people' accusation.

Getting strategic objectives right is ultimately a matter for directors' and managers' professional judgement. Unfocused ones need clarification, ambitious ones need tempering, irrelevant ones need to be dropped. Effective managers spend time on strategic objectives and strive to keep them clear and appropriate.

## 5.4 DEVELOPING STRATEGY

Most organizations need a structured process for periodically revisiting their longer-term strategy. They need to build an understanding, among board members, managers and staff, of the recent history of the organization and its desired future development.

The process of strategic planning is a powerful tool for uniting the board, the senior management team and staff behind a shared conception of future plans and priorities. It can re-ignite the mission and motivate staff to focus their contribution more sharply on new priorities. It enables senior management to concentrate resources on achieving agreed outcomes rather than dissipating them over many activities. This section is about the process of developing an overall strategy for the organization. The process may include working on the mission and will always involve the establishment of new objectives. Planning strategy for individual services is covered in section 6.2.

Strategic planning has had a very chequered history. (See, for example, H. Mintzberg, *The Rise and Fall of Strategic Planning*, 1994.) Originating in attempts by the corporate sector to produce ten-year plans in the 1960s and 1970s, it migrated to the third sector in the 1980s. More often than not, strategic planning promised more than it could deliver. Massive effort was put into preparing plans involving endless meetings and drafts of lengthy documents. With a huge sigh of relief, plans were approved by the board and then consigned to everyone's bookcase or filing cabinet. Within a year or two the plan would either have been forgotten or be so out of date as to render it irrelevant. People rightly became cynical about the whole idea.

However, people working in an organization do require a clear understanding of its objectives and strategies. Third-sector organizations, in particular, have fuzzy boundaries and countless opportunities to drift away from their primary purpose. They are working in an increasingly

## COMMON OBJECTIONS TO PLANNING

'We need a strategic plan to guide our development over the next five years,' said the recently appointed chief executive.

'There's no point,' said the head of services. 'I've been here for ten years, and the one thing I've learned is that you can't predict the future.'

'We can't predict everything,' agreed the chief executive, 'but many of the changes that will affect us, such as community care, contracting and local–government reorganization, have been agreed. We need to anticipate how we will respond to them.'

'But even if we anticipate change, plans always depend on increasing funding,' said the head of services. 'Planning is an academic exercise until we know where new funding will come from.'

'My experience is that we will raise the money only if we know what we want it for,' said the chief executive, recognizing that he was on to a good argument.

'Well, my experience is that we need to be flexible, able to adapt to new circumstances and not be constrained by the straitjacket of a plan,' said the head of services.

'That's true, but I don't see the plan as being fixed forever. It is a route map, and if circumstances change, we can adjust our plan. It will enable us to see clearly the implications of making these changes,' retorted the increasingly frustrated chief executive.

'This argument illustrates the very point I want to make,' said the head of services, sensing victory. 'Planning will raise too many tensions that are better kept beneath the surface. If we can't agree on the need for a plan we certainly won't agree on its contents.'

**The need for planning must be widely accepted for it to be a useful tool.**

turbulent environment and need to review their purposes and priorities more frequently than in the past.

The old type of corporate planning process, therefore, needs to be replaced with something that establishes broad directions and specific targets but does not attempt to tie them all down in detail. The process needs to give a framework within which people can develop detailed plans for individual services. It needs to establish priorities and overall timescales. It needs to be developed more quickly than corporate plans were prepared in the past; it needs a shorter time horizon; and it needs to be reviewed more frequently. Early corporate plans had a ten-year time horizon. This may be necessary, for example, in organizations with major building or capital programmes. But for many others the time horizon has fallen consistently, first to five years then to three years.

It also needs to be reviewed more frequently. A major review of strategy used to be on the agenda every five years. Now major reviews often happen every three years and sometimes every second year. Organizations working in more rapidly changing environments need more regular reviews than those in more stable environments.

In today's turbulent times planning should be regarded as a process of learning and discovery. It should aim to help people to understand how their part of the organization fits into the overall picture. From this new perspective, planning aims to build coalitions of people who can work together to achieve common objectives.

This section therefore focuses on the process of planning. It establishes the circumstances that need to exist for an organization to develop its strategy in a formal way. It explains how to plan the planning process, how to improve existing processes and finally it identifies common pitfalls.

## Preconditions for strategic planning

There are a number of circumstances in which strategic planning is either inappropriate or will not work effectively as a management tool.

1. **Organizations need to have sufficient independence to select their own objectives and deploy resources to achieve them.** If the organizational unit is an integral part of a larger system (usually a public bureaucracy), strategic planning may not be appropriate. In 1992 the London Symphony Orchestra had sufficient managerial and financial independence to prepare a strategic plan. The BBC Symphony Orchestra, however, was financially and managerially an integral part of the BBC. It did not have its own accounts or its own management, and its schedule was to a considerable extent determined by the demands of Radio 3. Strategic planning would have to be within the wider BBC framework.

2. **Commitment of the chair and the chief executive.** A high level of commitment, particularly from the chief executive, is an essential ingredient of strategic planning. If the chief executive is not seen to be in command of the strategic planning process and dedicated to using the plan as a managerial tool, scepticism will creep in and planning will not be effective. In a similar vein, the chair needs to be involved and committed to demonstrating to the board that planning is for real and not just a paper exercise.

3. **The senior management team needs to be stable.** If two or more senior managers are in the process of leaving, or if a major reorganization of the senior management team is imminent, strategic planning will be dominated by the inevitable politics of reorganization. It is not a moment for sitting back and dispassionately reviewing the organization and its prospects.

   Similarly, if new members have recently joined the team or a team has just been established, the dynamics of a group in 'forming mode' (see section 8.4) are likely to interfere with strategic planning.

4. **Lack of major crises.** If the organization is in crisis, or if one is imminent, short-term pressures will predominate. The loss of a major source of funding, fundamental divisions over future directions, resignation of a number of board members or dismissal of a senior member of staff are all circumstances that militate against effective planning. There needs to be sufficient stability in the organization, and a willingness of senior staff and board to be dispassionate, for planning to be effective.

5. **Distinguishing strategic and operational planning.** Organizations offering a number of different services need to make a clear distinction between strategic planning, the subject of this section, and operational planning, which is covered in section 6.3. Strategic planning is concerned with the direction of the organization as a whole and the allocation of resources to different services and activities. Operational planning is concerned with the practical shorter-term plans for each of those services and activities.

In strategic planning both the planning process and the substance of the plan are ultimately matters for the board and senior management, in consultation with the staff and sometimes service users and other stakeholders. In operational planning the board and senior management are responsible primarily for establishing the process, and individual departments and service managers are responsible for the content.

## Planning the planning process

The objective of strategic planning is to build a widely shared conception of the future of the organization and its managerial priorities, not to create a glossy document that sits on people's bookshelves. The key to effective strategic planning is therefore to focus initially on the process of preparing the plan and not the plan itself. Key elements of developing an appropriate strategic planning process are:

1. **Legitimizing the process throughout the organization.** People in significant positions in the organization need to be committed to planning. Their involvement in the decision to embark upon strategic planning and in the design of the strategic planning process is consequently an essential ingredient for success. Similarly, line managers and service-unit managers need to be involved in the design of the process if they are to engage with it at later stages.

2. **Clarifying who will be involved at different stages.** Ideally strategic planning should involve as many people as possible from the organization's different constituencies. However, there is a trade-off to be made. Consultation takes time. Not everyone can be involved in all the stages of carrying out a strategic review, identifying key issues and making strategic choices. Decisions therefore have to be made about whom to involve at different stages of the process, and how to involve them, to gain their commitment to the plan. Once these decisions have been made, everyone should be told how and when they will be expected to make their contributions.

3. **Integrating with other management procedures.** The strategic plan needs to fit with other procedures for agreeing budgets, submitting applications for grants and being prepared for performance reviews commissioned by funding bodies. Managers should anticipate having to make trade-offs because the timetable can never meet everyone's requirements. In practice, strategic planning, even in a small organization, is likely to take at least three to four months. In larger organizations, and in those where more extensive consultation

is required, six to nine months is more likely to be appropriate, and those planning for the first time should expect to add two or three months to allow time to learn how planning works and fits with other management processes. The key to successful integration is to ensure that the timetables for planning, budget-setting and making funding applications all fit together.

4. **Challenging conventional wisdom.** Strategic planning is not a process of describing what the organization already does in new management language. It is a process of challenging existing beliefs, checking whether assumptions still hold and developing new perspectives. This may require the involvement of outsiders and people who are close to the organization but not an integral part of it. Designing them into the process will help to ensure that there is independent challenge to conventional wisdom.

5. **Communicating strategy.** Communication is an essential ingredient for effective implementation. In third-sector organizations there are frequently many stakeholder groups who can contribute more to the organization if they understand its strategic priorities. These can include funding bodies, members, major donors, service users, branches, local centres, local committees and any other group that has a relationship with the organization.

6. **Developing systems to monitor strategic performance.** Once the plan has been agreed, both the board and management need processes for gathering data and reporting on the overall performance of the organization. This element is frequently forgotten. It takes time and effort to identify the precise measures that will be used to monitor performance, to collect the necessary data and to report regularly on progress.

## Preparing strategic plans

There is no right or wrong way to go about the work of preparing a strategic plan. The following guidance may help organizations to anticipate problems that they are likely to encounter.

Organizations that have not engaged in planning for some time and organizations with a relatively new senior management team find the internal and external reviews to be time-consuming. This is unavoid-

## THE INTELLECTUAL PROCESS

A strategic planning process usually incorporates the following common elements:

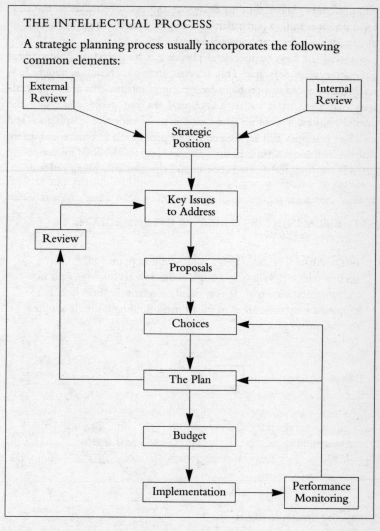

able, not least because a great deal of learning is taking place as the reviews are carried out. New data are discovered; much needed data may not be available or will be available only in a form very different from that required.

Even when basic facts and figures have been collected, it takes time to interpret the data and develop new insights into the changing circumstances. Allow time to draw out the critical threads of the strategic position and, in particular, to think hard, and as a group, about the key issues the organization needs to address.

One of the keys to successful planning is to confront choices about alternative ways forward. This is what strategic choice is about. It is tempting to avoid this problem by agreeing strategies that are so generalized that they meet everyone's aspirations but avoid addressing the critical choices. The other temptation is to be excessively ambitious and to adopt priorities that far exceed the organization's resources and, more usually, its management capacity. The techniques described in section 4.5 provide methods for making choices and consequently being realistic.

## THE PLANNING PROCESS AT INTERMEDIATE TECHNOLOGY

Intermediate Technology is a multi-million pound aid agency which develops and implements low technologies for non-industrialised countries. It was asked, at relatively short notice, to prepare a new strategic plan for its main funding body. It adopted the following process:

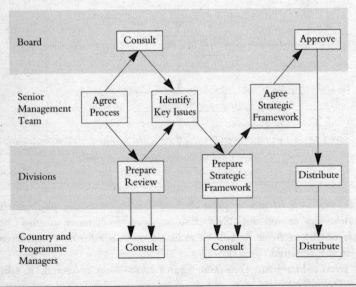

## Content of plans

The content of plans needs to reflect the outcome of the planning process. Long, dreary documents incorporating everything discussed are less useful than short, accessible documents that:

- reflect the organization's values
- communicate the key messages
- provide the basis for reviewing progress.

In smaller organizations the document is usually called the strategic plan. In larger organizations that have separate strategic plans for each of their services the document is sometimes called the 'strategic framework'. These set the overall context within which detailed operational and service plans will fit.

When it comes to preparing the plan itself, I have found the most useful documents:

- are **short** and to the point – say, ten to twenty pages
- **combine communication methods**, such as text, diagrams, bullet-point lists and charts
- are **inspirational** – demonstrating what will be done
- **avoid detail** – which can be documented separately.

## Requirements for top-quality plans

The best plans have the following characteristics:

- **They embody clear thinking and good judgement**. The key to successful planning is the synthesis of data to focus people on critical trends that will have a significant impact on the organization. This allows people to engage in clear strategic thinking. Penetrating thought and good judgement are the prerequisites for a powerful strategy.
- **They need to have clear measures of performance.** Good intentions are not enough. Plans need objectives with measures of performance attached to each. These should be a mixture of qualitative and quantitative measures.
- **They are specific but adaptable.** They should not be set in concrete or so inflexible that they cannot be adapted if circumstances change. But they should also not be so generalized that they mean anything to anyone.

## EXAMPLES OF THE CONTENTS OF STRATEGIC PLANS

### VSO's Strategic Plan for the 1990s: Investing in People

- About this plan
- Background
- Purpose, values and distinctive features
- Key directions
- Strategic issues
- VSO in 1997

### RELATE 2000: Meeting Client Needs

- The vision and the priorities
- Securing the marital counselling service
- Service developments
- Financing the plan
- Achieving the plan

### The National Consumer Council's Three-year Plan: Giving Consumers a Voice

- A national voice for consumers
- The consumer agenda
- Priority 1: public utilities
- Priority 2: public services
- Priority 3: high-street goods and services
- Priority 4: legal services
- Priority 5: credit and debt
- Working for change
- Resourcing the plan

## PLANNING THE FUTURE FOR OUTWARD BOUND

Outward Bound is a large national organization that exists to give people personal-development opportunities. It has five centres located in the mountains or beside the sea and a mobile inner-city programme. For many years its programmes were unique.

However, during the 1960s and 1970s local authorities and other charities began offering similar courses and in the 1980s companies also entered the field. The very success of the concept became the potential downfall of the organization. By the mid 1980s Outward Bound centres were looking out of date and there was uncertainty about their future development.

With a consultant's guidance the director assembled a team of headquarters staff (including himself and the heads of marketing, finance and the inner-cities programme) and the principals of the centres. They met for a full day once every six weeks for almost nine months. Team members investigated each of the student groups that the organization served (individuals, companies, public-sector bodies and other charities) to map out:

- numbers in each sector
- changing needs of students
- students' perceptions of Outward Bound
- future potential of each sector
- actions required to develop Outward Bound's service.

Draft plans were prepared, costed, discussed with the board and revised before a 'road-show' went round to each centre to consult front-line staff. The plans were revised again before being subjected to further board scrutiny and approval as the basis for future developments.

The process was not completed without difficulties. More than once, there was heated ideological debate about the underlying purpose and values of the organization. However, those fierce arguments provided some of the critical insights and understanding upon which the plans have been built.

More important than the plan itself was the fact that a group of people from all over the country were welded into a team which had a deep understanding of the future direction of the organization as a whole, and were clear about each other's priorities.

- **They focus on raising income as much as on spending it.** Strategies for raising money from donors are usually prepared separately from strategic plans. The two need to be brought together, particularly when donors can do more than dip into their pockets (for example, by joining in campaign work or volunteering).
- **They contain an implementation timetable.** Targets without a timetable are not real targets. Every plan ought to contain approximate dates by which key actions will be put into place.
- **The allocation of responsibilities is clear.** When a strategic plan is completed, key individuals need to be clear about what they have to achieve and by when they have to achieve it.

Finally, many organizations fall into the trap of assuming that planning will solve all the organization's problems. 'We can't agree that until the plan is completed', a common sentiment, is usually an excuse for avoiding a decision. Plans are not a panacea. They are a structured means for conducting a rational debate, and coming to agreement, about future priorities.

## 5.5 COMMON STRATEGIC DILEMMAS

When organizations are skilled at strategic planning they often discover that there are some fundamental dilemmas to be considered. These are common to many organizations, and they usually emerge at the strategic-choice stage.

Strategic choice is a key stage in developing future strategy. Making choices between alternative strategies is ultimately a matter of judgement based on the values and beliefs of the board and the staff. There are no right and wrong choices. The appropriate choice for one organization with its set of skills and aspirations may be entirely inappropriate for another organization working in the same field but having different capabilities and motivations.

The strategic dilemmas that appear time and time again are set out here to illustrate some of the common issues that organizations have to address. When the strategy-making process has reached one of these dilemmas, managers know the time has come to make judgements.

### 1. A little help for many or a great deal of help for a few

Many organizations can focus their resources on making a substantial difference to a limited number of people or spreading them out and giving a little assistance to many people:

- Organizations for homeless people have to choose between giving a few people extensive services, including a roof over their heads, psychiatric support, employment training and help in finding a job, or providing a basic shelter for a large number of homeless people.
- Aid agencies have to choose between an attempt to make a substantial difference by concentrating all their resources on a few communities or spreading their efforts across the many countries that desperately need their assistance.
- Disability organizations have to choose between offering substantial support to a few service users (perhaps people with the most profound disability) or a little assistance to the many people with a mild disability.

### 2. Treat the symptoms or the cause

Most organizations can identify fundamental causes of the problem they seek to address, but it is usually beyond their resources to do much about it:

- Health and disability organizations have to decide how much money to spend on alleviating the pain and suffering of people with the illness or disability and how much to put into research to discover the cause (and perhaps a cure) for the illness or disability.
- Social-service organizations have to choose between meeting people's immediate needs or working on the more fundamental causes of the problems. RELATE, for example, gives people counselling but also provides an education service to help people establish healthy relationships in the first place. The Samaritans can befriend people with suicidal thoughts, but they could also commission research into why people commit suicide.

### 3. Provide services or campaign for change

Many service-giving organizations start to campaign for changes in government policy or funding when they realize that their contribution will always be small by comparison with the size of the problem. Similarly, some campaigning organizations start to provide services to demonstrate what needs to be done:

- Disability organizations have to find a balance between providing services and campaigning. They recognize that they can potentially achieve so much more by changing people's attitudes towards people with disabilities than they will ever achieve through direct service provision. Campaigns for the rights of people with disabilities have consistently demonstrated the value of achieving policy changes. But these organizations also have to recognize that people need services now, as well as when the policy battle has been won.
- Aid agencies have to balance their lobbying activities with their practical projects. They recognize that, for example, successfully campaigning for write-offs of non-industrialized country debts will achieve much more than all the practical projects they fund – but it may take many years to achieve and people need help now.
- Medical charities have to choose between lobbying government to put more money into their field of research or using the money to fund their own research programme.

### 4. Focus or diversify services

Organizations can choose between concentrating on relatively few services and building their expertise in those tightly specified fields, or diversifying their expertise and delivering a wide range of services.

Many pressures encourage diversification. Funds may be offered for a new service; members or service users may call for new services to meet different needs, often as they get older and have different needs; and staff may push for new services because they offer new challenges and career-development opportunities.

Despite these pressures there are powerful arguments for focusing on particular services. Economies of scale mean services can be provided to more people at lower cost. Focusing leads to increased expertise in all aspects of the service:

- Colleges have to choose between systematically strengthening particular departments and programme areas and investing resources evenly across a number of fields.
- Campaigning organizations have to choose between spreading their efforts over a number of campaign fronts and focusing on the achievement of a few tightly specified objectives.
- Hospitals have to choose between putting new investment money in a limited number of specialities, gaining a reputation in these fields and,

perhaps, being able to offer a lower-cost service to purchasers and spreading the money over a wider range of specialities.

## 5. Hold virtuously to beliefs or be tempted by new resources

Many organizations face the dilemma of whether to hold righteously to their core beliefs or to compromise in order to gain new resources:

- Voluntary organizations have to choose between accepting funds from government initiatives and turning the money down because they are being seduced away from their core cause. In the 1980s many accepted money for employment and training projects that, in retrospect, consumed substantial management time and contributed little to help their organizations achieve their objectives.
- Organizations have to decide whether to accept sponsorship from the tobacco and alcohol industries. For environmental and health-care organizations, this is often difficult.
- Fundraising organizations know that pushing the emotive side of the cause (the starving baby, the child with disabilities) will raise more money. But it distorts the public perception of the beneficiary group when people want a fair chance in life, not charity.
- Housing associations have to choose between sticking to their core user group or bidding for money from the latest Housing Corporation funding scheme, which may divert management time (and financial resources) away from their historic purpose.

## Overcoming disagreements on strategy

Agreeing long-term strategy is not always plain sailing. I have worked with:

- a theatre where opinion was deeply divided on whether to put on a programme of more challenging plays or to produce popular plays that would improve its financial security
- a social-service organization, with service users from all socio-economic groups, where there was much disagreement about the principle of charging for the service
- a social-welfare organization in which funders and volunteers just could not agree about monitoring the effectiveness of volunteers' work.

## KEY ISSUES FOR FAMILY SERVICE UNITS

Family Service Units is a national organization that helps disadvantaged families through a network of centres that provide counselling, group therapy and community development.

At the end of an extensive review of corporate strategy, to clarify the alternative ways forward for the organization the FSU Planning Team summarized three strategic issues facing the organization as a whole:

1. *Focus on specified client group or general community needs*
FSU's reputation and experience lies in providing intensive support for families facing severe difficulties. Yet an increasing number of units are devoting resources to providing a variety of services to broader sections of their communities. FSU needs to decide whether it will be more effective if it concentrates on meeting the needs of a specific client group or if it aims to respond to the differing needs of a wider range of clients.

2. *Aim for a consistent approach throughout the country or aim to promote diversity*
Each unit has developed its own priorities and practices. FSU as a whole offers an enormous diversity of services. The dilemma is how to establish a clear identity and focus for FSU while retaining local responsiveness. Too much diversity makes it difficult to identify what is distinctive about FSU, and creates a confused message for potential funders. A too rigid model of service provision would limit the unit's ability to respond effectively to local need.

3. *Develop national standards for performance or encourage units to adopt their own*
There is great variation in the quality and management of FSU services. Expectations about standards are determined by each unit. To promote a high level of performance FSU could develop standards and performance measures that would be adopted by each Unit. Alternatively FSU could encourage local responses and accept different standards in different parts of the country.

These are just a few of the disagreements that can stop a strategy process in its tracks. Disagreements of this type often come down to different values and assumptions (see Appendix 2). Overcoming them may require:

- allocating time to enable representatives of the different viewpoints to explore the reasons for their multifarious views and whether they can find common ground
- use of an independent third party to act as a facilitator in a review of alternative ways forward and the consequences of pursuing different strategies.

Sometimes agreement is not possible. If talking and the use of independent outsiders cannot resolve the differences, some people may need to leave to allow the organization to move beyond a blockage and continue to function effectively.

More often, the disagreement results from misunderstandings and the allocation of insufficient time to talk through people's assumptions and viewpoints. In these circumstances time spent debating differences can be both motivating and rewarding. It can shed light on the 'messy' nature of these organizations and the fact that few issues have clear-cut solutions. It often leads to robust outcomes that provide firm foundations for the long-term development of the organization.

## SUMMARY OF KEY POINTS

### Choosing where to start

- Making organizations work more strategically should start by identifying whether work on strategic management, management processes, the management structure or governance arrangements will bring the greatest benefits.
- If strategic management is the priority, choices need to be made about which aspect to focus on.

### Developing the mission

- The mission can be strengthened as part of an exercise that involves many stakeholders in considering fundamental questions about the purpose, core values and distinctive competencies of the organization.
- It can also be an integral part of the strategic-planning process.

## Clarifying strategic objectives

- Strategic objectives are usually established as part of the strategic planning process. They are required for each key issue that emerges from the review.
- Strategic objectives need to avoid being wildly ambitious, highly generalized and gratuitous.

## Developing strategy

- New-style strategic planning establishes direction, priorities and key targets. Plans have a shorter time horizon and are prepared more frequently. They help people to understand how their work fits into the broader strategies.
- Preconditions for planning include: commitment of the chair and chief executive, a stable senior management team and lack of major short-term crises.
- Planning the planning process is critical. Key considerations are:
  - legitimizing the process
  - clarifying who will be involved at different stages
  - integrating planning with other management procedures
  - challenging conventional wisdom
  - communicating the new strategy
  - developing systems to monitor strategic performance.

## Common strategic dilemmas

- Many organizations face fundamental dilemmas about strategy:
  - provide a little help for many people or a great deal of help for a few
  - treat the symptoms or the cause
  - provide services or campaign for change
  - focus or diversify services
  - hold virtuously to beliefs or be tempted by new resources.
- These are best resolved by allocating time to discuss and debate alternative ways forward.

# CHAPTER SIX

# Making Management Processes Work

## 6.1 PROCESSES CONVERT STRATEGY INTO ACTION

Organizations need management processes to convert strategies into action and to enable people to work together effectively. People may agree what needs to be done, but organizations need processes and structures to achieve the mission and the objectives.

Managers are responsible for the design of processes. They have to create systems for planning work, managing people and monitoring achievements. In fact many managers spend a significant amount of their time on organization design, updating old processes, establishing new procedures, reorganizing the structure and setting up coordinating mechanisms.

This chapter focuses on the management processes that are required to make an organization work effectively. The next chapter looks at the design of management structures. They appear in this order because the processes are the most critical part of organization design. Organizations can work with imperfect structures – but poor processes seriously inhibit effectiveness.

A helpful analogy is to see the structure of an organization as the skeleton and the management processes and procedures as muscles and nerves that make it work. In the body, the growth of the skeleton is accompanied by development of the muscles and nerves. A similar relationship exists in organizations. Changes to the structure are inevitably accompanied by changes to the processes and procedures.

### Exploit skills by involving people

Most organizations have a predisposition towards involving staff and managers in their management processes. Some talk in terms of a consultative ethos; some proclaim their commitment to consensus decision-making and virtually all encourage cooperation between different parts of the organization.

There are many assumptions behind this predisposition. Third-sector organizations are staffed predominantly by people who often have strongly held opinions about what the organization should be doing. They expect to be involved in the management process and can make a valuable contribution when the processes encourage their participation.

People also assume that because they are working for a cause, rather than working just to earn a living, they have a right to be consulted on major decisions. People working closely with service users cannot avoid having strong feelings about the organization's work. They often understand service-delivery problems better than managers who work one step removed from the front line, or board members, who may be less directly involved. These staff feel a duty to ensure that management does not make mistakes, and that the best way to achieve this is to get involved in the management processes.

In some organizations, staff make the assumption that the opportunity to be involved in management processes is a reward for low salaries and long hours. The unwritten contract assumes that because people are sometimes not paid as well as their counterparts in the private sector, they should be rewarded through the power of participating in the big decisions.

Another assumption is rooted in the liberal and left-of-centre philosophies that are the predominant beliefs in some organizations. These beliefs lead to a presumption that organizations should be democratic and equitable. Some staff consequently assume that they should be involved at all levels in management and decision-making.

These committed and motivated people are an asset. They have a huge contribution to make to the effectiveness of the organization. It is management's task both to allow them to make it in an effective way and to establish clear boundaries to ensure that individuals are still held accountable for specific decisions. The processes for planning, managing and monitoring the organization's work need to be designed to enable and empower people to make an effective contribution to the major discussions and decisions.

Despite a frequent predisposition to involving people and all the rhetoric about consultation and consensus, many managers put insufficient effort into the design and implementation of processes that allow participation in practice. Concern about the cause itself predominates and the practical actions needed to create a well-managed organization fall to the bottom of the agenda. Those organizations that loudly proclaim their commitment to involving staff in management are sometimes the very ones that put least effort into the difficult task of creating streamlined and effective management processes that enable people to participate in practice.

## Identifying key management processes

Management processes are an essential element of organization design. The key processes for operational management of third-sector organizations include:

- service-level planning
- operational planning and budget setting
- people management
- participation and communication
- financial management
- performance monitoring.

Although there are many other management processes operating in organizations, such as developing fundraising plans, recruitment procedures, tendering processes and meeting cycles, this chapter focuses on the six processes that flow from the strategic management process described in the previous chapter. They fit together in a simple logic:

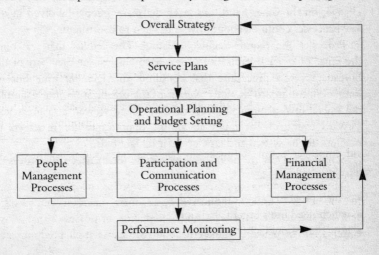

## *Processes need continuous development*

Some organizations strive continuously to ensure that their management processes are planned and monitored. They recognize that all these processes need to evolve in a deliberate way as the organization itself grows and develops. They aim for excellence in their management processes, just as they aim for excellence in their services.

It is, however, a never-ending task of development and adjustment. The design itself is often quite straightforward – the problems come with implementation. It takes time and effort to explain a new or changed process to everyone involved, to enable people to play their part in the process and to overcome unanticipated problems.

Then, when the new process is working, someone discovers that it does not fit with other management processes. The new financial-management information system, for example, that was implemented just before the chief executive reorganized the management structure, meant that managers still could not get information about costs they control. The idea that seemed so simple often turns out to be more difficult in practice.

Management has a fine tightrope to walk. The processes need to be developed continuously to meet the changing needs of the organization, to provide management and board members with better information and to avoid unnecessary bureaucracy. Too little change and the processes will lag behind the real needs of the organization. Too much change, on the other hand, can leave the many people involved in the key processes confused about how and when to contribute.

Processes also require regular updating. The activity that was once the envy of other organizations soon becomes just another part of the bureaucracy – a procedure that consumes management time but no longer contributes to the effectiveness of the organization. For example, the operational-planning process that was once viewed as a great leap forward eventually becomes an annual opportunity for managers to manipulate the system and rack up their budget bids.

Senior managers are ultimately responsible for management processes. They need to decide:

- which processes are working well
- which need most urgent attention
- how they should all fit together.

This chapter describes the processes, how to make them work and consequently how to improve the organization's effectiveness.

## 6.2 SERVICE PLANS

Chapter 4 established the need to define separate services and explained the concept of a service-delivery unit as a group of people responsible for delivering a service to a set of service users. Each service-delivery unit needs its own strategy, usually covering a one- to three-year period, which sets out objectives and how they will be achieved. The overall strategy sets the direction of the organization as a whole and defines the services that will be offered. The service strategies define the plans for each of these services.

Conceptually the process for developing service strategy is very similar to the corporate strategy process. It involves two stages, beginning with a review and ending with the preparation of a plan. At the review stage management gathers data about the external environment and the service itself to pinpoint key issues that the plan needs to address. Options can then be developed, choices made and a plan prepared.

However, service managers sometimes need help with their strategic thinking. Some may have been promoted from a service-delivery role to their first management post. Well trained in their own specialism, they are often unfamiliar with the task of bringing together service-delivery, human-resource, financial and other concepts to create a strategy. Some may feel that senior management ought to take responsibility for service strategy. Others are driven by seemingly never-ending demand for their service and feel that they do not have the time to stand back from the daily pressures of crises in the hostels, the refugees queueing desperately for advice or the deadline of the opening night. Senior management is responsible for providing service managers with the support they require.

Preparing the first review of a service is particularly difficult because it often requires definition of what the service is, the nature of the service-user population and the collection and analysis of data that may not previously have been drawn together.

## *Process for preparing service strategies*

Managers need to involve staff and, depending on circumstances, board members and volunteers in the preparation of a service strategy. Their involvement will lead to greater commitment to implemention of the plan and deeper understanding of how their service fits into the overall strategy.

A common approach involves staff and, if appropriate, board members in a discussion of how the review and planning are to be carried out and a series of meetings to consider the review data, define the key issues that need to be addressed and prepare the plan. The service manager may need to procure additional resources to ensure that staff have the extra time needed to help prepare the plan.

In larger organizations offering a number of services, senior management needs to develop and coordinate an organization-wide process for service strategic planning. This involves timetabling when the service planning should happen and how it will fit with the corporate strategy and budget-setting processes.

Tidy logic suggests that service managers should prepare their strategies when the corporate strategy has been completed. In practice, this is not always possible because the total timetable for preparing corporate and service strategies and then preparing operational plans and budgets becomes too extended. Senior managers may also need to spread reviews out so each can be given detailed attention. In addition changing external circumstances may require reviews of service strategy at times that do not fit neatly with the corporate planning timetable. An overall timetable is therefore required that results in each service considering its longer-term strategy about once every three years and does not require them to do their planning just after they have completed a budget cycle (because that is very demoralizing for staff).

Senior managers should expect to make a significant contribution to the content of service strategy. Senior managers are usually more experienced strategists. Their job is to provide the insight and judgement that can help to turn an adequate service strategy into an excellent one. This means being involved in helping managers to define the key issues and providing input into the shape of the emerging strategy.

## *Service reviews*

Service reviews should provide answers to the following questions:

### *External Issues*

**How are service users' needs changing?** Looking at rising expectations, and different ways of assisting them.

**What are the trends in the numbers of people requiring the service?** Reviewing demographics and the numbers requiring the service but not receiving it.

**Who are the competing suppliers and what distinguishes them?** Identifying other organizations (including private- and public-sector bodies) that provide similar services and understanding what is distinctive about your and their services.

**What are the relevant legislative and political changes that will affect the service?** For example, voluntarization of local-authority services and European legislation.

**What are the trends in funding for the service?** Including income from sales, government, donations and membership.

### *Internal Issues*

**Who are the current service users?** Segmented by such criteria as need, age, socio-economic group, and geography. In some cases the service users may be other organizations rather than individuals.

**How many benefit from the service?** Trends in the number of each type of user receiving the service.

**What are the benefits to service users?** Requiring an assessment of the quantitative and, equally important, the qualitative outcomes of services, where appropriate using service-user 'satisfaction' surveys.

**What skills are being used?** Identifying the critical competencies the organization requires to deliver the service.

**What have we learned?** Focusing on what the organization has learned about the users and the services provided to help change and improve the service in the future.

**What staff skills and staff training are required to improve the service?** Looking at different ways to develop people's skills.

**How much does it cost?** Pinpointing how much the service costs to provide, the overall subsidy required to finance the service and the cost and subsidy per user.

The data gathered needs to be distilled to pull out those items that are most critical to the future of the service and to identify information that needs collecting on an on-going basis.

Campaigning organizations can consider a similar set of issues for each campaign. External considerations include:

- changing public perceptions of the issue
- changed circumstances that affect the objectives of the campaign or the strategy for achieving objectives
- forthcoming political decisions that provide campaigning opportunities
- changing policies of each political party
- new coalitions required to make an impact on the issue.

Internal considerations include:

- the specific objectives of the campaign
- achievements to date
- effectiveness in the use of people and money
- learning about why some campaign objectives and not others have been achieved.

## Service strategies

The service strategy should be succinct, establishing objectives, articulating a strategy and setting out groups of actions needed to achieve the objectives. Typical contents might include:

- summary of the review
- description of the service
- summary of existing and potential service users
- objectives for the next three years
- the overall strategy
- specific targets
- timetable for implementation
- human-resource requirements
- financial-resource requirements
- sources of funding.

## 6.3 OPERATIONAL PLANS

The purpose of an operational plan is to link proposed activities with a budget. Most organizations put a huge amount of effort into establishing a budget. Many do not link the proposed expenditures with the activities planned for the next twelve months. The operational plan and the budget are therefore one short document that integrates activity and money.

In an ideal world, operational plans flow from strategic plans. Strategic plans give the broad direction for each service and the operational plans set out a programme of work for the next twelve months or, in a few cases, two years. Operational plans should focus on what will be done, by when, and what it will cost. They are vehicles for the discussion and agreement of future priorities. They:

- provide a basis on which to delegate work and responsibilities
- describe desired outcomes and, where appropriate, specific targets
- establish the activities upon which the budget will be based
- create a tool for measuring progress.

Most organizations benefit from having a process that requires managers of all services to prepare short, succinct plans. Whether they are called campaign plans, operational plans or work programmes, they provide a structure for the work and are important tools for communicating across organizational boundaries. They can apply equally to service-delivery parts of the organization and support services such as finance, personnel and information technology.

Although operational plans need to fit with strategic plans, there is no ideal architecture for the development and integration of the different types of planning that organizations undertake. Theoretically organizations could have strategic and operational plans at the corporate, departmental, regional and local levels. It would be a planner's paradise, but real work would grind to a halt. Choices have to be made. The current trend is away from complex networks of formal strategic and operational plans. The greatest value comes from an overall strategy at the corporate level and succinct strategies and operational plans at the level of individual services, which are tightly keyed into the overall strategies. Strategies and plans may exist at other levels, but there is often little value to be gained from the bureaucratic process of documenting them at every level.

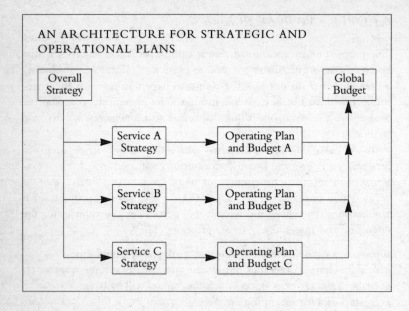

AN ARCHITECTURE FOR STRATEGIC AND
OPERATIONAL PLANS

## Operational planning process

Operational planning processes generally start with the board and senior management agreeing planning guidelines. These establish the parameters of the process. They may set broad targets and budget boundaries (for example, no additional subsidy). In a small organization the guidance need be only one side of paper on which the board sets out its aspirations for the next twelve months. In a large organization it will inevitably be more detailed because of the need for consistent budget data across services for the corporate budget-setting process.

Managers then work with their staff to prepare the plan, which again needs to be a succinct summary. The best plans are a few pages long, encapsulating critical thinking and proposed actions.

Draft operational plans and budgets need to be considered and agreed by line managers. Once approved, the documents need to be brought together into an overall operating plan and budget for the organization as a whole. This should highlight key proposals for the year, the timetable of major events and the budget. It should be approved by the board shortly before the start of the organization's financial year.

## Content of operational plans

Operational plans need to highlight:

- the number of people who will benefit
- the amount of help that will be given
- the quality standards
- the cost of each type of help given
- the implementation timetable
- mechanisms for reviewing performance and outcomes.

Ideally, operational plans should establish desired outcomes as well. In some cases this is relatively straightforward. It is easy to describe how many homes are to be built or to set a target for the number of people who should pass an examination or receive a qualification. In many cases it is more difficult. Outdoor education centres can plan how many people will attend their team-building courses, but it is more difficult to measure how they have benefited. Welfare organizations can plan to offer a number of counselling sessions, but detailed follow-up is required to measure the benefits that arise from this service. Aid agencies can aim to distribute a specific number of grants to projects in non-industrialized countries, but it is much harder to specify the desired achievements of the projects.

In some cases it is virtually impossible. Drug-prevention schemes cannot measure the number of people who have not taken drugs because of their preventative work. The Samaritans cannot measure whether the people who call subsequently commit suicide.

So while some organizations can measure the outcomes of their services, others have to be satisfied with measuring their output rather than their actual achievements.

The final ingredient of an operational plan is a budget that establishes:

- income to be raised from supplying the service
- the cost of providing the service
- the surplus generated or subsidy required.

## Common mistakes

The most common mistake is to allow the process to become too bureaucratic. A year or two after initial enthusiasm for the process, it is easy to fall into this trap. The process becomes so routinized that once a year everyone automatically cranks out a plan. People give it little thought and quickly come to see the plan as work that is needed to satisfy the system but not as a useful managerial tool. There is, to some extent, a degree of inevitability about this. All new processes have greatest leverage when they are first introduced, and this decays with time. This difficulty can be overcome by carrying out a brief review shortly after completion of the process to identify what went well, where problems were encountered and how the process could be improved next time.

Senior management, therefore, needs to see its task as continuously revitalizing the process. Each year the guidance needs to be adjusted to meet new circumstances. Managers need to be pushed harder to identify real benefits for service users, to seek ways of streamlining their services, to improve quality and to reach out to more people.

The second mistake is for senior management to require the plan well before the implementation dates. Long timescales are a particular problem in large organizations, where the operational plan for each service may need to be approved by departmental management, then the committees for each service, then senior management, then the finance committee, before finally being submitted as a global budget to the board. In the worst cases the plan is being prepared a year or more before its start date. This type of bureaucratic process needs to be streamlined to fit the fast-changing world of the 1990s. The scope needs to be agreed (for example, four pages describing benefits to users, actions, a timetable and a budget) so the minimum number of steps required to involve people in preparing and agreeing it can be established (see box).

## 6.4 PEOPLE-MANAGEMENT PROCESSES

People are an organization's greatest resource. In today's rapidly changing environment, human resources need more attention than they have ever before received. Organizations should work on the assumption that if their people are not developing as fast as the changes in the environment, they are losing their capacity to be effective.

Developing people requires both commitment from managers and the people being managed and the ability to help people learn how to

## OPERATIONAL PLANNING IN SENSE

SENSE provides pre-school education, post-16 education and long-term support for people who are both deaf and blind. Services are delivered regionally and their annual budget was £14 million in 1994/95. Every four years the organization reviews its overall strategy.

Their operational planning process works as follows:

| | |
|---|---|
| 21 October | Finance Committee agrees inflation and cost-of-living assumptions |
| 26 October | Senior management team agrees guidelines and timetable for operating plan and budget preparation together with assumptions on fee increases |
| 31 October | Fee increases agreed with purchasers |
| 3 December | Current year budget, expenditure to date and blank pro-formas mailed to senior management team members<br>Directors review plans with service managers and start to consolidate them into departmental and regional plans and budget bids |
| 9 December | Progress report to Governing Council |
| 17 January | All completed operating plans and budgets to be with Director of Finance |
| 18 February | Summarized national operating plan and budget mailed to senior management team |
| 27–29 February | Residential meeting. All Directors present plans for scrutiny by colleagues<br>Revisions agreed for submission to Governing Council |
| 22 March | Council agrees operating plan and budget |
| 1 April | New financial year begins. |

be more effective. Organizations cannot make this happen, but they can construct people-management processes that require all managers to give people management a greater priority.

These processes are particularly important in third-sector organizations because there is often a supposition that people development will somehow happen automatically. In some organizations it is assumed that people development requires little more than casual inquiries about the progress of their work. Nothing could be further from the truth. In practice developing people is a challenging task, and organizations need to do everything they can to help managers to become more effective at it.

Even in organizations that are committed to taking a systematic approach to people development, other pressures can push it to the bottom of the agenda. Surrounded by demands to deliver more services, campaign for change, respond to media opportunities and resolve the endless stream of short-term crises, the needs of the people who do the work are all too often neglected.

Organizations should seek to avoid:

- the efforts of energetic employees being dissipated across all sorts of internal issues rather than being focused on the specific objectives the organization needs them to achieve
- talented people deciding to move to other organizations when they still have a great deal to contribute
- poor performers being allowed to remain in post long beyond the time when they should have been moved on
- poor people management causing great personal upset and leading to reduced confidence in management.

Historically, organizations established people-management processes that had a strong 'top-down' flavour. There was a sense that people management was something managers did to their staff – they inducted them; they supervised them; they appraised them. Separate processes were established to enable managers to discharge these responsibilities.

This view is no longer adequate. All these processes need to be two-way dialogues in which managers and staff agree their expectations of each other and review performance together. Managers can learn from staff as much as staff learn from their managers.

There are four elements to people-management processes that need to be considered:

- recruitment
- induction
- supervision
- appraisal.

These processes all have the common objectives of ensuring that people develop their skills and abilities and that their efforts are directed towards the objectives the organization needs them to achieve. This section describes the overall architecture of people-management processes. Advice about managing people as individuals is given in chapter 8.

## *The recruitment process*

A recruitment process is required to ensure that best practices are applied in recruiting people for different jobs. This section focuses on the recruitment of managers. As there is no foolproof method of recruiting managers, the process needs to concentrate on systematically using procedures that maximize the probability of appointing the best person available for the post. Effective recruitment processes include:

- realistic timetables to review the job and recruit
- job descriptions that set out the purpose of the job, the principal responsibilities and reporting lines
- person specifications that describe the experience, skills, qualifications and personal qualities required, all divided into 'essential' and 'desirable' attributes
- a standard application form for each post, avoiding discriminating issues such as marital status and children
- a process for shortlisting applications against the criteria in the person specification
- an appropriate mixture of selection methods for the job, preferably including three different methods (see box overleaf)
- a mechanism to ensure that referees are asked specific questions about the applicant
- a system for monitoring the ethnic group, gender and disabilities of applicants, shortlisted candidates and people appointed and for taking action on the results.

## SELECTION METHODS

There are many views on the appropriateness of different selection methods. A recent survey of selection methods used by the public, private and third sectors showed the following methods were used to select senior and middle managers.

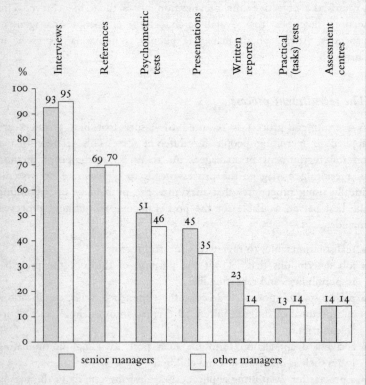

*Managing Best Practice 4: Recruitment and Selection*, The Industrial Society, 1994.

One practical test we use at Compass Partnership is to invite groups of four to six candidates to work on a case study. We watch them address a real client problem and assess their skills against agreed criteria. This is a useful way of allowing candidates an opportunity to demonstrate both their analytical skills and their ability to work as a team to solve a multi-faceted problem.

## *The induction process*

A process is needed to introduce new entrants and to acclimatize them to the organization's culture as efficiently as possible. The traditional approach of wandering around talking to people is not sufficient. Managers need to ensure that new staff go through an intensive learning process that:

- teaches them how the organization works
- clarifies exactly what is expected of them in their job
- explains the support and resources that are available to help them achieve their objectives.

---

### INDUCTION OF VSO FIELD STAFF

Field staff at Voluntary Service Overseas are responsible for VSO's work on the ground. They work from offices scattered around some of the poorest and most remote countries of the world. They receive an intensive two-week induction as part of their preparation. The programme is as follows:

**Week one**

| | |
|---|---|
| Monday | Introduction to VSO and the induction programme |
| | Description of how policy decisions are made and the role of VSO's Council and Executive |
| | Visit to Resources Centre |
| | Introduction to Personnel Administration |
| Tuesday | Payroll, pensions and insurance issues for overseas staff |
| | The Field Office |
| Wednesday | Overview of Recruitment Division, Central Applications Unit, Volunteer Assessment Unit, Postings Department, Training Department |
| Thursday | Overview of New Services, Evaluation and Communication of Overseas Experience, Press and Publicity Offices |
| Friday | Financial Management and programme funding |

**Week two**

| | |
|---|---|
| Monday | Field Office role and responsibilities, Overseas Division calendar and annual Country Plan |
| Tuesday | Exercise visiting potential volunteer employers Supporting volunteers. Appropriate and inappropriate interventions Dealing with sensitive and emotional issues |
| Wednesday | Developing new project-placement opportunities Evaluating the success of individual placements Budgetary control |
| Thursday | In-country training – support to expect from VSO Providing professional support to volunteers Addressing demands on Field Office from volunteers |
| Friday | Medical emergencies Roundup and evaluation of the programme |

The senior management task is to ensure that the organization has appropriate processes for the proper induction of staff at every level. Methods of ensuring it works well include:

- development of a checklist
- making support available from the personnel department
- asking new staff to review, with their manager, how they felt about the induction and what could be done to improve it.

## The supervision and development process

Most organizations need a system that enables all staff to meet one-to-one with their line manager at an agreed frequency. Absence of such meetings can quickly lead to the build-up of misunderstandings, differing perceptions and poor relationships.

The main purpose of supervision and development is to provide a framework within which managers and staff can:

- review work progress
- clarify priorities
- praise success

- deal with problems
- review areas where performance improvements are required
- raise personal concerns.

One-to-one supervision meetings should therefore clarify how the individual is progressing towards achievement of the desired outcomes and whether the organization has provided the necessary support and resources.

Establishing a supervision system should involve both the staff who are required to provide supervision and the people who will receive it. Their participation helps to build commitment to the supervision process and to incorporate it into everyone's work routines. Ideally, it should become part of the accepted culture that everyone expects to receive supervision. A series of workshops to tailor a supervision process to the organization's circumstances is a good way to build commitment. This should be followed by management decisions about the frequency of supervision and training requirements to support implementation.

Setting an example from the top is crucial. Chairs are responsible for ensuring that chief executives have one-to-one supervision, either by doing it themselves or by appointing someone else to perform this function. Managers who report to the chief executive should have supervision meetings with the chief executive before the process cascades down the organization.

Support for people who are anxious about one-to-one supervision helps to build confidence and commitment to the process. This can take the form of training, a helpline and an opportunity to review progress with senior management.

It takes a concentrated effort to establish the one-to-one supervision part of performance management, but, once established, it brings huge benefits in focusing people on the organization's priorities and ensuring that they have the resources and support they require.

## The appraisal process

Organizations need a process for periodically carrying out a thorough review of each employee's performance and the support that the organization has provided. Many call this the annual appraisal, though it can be more frequent, and it should not simply be a one-sided appraisal of each employee but a dialogue between employees and their managers.

The value of the appraisal is the opportunity it provides to stand back and take stock. It allows managers and each of their staff to:

- discuss each other's strengths and weaknesses in a blame-free environment
- review past performance
- agree targets for the coming period
- establish training and support requirements
- review personal-development opportunities.

Activities needed to establish a performance-review process are similar to those needed to set up a supervision process. A programme of short discussions among managers about the design of the process will help to build commitment and understanding. Once an overall scheme is agreed, tailor-made training designed to suit the specific circumstances of the organization is essential to give people the necessary skills. Everyone should be offered training before being required to carry out a review.

The appraisal process should roll out, starting with senior management and gradually expanding until it covers all employees. Top-management commitment is essential and needs to be demonstrated by senior management team members appraising the managers who report to them before anyone else is asked to carry out appraisals.

The reviews need to focus on the extent to which people have achieved agreed targets. They should avoid the common tendency to make generalized judgements about people's characters. Although it is easy to describe someone as honest, caring and loyal, the performance-review process needs to encourage managers and their staff to agree:

- the extent to which objectives for the past period have been achieved
- the extent of achievements not related to objectives
- the qualitative and quantitative targets for the coming period
- the training and support that the organization will provide
- the personal-development opportunities that will be offered to the individual.

Once established, periodic actions are required to prevent the process from becoming a bureaucratic necessity that does not add value to the organization. Changing the questions on appraisal forms, requiring people to link appraisals explicitly with strategic or operational plans and listing the types of support the organization can provide are all examples of ways to give the process renewed life.

## Performance management

The aims of supervision, development and appraisal are to ensure that people become, and remain, clear about what is expected of them and that the organization provides the resources and support that all employees need to do their jobs. A useful way of thinking about this is to consider the arrangement to be a 'contract' between the organization and the individual.

On one side of the contract organizations need all employees (and volunteers) to be results-oriented, striving to achieve their objectives. People need help to clarify exactly what they are expected to do, guidance as they learn how to do it, praise when they are successful and advice on making improvements when problems are encountered.

On the other side managers, staff and volunteers need support and resources from the organization to enable them to do their work effectively. They need sufficient people and money to do the task, training and coaching to enable them to do their jobs and regular guidance as the work progresses. They also need their manager to give them authority to do the work and clear instructions about when to seek advice.

The notion of a performance contract helps to untangle problems when performance falls below expectations or circumstances change. Performance contracts fail for two reasons. Either employees do not meet the expectations made of them, or the organization does not provide adequate support and resources. Often problems arise because both have partially failed to meet their side of the contract. Reviewing the situation from the perspective of both sides of the contract helps to avoid blame and to identify the actions needed for future success.

The performance contract integrates the processes of induction, supervision, appraisal and departure. It gives a sharp focus to the induction process by specifying as precisely as possible the performance expected of the post-holder. It provides the basis for a two-way dialogue at one-to-one supervision. It gives a base line for reviewing progress and problems at annual review meetings.

The concept of performance management allows supervision and appraisal to be tied together into one overall performance cycle that focuses on what individuals have done to help the organization achieve its objectives, how the organization has supported them in their work and what needs to be done to achieve further improvements.

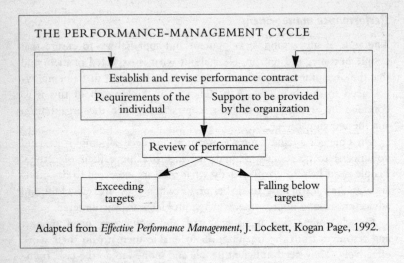

THE PERFORMANCE-MANAGEMENT CYCLE

Establish and revise performance contract

| Requirements of the individual | Support to be provided by the organization |

Review of performance

Exceeding targets

Falling below targets

Adapted from *Effective Performance Management*, J. Lockett, Kogan Page, 1992.

In this cycle supervision focuses on short-term performance require-ments, and annual review takes a longer-term view. Indeed, although it is common for supervision meetings to be at approximately monthly intervals and appraisal to be annual, the notion of a performance cycle allows the frequency to be varied according to circumstances.

## Moving-on processes

The last people-management processes to consider are the ones con-cerned with moving people on from the organization. Moving people on is particularly difficult in third-sector organizations because they continue to believe in the organization's cause even when they are not performing well or when the job has grown beyond their abilities. To make matters more difficult, it is sometimes the most committed individuals who become the greatest obstacle to the development of the organization's work.

It may be someone who is a renowned leader in their field but who is not able to manage a team, or a high-profile director who has lost the confidence of the board, or a junior manager who just was not able to do the task.

Whatever the circumstances, managing departures is always a sensitive issue in organizations whose work is often about looking after people. A poorly handled departure has ramifications for relations with funding bodies and possible loss of reputation if the issue gets into the media. More important, any departure is watched closely by other staff. If it is handled with kindness and compassion, staff gain confidence in management. If it is mishandled or seen to be unfair, people will begin to consider their own long-term future with the organization.

The key is to establish processes that are as clear and unambiguous as possible, before they are needed. Three situations need to be covered.

First, a **redundancy policy** is required to establish the terms that will be offered to people if their area of work is discontinued. It should be agreed by the board and must be referred to in employees' terms and conditions.

Second, a **disciplinary procedure** is required to overcome problems of poor performance that cannot be resolved and employee actions that are unacceptable. The exact process will depend on the size of the organization, but it should include:

- documentation of each step to be taken (for example, dates of verbal warnings, details of written warnings, the individual's responses)
- a review by senior management
- an appeal process.

Third, a process for **reviewing time-limited contracts** is required. It is increasingly common for chief executives and some senior managers to be appointed on contracts with set review periods. Contracts have the advantage of forcing the organization to be more systematic in reviewing performance. However, they also encourage employees to start looking for new opportunities when the end of the contract is on the horizon. Reviews ought therefore to happen at least six months before the contracts are completed to ensure that the organization does not unintentionally lose a good manager and, if the organization and the individual decide to part, that plenty of time is left to find a replacement.

When someone has left the organization through redundancy, dismissal or non-renewal of a contract, a thorough appraisal of the job may yield valuable insights. Organizations can fall into the trap of heaping so many responsibilities on a post, and giving the incumbent so little support, that failure was almost inevitable from the start. This is particularly the case with least-structured jobs such as the chief executive's post and entirely new posts (for example, the newly created post of director of fundraising).

A dispassionate review may reveal that the organization was at least as much at fault as the individual. It will avoid mistakes being repeated before a new appointment is made.

## Continuous development is the aim

Many organizations have historically given insufficient attention to developing people. This has left a legacy of poor management skills and an opportunity to make significant improvements. In these circumstances senior management needs to decide where to focus its energy.

Organizations with few people-management processes might start with the establishment of monthly one-to-one supervision. Organizations with processes that have lost their cutting edge might begin by aligning the content of annual appraisals more closely with the organization's current objectives. Organizations taking on significant numbers of new staff might focus on strengthening the induction process. This will encourage new recruits to see that linking individual performance with the organization's objectives is a priority for everyone.

The aim should be to get all managers to think about how they can improve the performance of the people who work for them. The discipline of meeting regularly provides an institutional framework. Focusing on achieving objectives that line up with the organization's strategy provides direction, but in the end there is no substitute for the insightful comments that help individuals to deliver improved performance.

## 6.5 PARTICIPATION AND DECISION-MAKING PROCESSES

Participation and communication processes are particularly important in value-led organizations. People who believe in the cause want to know what other parts of the organization are doing and they want to participate in decision-making. They need information to do this. They need to know about current activities, new developments, new appointments, new funding arrangements, changes to board membership and so on.

In small organizations most people glean the information they require informally. As organizations grow, increasing effort has to be put into ensuring that people know about different parts of the organization and are able to participate in decisions. Managers consequently have to develop processes and communication systems that enable people to contribute in appropriate ways.

The management of these processes is an easily forgotten topic. There is no imperative, such as the annual budget or the monthly supervision, to remind managers of their importance. It is often only when people start to complain – 'We've got communication problems,' 'We're never consulted,' 'We're never involved in decision-making' – that management starts to address the problems.

Sometimes these complaints are symptoms of an organization that has become directionless. More often they reflect the fact that management is not paying sufficiently close attention to managing and improving the critical internal processes.

It is important to recognize from the outset that there is no ideal solution. Perfect information and decision-making processes are a dream that no organization attains. There are nevertheless two extremes to avoid.

At one extreme there are organizations that have too few processes by which to keep people informed and consequently do not allow them to participate effectively in decision-making. These organizations tend not to have regular meeting cycles. They do not have a team-briefing system for information to move up and down the organization or an internal newsletter to disseminate key information to everyone who needs to know. They tend to have frustrated and poorly motivated staff.

At the other extreme there are organizations that assume everyone has a right to know everything and to participate in all decisions. These organizations are generally characterized by long papers, lengthy circulation lists, extended meetings and lack of clarity about where decisions are finally taken.

Managers are responsible for creating processes that ensure that their organization does not fall into either extreme. They have to make the trade-off between a natural desire to know about everything and be involved in all decisions, the time and cost of consulting people and making good decisions and the likelihood of getting better decisions that are easier to implement.

One way of finding the right balance is to think of the process as a cycle in which there are three Cs and one D. The three Cs are communication, consultation and consensus. The D is decisions. Managers are responsible for each of these processes and need to use different ones in different circumstances.

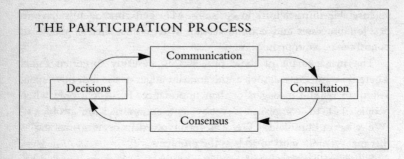

THE PARTICIPATION PROCESS

**Communication** is concerned with ensuring that people get the information they need to do their job effectively and can set their work in the wider context of the organization. People in every organization can say, 'We've got communication problems,' because it is an easy sentence under which to subsume many other problems. Nevertheless, managers do need to work to overcome the common problems of:

- people working away from the head office feeling cut off
- overloading the organization with news and facts but failing to communicate the essential information
- saying one thing and being heard to say something else
- information reaching some people but not others (for example, part-time employees and people on leave)
- giving insufficient information about why particular decisions were taken.

Managers are responsible for ensuring that organizations have internal communication systems that meet the organization's needs and do not overburden people with interesting but unimportant information.

Techniques for improving information flow around the organization include:

- regular team briefings in which essential information cascades down the organization in a series of short meetings, questions are answered and important issues are passed back up the line
- managers and staff conferences
- internal news-sheets
- meetings for user-groups (e.g., computer users, accounts users)
- summaries of decisions taken at board and senior management team meetings
- electronic mail.

Informal information flows are equally important. Organizations that promote openness and encourage managers to have lots of short conversations with people will find less need for more formal systems.

Managers can play a significant role in ensuring that people feel informed. However, they also have to take responsibility for discovering the information they need. The argument 'No one told me' is an excuse that managers should avoid. Good managers anticipate problems and seek out the information they require. They will, however, be better motivated if they believe that senior management is paying close attention to the need to keep people informed of:

- the overall performance of the organization
- major decisions
- departures and arrivals of new staff
- changes in board membership
- changes in the external environment
- major successes.

---

## TEAM BRIEFING IN RELATE

Once a month the director of RELATE prepares a briefing for staff and committee members. This briefing covers national issues. It is sent to regional managers and other senior staff, who add regional and departmental issues to the briefing before forwarding it to their staff, including the managers of local RELATE centres. Only additions are permitted as the briefing flows through the organization.

A typical briefing covered:

- arrangements for the AGM
- RELATE's response to the Lord Chancellor's Green Paper on Divorce Law Reform
- developing a new strategy for strengthening RELATE's public profile
- raising £30,000 from a zero-coupon charity bond
- latest demand statistics for counselling services
- a course for marriage counsellors in India
- a workshop for male counsellors
- new staff appointments.

**Consultation** is concerned with ensuring that people who will be affected by a decision, or who can help the organization to arrive at a better decision, can make their views known.

Consultation is an essential ingredient of management. The problems most organizations deal with are highly complex. Expertise and knowledge reside with many different people. Their contribution will often lead to better decisions. Furthermore, their commitment to implement decisions will be greater if they feel they have been consulted.

Consultation is also essential to hold together the coalition of stakeholders that constitute a third-sector organization. If funders, board, managers and employees have been consulted, they are more likely to back the decisions the organization makes, even if the decision is not the one they wanted.

Managers are responsible for the organization of effective consultation processes. Consultation is particularly important:

(a) on major strategic issues (such as the strategic plan, a change in the overall structure and the introduction of new information-technology systems)
(b) on issues that affect everyone directly (such as the grading of employees or new terms and conditions).

Consultation is particularly important in organizations with federal structures (see section 2.5) and member organizations. In both cases many people have a stake in actions that are initiated by the centre. They are more likely to be supportive if they have helped to shape decisions. Implementation will encounter fewer obstacles when members feel they have been properly consulted.

Consultation with trade unions and staff associations is particularly important. Where they have been established, they present another channel for seeking people's views. There may be certain issues (often related to staff terms and conditions) on which there is an agreement or a legal obligation to consult. In addition management can consult on other issues, provided it also consults through the line-management structure.

The keys to effective consultation are to be clear about:

- what people are being consulted on
- how they should make their views known
- when decisions will be taken
- who will take decisions.

The timetable for consultation exercises often presents dilemmas. Managers organizing the consultation process may have difficulty in completing the documents when they hoped to (because the issues are usually complex). So consultation often seems to start later than anticipated. Then, however much time is allowed, people being consulted frequently feel they are given insufficient time to consider the issues, consult their colleagues or members and feed back the conclusions. A

## CONSULTATION ON MENCAP'S STRATEGIC REVIEW

Mencap provides services and campaigns for people with learning disabilities. It has over 500 homes, 700 Gateway leisure clubs with 41,000 members and almost 500 local societies. Income of the national organization alone is almost £60 million per annum.

Following a period of very rapid growth in the early 1990s, Mencap carried out a major review of its overall strategy. The review concluded by seeking people's views on six major questions.

To obtain the views of the many constituencies that make up the organization, it launched a major consultation exercise, which included:

- mailing the review and feed-back forms to all local societies
- distributing the review to national and regional staff
- organizing a road-show in which one-day meetings were held throughout the country, each attended by a member of the senior management team or the chief executive
- producing a version of the review to consult people with learning disabilities (part of which is reproduced here)
- allocating time at a governing board meeting for a thorough discussion of the results of the consultation.

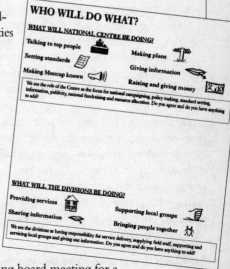

balance has to be found. Decisions have to be taken, as management does not always control the timetable. Sometimes things have to happen quickly. Nevertheless, much of the effort put into consultation is wasted if the people consulted feel that they have been given insufficient time to make a considered response. The trap of token consultation is one that managers need to avoid.

Consultation is not a panacea. Used appropriately, it helps to weld large groups of people together. But when it is over-used it easily becomes an excuse for avoiding decisions. Although it is difficult to argue against consultation, managers are ultimately responsible for making decisions, and sometimes these are more important than widespread consultation.

**Consensus** is about gaining agreement from a critical mass of relevant people to enable new courses of action to proceed. It is not an absolute requirement; it is always a matter of degree.

Many third-sector organizations are, quite rightly, proud of their desire to gain consensus on major issues. Consensus is particularly important on matters such as the overall strategy of the organization, the division of resources between different areas of work and the roles of the staff and the board. Without a reasonable consensus on these major issues, many minor decisions will grow into debates about the larger issues.

Gaining consensus necessarily takes time, and the larger and more complex the organization, the more time managers have to allocate to the maintenance of the consensus. Activities such as away-days, strategy-review workshops and informal discussion on major new issues all help to build and maintain the consensus that is needed for an organization to thrive.

However, a common mistake made by third-sector managers is to seek consensus on comparatively minor issues. The well-educated, liberal-minded managers who pervade the sector often believe that their staff expect them to discuss an issue until a consensus emerges. In practice, once the main arguments have been heard, most people expect managers to take decisions. They recognize that organizations can proceed only if managers take decisions when they are required. Managers therefore have to judge:

(a) which issues require a broad consensus
(b) when it is more important to take decisions, even if there is not a clear consensus.

People can be communicated with and consulted, and there may be a degree of consensus, but in the end organizations require processes for making **decisions**. This may sound obvious, but it is surprising how often decision-making processes and the way they operate are the cause of confusion and misunderstanding.

Every organization needs an annual cycle of key meetings in which to make decisions. This begins with the meetings of the board and its committees. They in turn set the broad timetable for meetings of the senior management team and departmental teams. This cycle of formal meetings is the spine of the decision-making process. When the cycle is well planned and clearly communicated to everyone involved it provides a framework to which people attach their understanding of how the organization works.

The cycle of meetings plays a role in communication, consultation, consensus and decision-making. In small or straightforward organizations all these functions may happen within the meetings cycle. However, as organizations become larger and more complex, meetings become overloaded. The processes have to be separated. More communication takes place outside meetings; consultation on major strategic issues is organized separately; and decisions are shaped over a period of time. Meetings in the annual cycle can then focus on formally confirming decisions that have been shaped in settings appropriate to the decision.

There is, however, a common danger in value-led organizations: that of assuming that everyone should be involved in as many decisions as possible. When this happens decision-making becomes very slow, and this itself becomes a source of frustration for staff, managers and committee members.

As a guideline managers should consider taking decisions on their own:

- on minor issues
- when decisions are required at short notice
- when other people are not affected
- when consultation has led to a clear consensus
- when people cannot agree and decisions are required or recommendations have to be put to a higher body (e.g., the board).

## 6.6 FINANCIAL-MANAGEMENT PROCESSES

The strategy has been agreed, the operating plan and budget fixed, people-management procedures are in place and participation is working well. The next process to review is the one that ensures that managers have the financial information they require to do their jobs.

Financial-management systems are important because they are one means by which organizations give people responsibility and hold them accountable for their actions. Good financial-management information is an essential corollary to delegation of authority. When organizations delegate responsibility, they can encourage people to be more accountable by providing timely information in the required formats. However, financial management is one of the corporate-management processes that cause the most anxiety among service managers, particularly when they are expected to take responsibility for income and expenditure but are not given the information needed to discharge that responsibility.

A management-accounting system designed to fit the organization's task is an essential feature of an effective organization. Unfortunately, many organizations give financial management insufficient attention and, as a result, money is wasted. Third-sector organizations often do not compare well with either the public or private sector in the sophistication of their financial-management processes. During the 1960s and 1970s manufacturing businesses made great improvements in their financial-management arrangements. Systems were developed to give line managers reliable, up-to-date, accurate accounts. Similar improvements were made by service businesses in the 1980s as banks, building societies and financial institutions started competing with each other.

This effort has continued with firms comparing themselves with their competitors and, more recently, with wholesale reviews of business and management processes to find even more efficient ways of producing superior quality at lower cost.

Third-sector organizations are beginning to feel the winds of competition blowing in their direction. Those that tender for work in the contract culture and those that are facing greater competition for donations require top-quality financial-management systems.

This section explains the essential requirements of a management-accounting process that will help managers to get a better grip on the income and expenditure for which they are responsible. It is not about the financial-accounting system that organizations have to meet their constitutional and legal duties to report as companies, charities or friend-ly societies. It is about the information that managers and trustees need in order to manage their organizations.

## Management accounting is a service

The essential elements of a good financial-management process are straightforward. Organizations need a budget, a system that records income and expenditure and provides up-to-date accounts relevant to each level of the organization. Service managers need information about the income and expenditure that they control and the subsidy that they require. Departmental managers need summaries of the services for which they are responsible. Senior management and the board require an overview of income and expenditure, a balance sheet and a cash-flow forecast.

That is the ideal, but it takes hard work to achieve it. A series of common problems ensure that many managers do not have the informa-tion they require in an appropriate format. These include:

- management accounts that arrive late – sometimes thirty to sixty days after the month end, when seven days is quite achievable
- accounts that are inaccurate – as a result of misallocation to budget-holder accounts, late payments or early receipts
- overhead costs that are not separated out of service managers' accounts, so they cannot distinguish between the costs they control and the ones that they do not control and should not be held accountable for
- expenditure that is not subtracted from income, so managers cannot see at a glance whether their service is generating a contribution to overheads or requiring a subsidy
- costs that are incurred continuously (e.g., heating) but charged infre-quently and not accrued, so accounts look good until that bumper invoice hits the system
- budgets that are not varied month by month to take account of cyclical demand or skewed expenditure patterns
- accounts that are produced in a standard format that suits the accounts department's computer system but not the needs of service managers
- information needs of different users, such as board members, senior management and service managers, that are not distinguished to help them focus on their responsibilities.

To overcome these problems, the organization needs to see the management-accounting process as a service that has to meet the different needs of its different users. The users include the board, the directors and managers, each of whom needs financial information for different purposes.

The job of the management-accounts service is to work with each

---

## FINANCIAL-MANAGEMENT INFORMATION AT SENSE

SENSE provides a dozen different services for children and young adults who are both deaf and blind. Income of £14 million comes from statutory sources, foundations, companies and donors. It is structured into geographical divisions.

**The board and the senior management team receive:**
an overall financial statement showing income, expenditure, surplus (and deficit) figures for each main service for

- last month
- the year to date.

**All figures show:**

- budget
- actual
- variance

alongside each other for easy comparison. These are set beside the annual budget with notes explaining unexpected differences.

**Regional and departmental directors receive:**
Income and expenditure statements broken down into cost centres, with budget, actual and variance figures for easy comparison.

**Service managers receive:**
Cost-centre reports broken down into single budget codes with budget, actual and variance figures.

On request, any manager can receive a nominal account listing of all transactions on a single budget code. Managers at regional centres can access this directly from their own terminals.

user group to agree what their needs are and how they can be met. Appropriate formats, frequency of reporting and levels of detail should be established so users get what they need (consistent with the cost of producing the information, of course). Training and support is often also required to help people understand how figures are derived and how to analyse the reports they receive.

Organizations with a number of different services funded both from their own income and from central subsidy need to produce management accounts for each service. These should identify income, expenditure and subsidy attributable to that service. The best way to do this is to lay out the accounts in what is known as the contribution approach (which is explained in Appendix 3).

## Characteristics of an effective financial-management process

Getting useful information to each level of management requires continuous effort. Every new development, and every change in management structure, has implications for the financial-information system. The aim should be to keep the system bang up to date with developments in the organization.

Once the process has been agreed it needs to provide information that is:

- accurate
- appropriately formatted
- timely.

## 6.7 MONITORING STRATEGIC PERFORMANCE

Value-led organizations are becoming increasingly aware of the need to monitor performance. Funders want evidence of outputs and outcome; boards want to know the extent to which objectives are being achieved; and managers need the information to enable them to take corrective action.

Organizations have consequently begun to establish systems to collect and report performance data. However, much of these have been at a very low level, relating primarily to the outputs of individual services (for example, the number of calls on the helpline or the number of visitors to the castle). The more challenging task is to measure the over-all performance of the enterprise. To do this an organization needs to know what it has achieved for the population it serves so it can justify its efforts to itself and its funders.

At present many organizations do not have a system designed to cap-ture data about strategic performance. They do not know, for example, whether they are reaching a growing or declining proportion of their relevant population. Even if they know the numbers of people using different services, they do not know precisely what they have achieved for each group. And when the data are collected, many organizations do not have a management process that enables the board and senior man-agement regularly and systematically to review the information and to take action on the results.

While there are good reasons for this, effective organizations strive to develop and improve systems to monitor strategic performance. This section describes what should be done to establish such a system.

## Overcoming obstacles

There is a mountain of academic literature about measuring the perform-ance of organizations. Most of it describes the problems. Very little is dedicated to offering practical solutions.

Performance monitoring requires careful thought. Since it is hard to pin down the objectives of third-sector organizations, people may dis-agree about what to measure. Indeed, heated arguments about perform-ance measures often have their roots in differences of opinion about objectives.

Ask, for example, what the organization for homeless people achieved last year and it might say it opened its doors to 250 people, each of whom stayed an average of six weeks with a bed occupancy of 90 per cent. Impressive performance at first sight. Yet, when one delves a little deeper one discovers that half the residents were the same people who each came ten times during the year. The other half were people who had been at the centre for more than two years – visitors who became permanent residents by default. If the objective was purely to provide a roof over people's heads, the organization was doing well. Beds were being used efficiently. If the objective was to help people overcome their inability to find and remain in independent accommodation, its performance was appalling. Neither group was receiving an effective service.

The second issue that has to be addressed is that different stakeholders want the organization to measure different things. The artists in the opera company, for example, want to measure the critical acclaim they receive. The education authority (a funder) wants the company to measure the number of schoolchildren the organization reaches. And the board wants to measure the annual growth in seat occupancy for different types of production.

Third, there is the issue of the measurements themselves. Quantitative measures, designed as they are to be objective, can always be criticized because they never precisely capture the essence of what the organization is trying to do. For example, the church may measure attendance but may really want to know the extent to which church-goers were satisfied with the quality of the services.

Finally, there is the issue that qualitative measures can always be criticized for being subjective. Musicians and actors can admire the quality of a performance while disliking the artist's interpretation.

## Establishing a system

Despite the inherent problems of measuring strategic performance, organizations do need a system. This has to start by accepting that multiple and sometimes conflicting performance indicators are required. The system should have three objectives:

1. It should provide indicators of achievements. These can measure outputs (for example, number of people trained, cases handled or grants given) but preferably should relate to outcomes (for example, students passing exams, people finding permanent accommodation, people with disabilities successfully seeking employment). Even better, they should relate to value added by comparing service users before and after receiving the service. This enables organizations to take account of the fact that some 'cases' are easier to solve than others. (For example, schools are beginning to record pupil achievements at different stages, so that they can measure improvement rather than absolute attainment, which depends heavily on the quality of the intake.)

2. It should enable the organization to re-allocate resources. To do this the system needs to draw together information about costs and outcomes so that judgements can be made about value for money.

3. It should measure quality, so that management can take action to improve the services they provide. Examples might include annual surveys of user satisfaction or independent appraisals.

Having decided the objectives, a system needs to be established to capture the required data. The organization's information systems

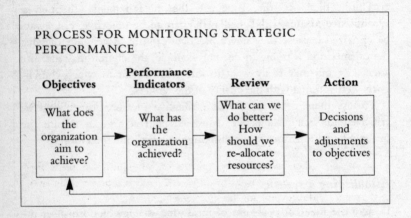

PROCESS FOR MONITORING STRATEGIC PERFORMANCE

| Objectives | Performance Indicators | Review | Action |
|---|---|---|---|
| What does the organization aim to achieve? | What has the organization achieved? | What can we do better? How should we re-allocate resources? | Decisions and adjustments to objectives |

PERFORMANCE INDICATORS AT THE ROYAL NATIONAL INSTITUTE FOR THE BLIND

The RNIB (income £47 million) provides over sixty separate services for visually impaired people. It has developed a corporate performance-monitoring system that aims to draw together:

- the number of people assisted by each service
- the outcomes of services (where this information can be captured)
- the cost of providing the service
- the subsidy that RNIB invests in the service.

Some services also collect data on quality from service users. This information, with a commentary on the significant trends, is circulated regularly to senior management and the governing board.

should be designed to enable managers to pull together information that often resides in different parts of the organization and, as often as not, in a format different from that required.

Having resolved data issues, the organization needs a management process that ensures that the board and senior management regularly review corporate performance against the agreed objectives and use it to agree the actions that are needed to improve performance.

## SUMMARY OF KEY POINTS

### Processes convert strategy into action

- Processes enable managers to plan, manage and monitor work, and they encourage people to contribute in effective ways.
- Keeping processes relevant and up to date requires continuous attention from management.

### Service plans

- Service plans describe the objectives, strategies and plans for each service the organization delivers. They are prepared in two stages – the review and the plan.
- The process for preparing service plans needs to be coordinated at the corporate level.

### Operational plans

- Operational plans link proposed activities to budgets.
- The process starts with board-approved guidelines and ends with agreement of a budget for the year ahead.

### People-management processes

- The critical people-management processes are recruitment, induction, supervision and appraisal.
- These can be combined to form a performance-management cycle that focuses people on producing results that fit with the organization's objectives.
- Problems with individuals' performance often result from a combination of employees not meeting expectations and the organization providing insufficient support and resources.

## Participation and decision-making processes

- The processes that enable people to participate meaningfully in management are communication, consultation, consensus and decision-making.
- Managers have to decide whom to consult, and when consensus cannot be achieved they need to take responsibility for making decisions.

## Financial-management processes

- Management accounting is a service that has to meet the needs of different user groups.
- Front-line managers need accurate, timely and relevant information on the income, expenditure and contribution or subsidy of their service to enable senior managers to make them accountable for the finances of their units.

## Monitoring strategic performance

- Organizations need systems to gather information and report on their overall performance to the board, management and other stakeholders.
- Most organizations require a number of measures and a mixture of quantitative and qualitative indicators. Managers need to strive continuously to improve the organization's ability to monitor its strategic performance.

# CHAPTER SEVEN

# Creating Flexible Management Structures

## 7.1 CHANGE BY CONTINUOUS ADJUSTMENT

Management processes make organizations work, but they need to be built on a structure.

Structures are central to our understanding of organizations. When people describe their organization they talk about being structured into five departments, or having nine regions. Structures define the way the parts of the organization should fit together.

However, it is well known that the structure itself is seldom a fundamental determinant of an organization's performance. It is all too easy to blame the structure for all sorts of management problems, to invest great effort in designing and implementing a new structure and to cause much personal *Angst* during the transition. Months later the original difficulties reappear because underlying problems have not been resolved.

Nevertheless, organizations do grow, new ventures are established, new posts are added and spans of control become elongated. Within a relatively short period, what looked like a rational structure quickly becomes incoherent to people inside and outside the organization. In these circumstances structural change is required.

In the past, structures were seen as relatively fixed and changed infrequently, usually in one grand effort to finally get it right. This view is no longer appropriate. The environment in which organizations operate is changing much more rapidly. New sources of funding, new methods of delivering services and the need for greater efficiency all mean that organizations need to be highly flexible. The aim, therefore, is not to design the ideal structure but to inculcate into the organization the assumption that continuous adjustments to the structure are an essential part of effective management. Those organizations that are flexible will be better able to adjust to the more uncertain and more demanding environment than those that have more rigid arrangements.

This approach enables management to move beyond the traditional approach of reorganizing to catch up with changing circumstances. It encourages managers to anticipate future needs and organize around them. Growth, changing priorities and new funding methods all require new structures. Management's task is to anticipate and adjust the structure in preparation for these new demands.

This chapter explains:

- the need to overcome obstacles to change
- options for management structures
- common dilemmas in organization design
- how to implement changes to the design.

## Overcome conservatism

It is an ironic truth that many organizations, committed as they are to change and development, are extraordinarily conservative when it comes to changing themselves. Indeed, the more radical the organization, the more entrenched can be its views of its own management. The campaigners whom the public see thumping the table in a TV interview can be very conservative when it comes to radical change in their own organization. They see no reason to change; they have the comfort of their cause – and anyone who challenges their role in the organization is seen as challenging the importance of the cause itself.

Similarly professionals with expertise in fields such as health care, education and social work have the protection of their profession. Change can be opposed because it is seen as a threat to professional independence. The aspiring organization designer can face an up-hill task. Evidence of organizations that have arrangements that have long passed their 'use-by' date is everywhere:

- small organizations committed to consensus-style management, with everyone having a say in everything, grow beyond the point where this is possible. They find it extraordinarily difficult to accept the notion of dividing managerial responsibilities and making individuals accountable for their performance
- medium-sized organizations continue to operate with one person attempting to coordinate everything when a senior management team is required to manage across departmental boundaries
- the hierarchical structures of some long-established organizations mean that decision-taking is torturously slow even when urgent action is required – for example, to stem falling membership.

Some organizations are easier to change than others. The pressures for change are strongest in organizations funded by the sale of their services. Here, market forces work to demonstrate a clear linkage between the need to change and the organization's survival. The pressures are weakest in donor-funded organizations where money may continue to flow in long after the organization has lost its cutting edge. Campaigning organizations, Churches and aid agencies need to put extra effort into changing their organization if they are to maintain efficient structures for changing circumstances.

Choice of design ultimately boils down to one person's judgement against another's. Typically the protagonists for change will argue in terms of increasing efficiency and improving the organization's attractiveness to donors, and those in favour of the *status quo* will argue that the proposed changes breach important values held by the organization, such as a commitment to consensus decision-making. Usually there is more than a grain of truth in both positions, so before long urgently required change becomes stuck in a quagmire of competing arguments. A strong-willed board or the advice of a consultant may be the only way to bring about change.

## 7.2 DIFFERENT MANAGEMENT STRUCTURES

The term 'management structure' refers to the way in which paid management and staff are organized. A useful way to think about the building blocks of the overall management structure is to consider the theoretical alternatives, recognizing that in practice most organizations need to be a mixture of each type as their preferred solution.

Since there is no ideal solution to the many dilemmas of organization structures, many organizations have one or two functional departments (such as finance and fundraising) and structure the other departments by type of service user, by service or by geography.

The main issues to consider when designing the structure include:

- the size of the senior management team
- inter-departmental links
- current managers' skills and experience.

The theoretical alternatives for dividing an organization into divisions, departments or units are:

| Structure | Examples | Advantages | Disadvantages |
| --- | --- | --- | --- |
| By function | Services<br>Finance<br>Fundraising<br>Human resource<br>Public relations | Reflects different functional skills required to manage the organization | Risks senior management teamwork being dominated by internal rather than service issues |
| By service users | Young people<br>Adults<br>Elderly | Focuses the organization on the particular needs of each client group 'Market oriented' in business language | Less suitable when service delivery is dependent on a limited pool of professional skills |
| By services | Education service<br>Housing service<br>Accident & emergency<br>Benefit rights service | Focuses on professional skills needed to deliver the service Recognizes different nature of services | Cumbersome for service users who need to access different services |
| By funder | Contract services<br>Charitable services<br>Sales-funded services<br>Membership services | Focuses the organization on its funders Separates out different logic that applies to charitably fund-ed services | Risks fragmentation of service delivery |
| By geography | Countries<br>Regions | Puts decision-making close to ground Allows for regional differences | Danger of over-stretching professional skills |

## ALTERNATIVE STRUCTURES FOR VOLUNTARY SERVICE OVERSEAS

VSO has 1,600 volunteers working on overseas assignments in fifty countries. In a typical year 75,000 people inquire about volunteering, 8,000 apply, 2,000 are interviewed, 1,200 are selected and 900 are placed. VSO gives training to volunteers before they leave and support while they are abroad. It also uses volunteers after they have returned and provides public education about its work. During a review the organization considered four structural options, simplified here for clarity:

| By region | By service |
| --- | --- |
| Africa | Services for poorest countries |
| Asia | Services for more developed countries |
| Latin America | |
| Eastern Europe | Reconstruction programme |
| Fundraising | Cultural and sports programme |
| Central services | Fundraising |
| | Central services |

| By volunteers' profession | By function |
| --- | --- |
| Education | Overseas |
| Health | Recruitment and education |
| Business development | Fundraising |
| Natural resources | Communications |
| Central services | New services |
| | Finance and administration |

Following discussions among senior management team members and consultation with staff, the director and the board decided to retain and adjust their functional structure because they wanted to increase accountability for achieving departure targets, give special attention to the development of new services and maintain a creative tension between education and fundraising.

## Size of the senior management team

The first issue to determine when structuring an organization is how many people should report directly to the chief executive. The main considerations are:

- **the rate of change in the external environment:** more rapid change requires faster responses by the organization and calls for a smaller senior management team that can meet at short notice and take quick decisions
- **the complexity of the organization:** more complex organizations require smaller senior management teams so that members can spend more time together coordinating activities and coping with the complexity

---

EVERYONE WANTS A SEAT AT THE TOP TABLE

Every department can make a compelling case for having a seat on the senior management team.

Regional Managers argue, 'We deliver the services – without us the senior management team moves into an ivory tower, utterly removed from practical service management issues.'

The Fundraising Department makes the case: 'We need to be on the team to represent the donors' views.'

The Communication Division reasons, 'Unless we are on the team we will not get our public image right, so we won't be able to raise the money or win the campaign.'

The Research Department suggests, 'We hold the keys to long-term success. If we're not on the team, investment may be wasted.'

The Personnel Department pleads, 'People are our main asset; human-resource management must be represented.'

The Development Team believes, 'We represent the new initiatives that are critical to the long-term future – they cannot be demoted to a second-tier position.'

And so on. The only department that seldom has to argue its corner is Finance.

**Tough choices have to be made to create a workable team.**

---

- **the stability of the senior management team:** when a group of managers have been in a post for a few years, and understand each other's assumptions, styles and skills, teams can be larger
- **past experience of the senior management team:** when experiences of members of the team are divergent – gleaned, for example, from private, public and the third sectors – large senior management teams are difficult because members base their judgements on different assumptions.

---

SENIOR MANAGEMENT STRUCTURE OF UNITED RESPONSE

United Response is a rapidly growing organization with an income of £12 million and 1,100 staff, providing a range of services for people with learning disabilities. Its senior management structure is as follows:

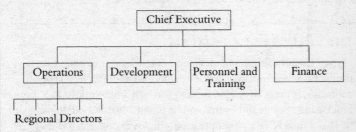

This group is divided into three teams:

a **national management team**, consisting of all these managers, which meets three or more times per year

a **strategic planning team**, which includes the four headquarters-based directors. It meets monthly and is responsible for the strategic management of the organization. It is chaired by the chief executive

an **operational management team**, which includes the regional directors and the development director. It is chaired by the operations director who is also the deputy chief executive, and meets monthly.

Although the size of the senior management team depends on circumstances, many chief executives find that teams of between five and seven people (including the chief executive) are optimal. More complex organizations in rapidly changing fields need to be at the smaller end of the spectrum. Simpler organizations with more stable management teams can have larger senior management teams.

In taking decisions about size, a choice has to be made between the desire to maximize the opportunities for team members to participate in decision-taking (which requires a smaller team), the need to bring specialist knowledge to the team's deliberations (requiring a larger membership) and the need to involve different stakeholder groups (also pushing up the size of the team).

## Inter-departmental links

In many organizations the horizontal links between different parts of the hierarchy are much more important than the hierarchy itself. These are the connections that make the organization work.

---

### THE STRUCTURE OF OXFAM

Oxfam funds health, social-development, agriculture, education, production, humanitarian and emerging programmes in seventy countries. It raises over £86 million through a network of 840 shops, fundraising appeals and events and its highly regarded catalogue.

It is a hugely complex operation employing over 2,500 staff. There are many inter-dependencies within the organization:

- fundraising has to work closely with campaigning
- trading imports products from overseas operations
- shops have to coordinate with area fundraising teams
- finance, personnel and administration have to support all areas of work.

It is structured in four divisions:

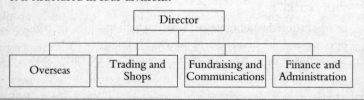

While many of the linkages come from the management processes (see Chapter 6), some can be built into the structure.

**Time-limited task groups** are an important way of bringing together the necessary skills to solve particular problems. Given an objective to achieve, agreed resources, a timescale and a leader, the task group is a highly effective cross-departmental link. However, it does have a tendency to develop a life of its own. Groups often recommend that further research is required or that they need to continue to monitor outcomes. Rigorous challenge is often required to check why nobody felt strong enough to say, 'We've done our work. It was enjoyable. Now other things are more important.'

**Coordinating groups** are another way of creating integration. By establishing a permanent group with specific responsibilities that cut across the hierarchical structure, management encourages cross-departmental linkages. However, these are more tricky to manage because the power base usually resides in the hierarchical structure.

These types of linking mechanism require skilled management if they are to be effective. The essential elements of such management include:

- a limited number of clearly specified objectives, which are kept under regular review
- leadership responsibilities given to one person, who is accountable to the line-management structure
- well-defined expectations about the way group members will report back into the line management structure
- distinct boundaries for the role of the group, to avoid gradual drift into activities that are outside the group's brief
- a focus on action, to prevent the group from becoming a talking shop that does not add value to the organization's work.

## Current managers

The final determinant of management structure will always be the current managers. Their skills and their development needs cannot be separated from the structural issue. Holding on to talented people, giving them growth opportunities and widening people's experience are all-important issues. The aspiring structure designer needs to remember that the people are the organization and that the primary purpose of the structure is to create arrangements that enable people to work together effectively in order to achieve the organization's objectives. Structures

## TEAM WORKING AT INTERMEDIATE TECHNOLOGY

Intermediate Technology (IT) is a large (£7 million per annum) multi-national agency that develops and promotes the use of appropriate technology in non-industrialized countries. It has offices in seven countries (Bangladesh, Kenya, Peru, Sri Lanka, Sudan, UK and Zimbabwe) and has work programmes for food production, building materials and shelter, energy, agro-processing, mining and small enterprise. The problems of coordination are immense.

For many years, management structure was organized around technology-driven programmes of work directed by the UK headquarters. Recently, the group has reorganized with the objectives of :

- becoming a truly multi-national organization
- decentralizing responsibilities for project work and management to country offices in the South
- making the organization more accountable to people in the countries in which it works
- focusing the UK office on propagating learning among other development agencies and providing programme support for country offices
- moving away from a highly departmentalized, hierarchical structure towards one based on team-working, cross-linkage and a high degree of interaction and cooperation.

The new senior management team meets twice a year and does much of its work in smaller teams, since travel time and costs are huge. The UK office has twelve units, two of which (publishing and consultancy) are semi-independent commercial subsidiaries. All report to the UK Director.

The International Secretariat was specifically designed to provide functional support to the line-management structure. It assists the chief executive and the senior management team and has no line authority.

To glue the whole structure together, IT has a series of cross-departmental teams. Each technology area has an international technology team drawn from people working with that technology in each country office and incorporating communication specialists when required. These teams are coordinated by international programme managers who do not have line-management authority.

IT also has two permanent activity teams in the UK, one to advise on project approvals and the other to advise on strategic planning. It also has time-limited project teams, which are set up to resolve specific problems and then disbanded.

The structure is evolving and early indications are that it is meeting the complex demands of their organization effectively.

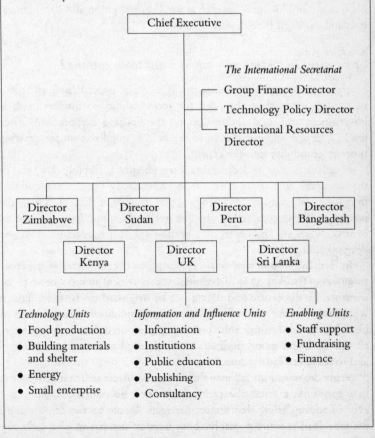

Chief Executive

*The International Secretariat*
— Group Finance Director
— Technology Policy Director
— International Resources Director

| Director Zimbabwe | Director Sudan | Director Peru | Director Bangladesh |

Director Kenya    Director UK    Director Sri Lanka

*Technology Units*
- Food production
- Building materials and shelter
- Energy
- Small enterprise

*Information and Influence Units*
- Information
- Institutions
- Public education
- Publishing
- Consultancy

*Enabling Units*
- Staff support
- Fundraising
- Finance

that are perfect on paper are of no use if they do not capitalize on the available people.

Judgement by the chief executive and board members about individuals and their potential is therefore often the most crucial element of an effective design.

## 7.3 MORE DESIGN DILEMMAS

Organization design is an art, not a science. There are no right and wrong answers – just more effective and less effective arrangements. Two common dilemmas revolve around centralization and decentralization and the need for a deputy director.

### Some want to centralize – others want to decentralize

Many organizations believe that this is a critical issue. People in favour of centralization argue the need for accountability to funders (such as government and local authorities and the housing corporation). They see lack of skill and experience in the field as good reasons for drawing more responsibility into the centre.

People in favour of decentralization argue just as forcibly that local or departmental differences have to be recognized. They point out that front-line staff can deliver effective services only if they are given the power and resources to do the job relatively unhindered by central control. They see the centre as a bottle-neck that hinders progress and development.

In fact, the argument about centralizing or decentralizing is generally misplaced. The key is to determine which critical matters need to be managed by the centre and which can be delegated to the field. This is what business calls the loose–tight organization. A few matters need to be tightly controlled from the centre (e.g., resource allocation and overall strategy), and many things can be delegated to front-line managers and subjected to loose control.

Many organizations fall into the trap of not decentralizing activities as they grow. As a result the centre becomes a bottle-neck. Despite the ever-increasing effort that senior managers devote to the organization, the workload grows inexorably. They need to determine what tasks can be decentralized. It is seldom whole areas of work. More often it comes down to decentralizing certain aspects of each area of work. The management-accounts computer needs to be centralized, but data input and report generation can be localized. Service standards need to be agreed centrally, but application is a local responsibility. The overall budget is a central responsibility, but despite the temptation to meddle, the detail should be delegated to front-line managers.

At the same time the centre of many organizations fails to control those issues that are the critical determinants of success. The centre should have a tight grip on the overall allocation of resources to different objectives or services; it should be very clear about what specifically is being achieved for each group of service users, and it should know what it costs to achieve the benefit. Unfortunately, often the centre does not gather information in ways that allow it to control these critical variables.

Commissioning a review to determine which management issues should be centralized and which decentralized will sometimes shed more light on management problems than restructuring exercises. A review provides for managers the basis on which to have a systematic discussion about the allocation of work and consequently to delegate more responsibilities and release the log-jam that often occurs at the top of the organization. The most common problem I encounter is capable middle- and front-line managers who need to be given clearly specified boundaries to their work and then be held accountable for achieving rigorously defined targets. It is always tempting for senior managers to involve themselves in the detail of the services to the detriment of their primary task of setting objectives and boundaries and delegating practical responsibilities to their unit managers.

## The deputy director dilemma

Overstretched chief executives sometimes yearn for an efficient deputy – 'someone to deal with all the detail that comes across my desk'. The pressures are very real – delivering services, campaigning for new laws, raising the money and reporting to multiple stakeholders all make the chief executive a busy person. Sadly, in many circumstances the seemingly simple solution of a deputy does not work as intended.

There is much confusion about deputies because people use the same word to mean different things. The four types of deputy are the following.

1. The person who already has a line-management responsibility but 'deputizes' for the chief executive when he or she is away.

   This is a common and sensible arrangement, which gets difficult only when the chief executive does not give the deputy adequate authority, when the deputy has a different agenda from the chief executive or when managers prefer being managed by the deputy.

2. The person who accepts responsibility for a group of services (for example, finance, personnel, administration, information systems) to reduce the chief executive's workload and span of control.

   This is one way of overcoming the problem of the overloaded chief executive. One consequence of this arrangement is that people have either to accept three 'tiers' of managers on the senior management team or to expect that people who are excluded may feel demoted and frustrated. Neither alternative is entirely satisfactory unless there is a great deal of trust and goodwill between all team members.

---

SENSE

Following a review of the management structure, the chief executive of SENSE decided to reduce his span of control by grouping all the business affairs of the organization under a deputy chief executive. This arrangement enabled the organization to grow rapidly, its income increasing from £2 million in 1987 to £14 million in 1994.

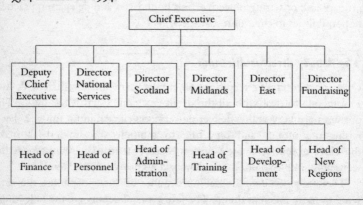

3. The 'floating' deputy director who has no line responsibilities but is used as a fixer and given specific time-limited tasks to reduce the burden on the chief executive.

   Successful operation of this arrangement depends on good working relationships between the deputy and other members of the team. The deputies need to work very closely with departmental heads to prevent them from feeling that she or he is interfering in their responsibilities. The potential for trust to break down is high!

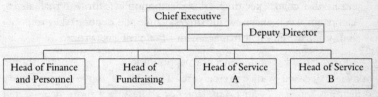

## INSTITUTE FOR THE STUDY OF DRUG DEPENDENCE

ISDD is an independent institute that collects, interprets and disseminates information on all aspects of drug dependency. Its director was a well-known authority on the subject and spent much of his time outside the organization. He supervised the professional content of the work of the unit heads. The deputy director took responsibility for the day-to-day management of the organization. He was responsible for financial and personnel aspects of their work.

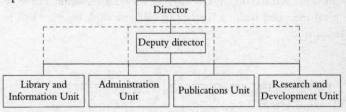

This solution was devised to suit the people at the institute and the particular combination of skills needed at that point in the organization's development. However, it is worth noting that the success of this type of solution depends on people's willingness to separate professional and managerial issues and on not bypassing the deputy when they disagree with his or her decisions.

4. The deputy who line-manages the staff and allows the chief executive to focus on external relations and overall strategy.

This works only when there is complete trust between the chief executive and the deputy and when senior managers do not bypass the deputy to get decisions from the chief executive. It can be successful when the two individuals have been working together for some time and the arrangement evolves. It works best when people are quite clear about the different roles of the two posts. This may mean the chief executive taking responsibility for external affairs, campaign work and new initiatives, while the deputy takes responsibility for the efficient management of current operations.

Organizations considering the appointment of a deputy should take this decision with extreme care. The idea of appointing a deputy director is sometimes an excuse for not addressing a more deep-seated problem in the organization. It may be that the chief executive is not delegating effectively, is failing to appoint capable senior staff or is not getting the senior management team to share responsibility for the organization as a whole. It can also result from the waning interest of chief executives or their unwillingness to do parts of the job that they do not enjoy. In any of these circumstances tackling the root cause of the problem can be more productive than appointing someone to a post that will often be a very difficult role to fulfil satisfactorily.

In circumstances where it is appropriate to have a deputy, the success of the appointment is heavily dependent on the relationship between the director and the deputy. Ideally, they should know each other well, be loyal and open with each other and able to work together in a pragmatic way.

## 7.4 IMPLEMENTING CHANGES TO THE STRUCTURE

Making major changes to the management structure is a sensitive and time-consuming task. Getting agreement to the process, developing options, consulting the board and staff and dealing with the human implications all consume effort and energy. It is a major decision that should not be taken lightly. Furthermore, as has already been stressed, the cause of ill-defined management problems may not be the structure anyhow. It is always worth checking whether other less tangible issues, such as an unclear strategy or poor management processes, are the real problems that need addressing.

Alternatives to changing the management structure include:

- improving management processes (see Chapter 6)
- changing the meetings structure (see section 6.5)
- creating cross-departmental teams (see section 7.2)
- changing one or two key people (see section 6.4).

Another consideration is the relative importance of strategy and structure. In most circumstances organizations should avoid changing their structure and the strategy simultaneously. A major review of strategy requires that managers work closely together in a dispassionate way to consider alternative futures for the organization. This cannot happen effectively if some managers are worried about the effect of a reorganization on their work and, more critically, whether they will have a job in the new structure.

Senior management has to decide which to tackle first. In some cases a new strategy may be needed before decisions about the structure can be taken. In others, the structural problems may be so pressing that management has to accept the current strategy and wait until the new senior management team is established before working on it. Although logic suggests that structure should follow strategy, sometimes it is necessary to get the right people in place in order to develop a top-quality strategy.

Since major structural adjustments are disruptive, managers should try to avoid 'big bang' changes. If the chief executive and the board have a view of the structure needed to deliver the strategy, they can use opportunities provided by growth, departures, retirements and promotions to make a series of alterations to create the desired structure.

When the structure lags far behind the organization's needs major change becomes unavoidable. In these circumstances chief executives should be prepared for the issues that frequently arise. First, the interests of each individual involved in the change (for example, for promotion, for a new role or for more status) are almost never the same as the interests of the organization as a whole (for example, for a more streamlined structure or a smaller senior management team).

Second, in some organizations there is the expectation that there will be democratic consultation over every aspect of the changes proposed. In most cases consultation leads to better decisions and greater commitment to implementation. But consultation about future structures has to be handled with precision and sensitivity because some structures may not include all existing posts.

It is virtually impossible for anyone involved in the process to separate entirely issues concerning the structure from issues related to individuals' skills and abilities. This issue becomes particularly important when some people are perceived to be under-performing. In these circumstances widespread consultation with the people who report to them may be inappropriate.

## Stages of a major reorganization

The work of making major changes to the organization structure can be divided into five stages. Some stages can be combined together in smaller organizations, in ones with a less consultative tradition and when the reorganization involves fewer people. They are set out separately here to clarify the logic behind the process.

**Stage one: agree the process.** The chief executive should seek agreement with the board that a reorganization is necessary. Since reorganizations are a sensitive issue, this is likely to require preliminary discussion with the senior management team and, sometimes, an announcement to other staff that the issue of structure is to be put on the agenda. The chief executive should agree with the board:

- the major reasons for considering a restructuring
- the scope of the exercise (involving all departments or just a few; involving senior management or more junior levels as well)
- the way the review will be carried out and when staff and board members will be consulted (i.e., the process)
- how final decisions will be taken (for example, by the board, based on a recommendation from the chief executive)
- the timetable for consultation and decisions.

This preparatory stage is vitally important. The aim is to ensure that everyone involved is clear from the start why changes are necessary and how they will be consulted. It will also help to clarify that, while there will be consultation, a final decision will be taken by the chief executive and the board. In many circumstances a chief executive will want to retain the right to propose a preferred structure to the board. But the board may also want an input into this sensitive decision because it affects the overall balance of power and the importance attached to different activities. Ultimately the best decisions are those for which the board and the chief executive together agree their preferred structure. When agreement is not possible, it is nearly always inappropriate for the board to impose a structure on the chief executive. This allows her or him to blame the board if things go wrong.

**Stage two: instigate a review.** A review needs to be carried out to pinpoint specific problems with the organization design. This may involve looking at management processes as well, since it is difficult to separate the two issues. The review may conclude with a short list of key issues that the reorganization needs to resolve. The review is a vehicle for gaining agreement among staff and board about the exact nature of the structural problems. It should also be used to establish clear reasons for changing the structure. In straightforward circumstances, stage one and two can be combined.

**Stage three: develop options.** Options need to be created and the advantages and disadvantages of each set out. At this point options should be about principles (for example, to structure around services, regions or functions). Detailed organization charts are generally inappropriate because they encourage people throughout the organization to consider their own positions rather than the principles.

**Stage four: prepare a detailed structure.** The preferred option needs to be worked up into a detailed structure, fitting individuals into the structure, so that management can identify:

- posts that will remain unchanged
- posts that disappear
- posts that change partially
- entirely new posts.

At this stage individuals who will be affected need to be spoken to by their line managers and told of the implications if the reorganization proceeds as planned. An implementation timetable should be attached to the proposals.

**Stage five: take decisions.** The chief executive needs to take decisions in consultation with the board and the senior management team. Individuals affected need to be informed personally of the implications for their jobs before general announcements are made.

Appropriate consultation is an important element of a successful reorganization and a legal requirement in some circumstances. There will always be people who gain and those who feel they have lost out in the changes. But if the chief executive has been demonstrably fair in the process, there is less cause for complaint. Consultation with staff and trade unions can be undertaken between any of the five stages. However, since some stages may have been combined, it would be appropriate to arrange either one or two rounds of consultation, often after the review stage and after the options have been prepared.

When preparing for a reorganization:

- ensure that people understand that there are no ideal solutions – compromise is always necessary
- recognize that people currently in the organization will be a significant influence on the appropriate structure – clean-sheet-of-paper exercises are seldom possible
- ensure that the board supports the proposals
- consult openly with the trade union or staff association
- be willing to see changes through – this is not a time for vacillation.

Common mistakes include:

- springing surprises on people
- reorganizing too many levels in the organization at the same time
- using restructuring primarily to solve other problems (such as an under-performing member of staff)
- being heavily influenced by lobbying from powerful individuals or groups.

## Criteria for change

The absence of profit as a primary objective means that there is no simple logic to help managers drive through necessary changes. Consequently, adjustments to the structure have to be evaluated against other criteria. The value of criteria is that they help to focus people's minds on what the change is designed to achieve. They provide a framework for making difficult decisions. The debate moves from abstract ideas about structures to a discussion of change in the context of desired outcomes.

Management can evaluate alternatives by considering whether the changes will:

- enable services to be significantly improved – for example, by integrating the delivery of fragmented activities
- strengthen the organization's fundraising capability – for example, by separating out types of fundraising that require different skills
- enable the organization to deliver its strategy – for example, by grouping services together in a different configuration
- create teams with greater potential for high performance – for example, by streamlining senior management
- reduce divisions between service delivery or campaign departments and support functions such as fundraising, finance and personnel
- strengthen coordination across the organization's boundaries – for example, by having integrated units at a lower level in the structure
- incur costs that are small in relation to the anticipated benefits.

However, even with such criteria there is no way around the unsatisfactory truth that organization design is a matter of opinion and judgement and that ultimately the board and the chief executive are responsible for making decisions about the overall structure.

## SUMMARY OF KEY POINTS

### Change by continuous adjustment

- Management needs to inculcate into the organization the assumption that continuous adjustments to the structure are essential in today's turbulent world.
- Third-sector organizations need to overcome their innate conservatism and develop structures that anticipate future needs.

### Alternative management structures

- Organizations can be structured by function, service users, services, funders and geography. Usually they are a mix of two types.
- The key issues to consider are:
  - the size of the senior management team
  - inter-departmental links
  - current managers' skills and experience.

**More design dilemmas**

- Arguments about centralizing or decentralizing need to focus on creating a loose–tight organization, with some matters closely controlled by the centre and others firmly delegated to the field.
- Appointing a deputy director is seldom straightforward. Chief executives need to decide whether the underlying problems would be solved by appointing one. They then need to select the type of deputy required to resolve the problem.

**Implementing changes to the structure**

- Chief executives need to decide whether they can achieve the desired structure using opportunities created by retirements, departures and promotions or in one 'big bang'.
- The process for changing the structure needs to involve a review, options and a proposal. Consultation is an essential element of the process.
- Establishing criteria helps to evaluate proposed changes in a structured way.

CHAPTER EIGHT

# Concepts for Managing People

## 8.1 MANAGING PEOPLE IS AN ART

Until recently management was often assumed to be part of the culture of business. It implied profit-seeking values and a desire to manipulate people. Nowadays the notions of management trip off people's tongues as easily as the language of social policy or political campaigns. However, while the ideas of management are widely accepted, many organizations have a long way to go to put them into practice, particularly when it comes to the professional management of people.

As organizations have grown larger and more complex, managing people has become an increasingly significant issue. The challenge of managing hundreds and sometimes thousands of people, often working from many different locations and even many different countries, should not be underestimated.

The organization-wide processes for managing people were described in section 6.4. This chapter looks at the four people-management concepts that I believe are most useful to individual managers at all levels of the organization:

- managing your boss
- getting performance from teams
- delegating work
- developing and supervising people.

I use the term 'manager' to apply to all levels of management. The next chapter divides management roles into different levels and looks at the specific responsibilities that chief executives, divisional directors and managers have to discharge.

Organizations that are not good at the art of managing people are characterized by:

- too many decisions coming up to the top
- managers being unwilling to take responsibility for particular areas of work
- individual aspirations being put before team achievements
- personality issues predominating over professional management.

Organizations that get best value from their people:

- demonstrate through the actions and behaviour of the board, the chief executive and the senior management team that professional management of people is a high priority
- invest in processes that encourage good people-management practices
- offer managers training to strengthen people-management skills.

To manage people effectively, managers have to learn a group of skills and be able to apply them habitually. Books can explain the theory and unpack the components of effective people management, but practice is the only way to develop the skills. An artistic parallel explains the point. Aspiring pianists who read all the books about piano playing start to learn the art only when they sit in front of the keys, try to play and learn from their mistakes. People management is similar.

There are great benefits to be derived from improved people-management practices. The core of the third sector almost certainly employs over half a million people – more than many other industries. Finding ways to enable this army of people to work productively is a challenge for management.

## 8.2 MANAGING YOUR BOSS

The term 'boss' feels slightly uncomfortable in a third-sector setting, probably because of the implication of being 'bossy'. However, as no other term is quite so clear, this section uses 'boss' to refer to the person to whom you report.

Managing your boss (an idea propounded by John Gabarro and John Kotter in *Harvard Business Review*) is the foundation stone of being a good manager. It is possible for managers to be excellent at all the other aspects of management but fail because they forget to manage this crucial relationship.

Everyone has a boss, from the chief executive who reports to the chair to front-line providers who report to their supervisor. Some people have two bosses; regional and branch managers often report to a line manager as well as the chair of the regional or branch committee; departmental managers sometimes report both to a manager and to a committee chair. They have the additional challenge of managing two sets of relationships simultaneously.

Managers can do their job only if they have an effective relationship with their boss. Each is dependent on the other. Bosses need help, guidance and advice from the managers in order to do their jobs. They need confidence that they can depend on their managers. Similarly, managers depend on their bosses for guidance and support. Managers need to understand how their work fits into the wider context; they need information from their boss and, most of all, managers need their boss to help procure the resources needed to achieve their objectives.

Poor relationships between bosses and managers are often put down to personality conflicts. 'I don't get on with the boss' is a common sentiment. However, this description of the problem sometimes conceals simple misunderstandings about the mutual dependencies in the boss–manager relationship. Managing a boss is not about political manoeuvring to seek advantage. It is a process of working with him or her to obtain the best results for the department and for the organization as a whole.

The first step in managing bosses is to **understand their context**. This means having a sense of their priorities, their aspirations and the battles that are being fought at a higher level. It means tapping into their information systems, networking with other managers and asking questions when the broader context is not clear.

The second step is to **understand their strengths and weaknesses**. Successful managers recognize that all bosses are different. Some are full of creative ideas but need guidance to come to decisions. Some are decisive but need to have all the options developed for consideration. Some are good at networking outside the organization but need to be briefed on developments within the organization. Managers who understand their bosses actively exploit their strengths and support them in their weaker areas.

The third step is to **understand bosses' preferred working methods**. This requires watching their behaviour and gaining insights into the way they work. Some people prefer to learn about things on paper; others prefer a verbal report. Some like solitary time to think;

## TWO MANAGERS AT CITY HOUSING ASSOCIATION

Jane, the chief executive of City Housing, was formal and well organized. She paid attention to detail and liked to have written reports and formal meetings with set agendas.

Nick, a flamboyant and creative manager, preferred a more informal and intuitive style. He had great difficulty with the chief executive. Their meetings were always fraught with problems as the chief executive tried to piece together the information she thought she should have had before the meeting. Nick often felt that Jane was meddling in the detail when what he wanted was guidance and support. Despite being an excellent manager of his staff, he eventually left the organization.

Juliet, another manager, worked hard to manage her relationship with the chief executive. She asked what information Jane would like to have before they met. She noticed that the chief executive was most effective when she had time to think about issues before a meeting. Although it took time to prepare the paperwork, her department grew and flourished because it was able to exploit both her own and her chief executive's talents.

others prefer to work things out together. Some are lateral thinkers; others are better at making quick judgements. Managers can get better value from their boss if they understand their working styles.

Managers can conceive of their boss as a resource that needs to be used effectively. Bosses' time is always limited, so it needs to be used judiciously. Wasting time involving them in detailed issues which managers ought to resolve on their own is a common mistake. Briefing them on the issue and the action taken can be more helpful. Similarly, judging when an issue needs their attention, preparing thoughts about the problem and knowing what to ask helps make effective use of their time.

All relationships have frustrations. The successful manager learns how to handle them. People who rebel against their boss and undermine him or her are not creating the conditions for succeeding in their own job. Similarly, people who bottle up all their frustrations and do not share their concerns with their boss are storing up problems for the future. Effective managers work hard to address their frustrations with their boss in constructive ways. They praise their boss when she or he has done things well. They offer to support their boss when he or she needs assistance. They raise anxieties openly and make positive suggestions about ways of improving the relationship.

In summary, one of the priorities for any manager is to understand the broader context in which their boss is working, to discover their boss's preferred working style, to use their boss to help with tasks they are good at and to look elsewhere for the support their boss is unable to provide.

## 8.3 GETTING PERFORMANCE FROM TEAMS

In addition to creating relationships with their boss and sometimes with committees, managers also have to create relationships with the people who work for them. More than anything, managers need to create and lead a team of people who are dedicated to achieving agreed objectives.

Ultimately, managers' success depends on getting high performance from their teams. Their job is to release the potential that is within team members and to ensure that the results of the team as a whole are much greater than the sum of the parts. Teams are important not only in the line-management structure but also as an essential integrating mechanism across the departmental structure.

When teaching about teams, Ashridge Management College, a research and management school, summarizes the characteristics of highly effective teams as groups that are:

- persistent in pursuit of their goals
- inventive in overcoming obstacles
- committed to quality in all aspects of teamwork
- inspired by a vision
- action-orientated
- committed to the success of the organization as a whole
- able to distinguish the important from the urgent
- willing to take risks and be innovative and creative
- always looking for ways to do things better.

This, no doubt, reflects many team leaders' intentions. However, two special characteristics of value-led organizations have to be overcome to attain this ideal. First, there is the fact that the sector attracts

## LIFE CYCLE OF A TEAM

Many theorists believe that groups develop in a series of stages. The idea was originally put forward by B. W. Tuckman and has been neatly summarized by Charles Handy.

'Groups mature and develop. Like individuals and organizations, they have a fairly clearly defined growth cycle. This has been categorized as having four successive stages:

1. **Forming.** The group is not yet a group but a set of individuals. This stage is categorized by talk about the purpose of the group. The definition and the title of the group, its composition, leadership pattern, and life-span. At this stage each individual tends to want to establish his or her personal identity within the group and make an individual impression.

2. **Storming.** Most groups go through a conflict stage when the preliminary, and often false, consensus on purposes, on leadership and other roles, on norms of work and behaviour, is challenged and re-established. At this stage a lot of personal agendas are revealed and a certain amount of inter-personal hostility is generated. If successfully handled, this period of storming leads to a new and more realistic setting of objectives, procedures and norms. This stage is particularly important for testing the norms of trust in the group.

3. **Norming.** The group needs to establish norms and practices: when and how it should work, how it should take decisions, what type of behaviour, what level of work, what degree of openness, trust and confidence is appropriate. At this stage there will be a lot of tentative experimentation by individuals to test the temperature of the group and to measure the appropriate level of commitment.

4. **Performing.** Only when the three previous stages have been successfully completed will the group be at full maturity and be able to be fully and sensibly productive.'

From *Understanding Organizations*, Charles Handy, Penguin, 1994.

Some theorists have added two further stages – **re-forming** to account for changes in the group's membership and **mourning**, the necessary process of properly marking the end of a group's life.

an extraordinarily wide range of characters to its organizations, many of whom are intelligent, charismatic and opinionated but sometimes obstinate when it comes to being a team player.

Second, managers have to understand that their role is different from that of other members of the team. The democratic values of some organizations and the deeply held desire to represent users' views can spill over into team behaviour. Sometimes managers start from an assumption that their primary duty is to represent the views of their staff or service users. They put their loyalty to their staff or service users ahead of their role as a member of a more senior team in which they have to make trade-offs between the interests of different parts of the organization. They feel more accountable to the people they represent than to the more senior team. They find it hard to accept collective responsibility for management decisions and to support those decisions when they have to report back to their own team.

Managers therefore need to understand the techniques that they can use to create teams that perform well. This section briefly introduces some of the behaviours and actions that managers can apply.

## Creating the team

The first issue to consider is the **size of the team**. Teams that are too small may not contain all the skills required or generate enough variety of thought. Teams that are too large are cumbersome and frustrating for members.

Larger teams are appropriate when:

- some of the posts are similar (for example, managers of similar centres or regions) because they will have common problems
- members are experienced team players who require less support, supervision and coaching
- a wide range of skills is essential to the team's effectiveness (for example, resolving very complex problems).

Smaller teams are appropriate when:

- there is high interdependence between members (for example, an assessment and rehabilitation centre where tight coordination is required) – they need time to work closely together
- the team works in a rapidly changing environment (for example, a campaign team) – people will need lots of short meetings.

Any rule has exceptions, but, for many situations a team of between five and seven people is a common compromise.

The next issue to consider is the **characteristics of members**. For teams to perform to the highest standard people have to work closely together, support each other and put team needs before their own. A balance has to be found between having people with similar backgrounds and experience who work together well but only see issues from one perspective and having a more heterogeneous team drawing on people with different skills. Heterogeneous teams may experience more conflict but they can ultimately be more productive.

---

### REORGANIZATION OF A MANAGEMENT TEAM

In 1991 a British aid agency recognized the need for radical change in its management. Senior management team meetings were lengthy and often inconclusive, personal relationships were poor, meeting discipline was deteriorating.

'It's because we can't agree whether our primary objective should be emergency aid, long-term development, empowerment of local people or institutional change,' said one group. 'If only we can agree on our fundamental purpose, our problems will be solved.'

'The problem is we aren't sticking to our strategy,' argued another group. 'We spent a year agreeing a strategic plan, but we never use it to guide our decisions.'

'We can't work together as a team,' argued a third group. 'We need training in team development and facilitation to help us discover ways of working together.'

In practice none was right. The central problem was that the team of nine people was too large and too heterogeneous to work together. Too many big personalities, each in charge of a large division, just could not cooperate effectively.

Reorganized, the team became a group of five people. The combination of a smaller team, three of whose members were recruited from outside the organization, was enough to break the mould and establish new ways of working together.

Then there is the issue of **sensitivity and trust**. People who get along well, who trust each other and are sensitive to each other's needs are more productive than people who are suspicious of each other. Research has shown that compatibility is important and becomes more crucial as the task becomes more complex.

The fourth aspect of creating an effective team is allowing **time for people to get to know each other** both professionally and personally. Teams are more effective when people understand each other's personal backgrounds and personalities. They work more efficiently when members have a deep understanding of each other's strengths and weaknesses. This can take months, often years. Time for team 'away-days', social events and, particularly in the forming stage, lots of team meetings all help to provide the foundations for a high-performance team.

## Changing team membership

Sometimes managers need to change the size, structure or membership of a team in order to improve its performance. Teams can be restructured but, as Chapter 7 demonstrated, this does not always have the desired results. Another option for changing team membership is to make judicious use of opportunities created by people leaving or retiring. A departure gives managers the space to reconsider everyone's responsibilities and either reduce or enlarge the team.

Another, more subtle, option is to **change the definition of the team**. Team membership can be adjusted by redefining the scope and purpose of the team and incorporating or excluding people to increase its effectiveness. For example, if a team is too small and the organization has talented people who are not on the team, it can be expanded for certain types of meeting. A quarterly review of strategy, for example, or a series of planning meetings provide an ideal opportunity to enlarge the team. Alternatively the team may be too large. In this case it may be necessary to reduce the frequency of meetings and create a smaller group to coordinate activities between meetings.

Creating a team with an appropriate size and composition is an essential prerequisite for getting performance from it. However, there is a trap to avoid. Some managers mistakenly assume that getting the right group of people is their most important task. They continually adjust the structure and the membership of the team – not recognizing that **each adjustment is a disruption** to team dynamics. Developing appropriate team behaviour and coaching members to help them become better team players can have more effect than adjusting team membership. Each time team membership is adjusted, its behaviour takes a step back in the forming, storming model (see box), a consequence that is sometimes overlooked. In short, oversize or undersize teams with good team behaviour can be more productive than a team with appropriate size and composition and no accepted ways of working.

## Developing the team

**Teams need objectives.** Everyone on the team needs to be quite clear about what the team is trying to achieve. The team needs both to have words that define the objectives and to be clear about the context in which they have to be achieved. The objectives need to be understood from many different perspectives and from the different viewpoints that each team member brings.

Ideally, all team members must be directly involved in agreeing the objectives. Everyone needs to believe in them too. It is easy to support the words, but the high-performance team needs people who are motivated to achieve the objectives and demonstrate by their behaviour in and outside the team that they believe in the objectives. This can be achieved only by working on the objectives, taking time away from the office to explore the options and develop the thinking. Objectives can then be tested on other groups (up, down, across and outside the organization) to make them more robust.

**Teams plan together.** Successful teams spend time planning their work. Sometimes individual members of subgroups will prepare plans for achieving a particular objective and bring them to team meetings. In other situations planning the work will be done in team meetings. If the team has been created to undertake a specific project, it may well identify the factors that are critical to the project's success (see Eastlink Housing box). Whatever the circumstances, effective teams are clear about how the objectives will be achieved.

**Teams need coaching.** Managers are responsible for setting the standards for team behaviour. As well as guiding the team in its work, managers encourage members to contribute constructively. They praise good team behaviour, they criticize poor contributions and they help people to improve their work.

## EASTLINK HOUSING PROJECT TEAM

Project teams enhance their effectiveness by identifying the factors that are critical to their success. These are the limited number of action areas that are both necessary and sufficient to achieve the objectives.

Working to identify the actions, boil them down to a manageable list and check that they are both necessary and sufficient provides team members with a deeper understanding of objectives and how they will be achieved. Descriptions of critical success factors usually begin with the words 'We must . . .' or 'We need to . . .'

Eastlink Housing Association put together a cross-departmental team to manage a major conversion project. They established the following objectives and critical success factors.

### Objective

To convert three old people's homes into local centres for frail elderly people over the next three years.

### Critical success factors

- We must raise a total of £3.6 million from statutory and charitable sources to complete the project.
- We must create an in-house development team of three people dedicated to this project alone for at least two years.
- We must find superior-quality accommodation for existing tenants and give them a minimum of six months' warning of the move.
- We must recruit people with expertise in managing centres for frail elderly people to start work four months before each centre opens.
- We need to create new management committees for each centre incorporating the seven specialist skills identified as critical to their success.

**Teams need good administration.** Preparation for meetings and communication outside meetings are essential elements of effective teams. The major topics for meetings need to be planned, so papers can be commissioned, reviewed by the manager and distributed in advance. Timing of meetings, appropriate venues and circulation of action notes may all be details, but they are crucial elements of an effective team.

## Leading teams

Finally, study after study has shown that the most effective teams are those that have strong leadership that is sensitive to team members' needs and not dominant or authoritarian. Team leadership is an art. It requires the adroit use of different skills in different circumstances. The critical elements of effective team leadership can be summarized as follows:

**Start modestly.** Managers should set modest objectives at the beginning, build the team's confidence in itself and then increase expectations. If leaders are too ambitious, they risk losing credibility when the objectives are not achieved.

**Promote the mission.** Teams are motivated by missions. They need to feel that their work is vitally important and be able to set it into the broader context of the organization's overall objectives. Managers should emphasize the value of the work being done and remind people that bureaucracy and management are only necessary activities to achieve the broader mission.

**Encourage openness.** Teams under-perform when individuals have private agendas or when one group is making assumptions different from another's. Managers need to tease out private issues and ensure that their own agenda is open and explicit.

**Support each other.** Members of high-performance teams take particular care to support each other. They build on each other's arguments in meetings, show concern for each other's welfare and assist each other in their work. Managers set the tone by being seen to support team members.

**Face up to differences.** Managers with strong teams encourage differences of opinion. They expect members to make their differences clear but to be willing to compromise when decisions are required. They also expect team members to support decisions once they have been made.

**Review performance regularly.** Managers set aside time for the team to review its own performance. They identify behaviour that worked well and review situations where improvements could be made. They encourage critical discussion of the team's performance and expect the team to agree actions to improve team performance. They remind the team of agreed actions when behaviour slips below expectations.

**Encourage systematic decision-taking.** Teams make better decisions if they are systematic about gathering information, diagnosing problems, seeking opinions and evaluating options before taking decisions. Effective leaders encourage a rigorous approach to decision-taking.

**Make the team visible.** Managers promote their teams both inside and outside the organization. They communicate up, down and across the organization, ensuring that their team's work engages with the rest of the organization.

**Encourage action.** Managers encourage action. They clarify what needs to be done and ensure that agreed actions are followed through.

**Celebrate success.** Managers ensure that successes are celebrated. They mark achievements with praise, publicity and parties.

## 8.4 DELEGATING WORK

Delegation is the art of sharing work among the team, giving people the latitude to make decisions but retaining responsibility for achievement of the task.

There are many forces that work against delegation in value-led organizations. Managers are often highly motivated by the nature of the work they are doing. They believe in the cause they are working for, put in long hours and enjoy the detail. It is very tempting not to delegate enough in these circumstances.

Then there is the fact that staff feel overloaded. They too are committed to the cause and often believe that they could not work harder. So, before work can be delegated, managers have to find ways to help their staff review priorities and stop doing some things that they believed were important in order to create the time to do the new work the manager wishes to delegate to them. The issue is usually not lack of willingness but the ability to set priorities that are consistent with the manager's view of their relative importance.

Frequently there is the pressure of time. The work needs to be done quickly, so the easiest solution is for managers to do it themselves. It takes time to brief someone, explain what is required and help them to adjust their priorities, so it often appears easier just to do the task. This, however, is a recipe for overload. Effective delegators anticipate the need for the work and decide how it can be done before they are trapped into doing it themselves.

Another obstacle to delegating is the fear that the staff member will not be able to do the task. Sometimes this may be entirely justified and the task should not be delegated to that person. But sometimes managers have to take small risks to give the person to whom the task is delegated an opportunity for learning.

Successful managers delegate as much as they possibly can. They delegate in stages as people's skill and experience grows; they monitor the delegatee's performance; and they maintain the level of control needed to ensure a successful outcome. They start by delegating low-risk tasks, and as the person's experience grows higher-risk tasks are delegated.

To delegate effectively, managers have to trust their staff and be confident that they can do the delegated tasks. Simultaneously they must reduce the amount of direct control they have over the way the individual does the task. Once the boundaries have been agreed, managers should hand over control to the delegatee. The less control they retain the more the delegatee will feel responsible for completing the work to the required standard.

However, delegation is not simply a matter of handing over tasks to other people. It is the skill of giving people additional responsibilities that are within their abilities and providing appropriate advice and support until that person is able to take greater responsibility for the task. The amount of work that can be delegated depends on the person's experience, the confidence of the manager and the risk attached to the task.

## Learning the art of delegating

Becoming an effective delegator requires a certain attitude of mind. Good managers instinctively think ahead and ask themselves how to achieve each task for which they are responsible. Anticipation is a critical ingredient. Managers have to allow time to brief the people being delegated the tasks and to allow them to fit the work into their already busy schedules. They have to allocate time to review progress, give advice and to support the delegatee.

Managers also need to clarify why they are delegating tasks. They can delegate:

- **to make better use of time:** managers are paid to manage, not to do the work. They have to create time to discharge their many managerial responsibilities and this invariably means delegating as much work as their staff can handle.
- **to give staff development opportunities:** all staff need to develop their skills and abilities. Giving staff responsibility for additional tasks is an ideal method of enabling and encouraging professional development. It provides new challenges within carefully identified boundaries.
- **to use people's skills:** staff have strengths in areas where the managers may have weaknesses. Managers delegate to maximize the use of staff members' skills.

---

## DELEGATING WORK IN THE TRADE UNION

'I know I need to delegate more,' the union official told the management consultant. 'I've read all the books on it and even attended a course. It's just not that straightforward.'

'You need to sit down with each member of your team and agree what can be delegated. I'll help by providing an independent perspective,' said the consultant, spotting an opportunity to sell his time.

'That isn't the problem,' said the union official. 'My difficulty is that all the committee members expect me to deal personally with every problem. Committee chairs in particular feel that their status is not being recognized if I delegate their problems to my staff. Chairs feel they can do the job they have been elected to do only if they deal with me.'

'Well,' said the consultant, 'we'll have to think about how to persuade them to allow you to delegate.'

**Delegation is seldom straightforward.**

Some activities cannot be delegated. **People-management responsibilities**, such as supervision, appraisals, chairing team meetings, discipline, praise and resolution of disputes, are responsibilities that managers should retain in all but the most unusual circumstances. **Policy-making** cannot be delegated. The work of preparing papers, doing research and making proposals can be delegated, but decisions on matters which have widespread repercussions cannot be delegated. **Crisis management** usually requires judgements to be made from a broader perspective. These situations can seldom be delegated. Matters involving **confidential information**, such as sensitive personnel information, cannot be delegated. Finally, the **rituals** of celebrating successes, rewarding long service and representing the organization or department at major occasions should not be delegated.

## Improving delegation skills

Good practice in delegating involves:

- creating a well-informed team of people who understand the broader context into which their work fits: when tasks are delegated, people will understand why the work needs to be done
- giving people appropriate information about the task. Hard information about what needs to be achieved is as important as soft data about the people and problems that might be encountered
- being clear about the objective but allowing the delegatee to take the initiative in how it is achieved
- being clear about available resources and the timescale for achieving the result
- being honest about the task and what it will involve
- leaving no confusion about accountability for the work
- giving credit for a job well done and taking responsibility if it does not go well
- using mistakes as learning opportunities and not as reasons for allocating blame.

Delegating is a skill that is learned with practice. It is an essential ability that managers need to grasp. Too often managers either fail to delegate and overload themselves or delegate without providing the support and guidance that is needed to produce the required outcomes. Managers need to practise delegation so it becomes an instinctive way of working.

## 8.5 SUPERVISING AND DEVELOPING PEOPLE

The final set of ideas that needs to be introduced in this chapter concerns supervising and developing people. Organizations depend, more than anything else, on the quality of their people. Developing their skills and abilities is consequently a critical, and often forgotten, management task. Organizations that strive to develop the capabilities of their staff attract more talented people who grow personally and perform to higher standards. Organizations that neglect this crucial area have higher staff turnover, a less motivated workforce and achieve less with the resources at their disposal.

Supervision is concerned with:

- managing people to perform their work tasks
- providing a structured opportunity to review progress and problems.

Developing people is concerned with extending their skills and experiences:

- to enable them to be more effective in achieving the organization's goals
- to give them opportunities for personal growth.

The two have been brought together because a regular meeting can be used to perform both functions.

The overall process that organizations need to put into place to enable and encourage supervision and development was described in section 6.4. This section focuses on the principles that managers need to consider when discharging their supervision and people-development responsibilities.

### *Personal development*

Personal-development experiences come from many sources:

- the nature of the work that people are doing
- the teams that people are working with
- the supervision and appraisals that people receive
- the training that people receive
- the books that people read!

## RECOGNIZING DEVELOPMENT NEEDS

By observation, working together and discussion you will have a sense of someone's strengths and weaknesses; you will also come to know the areas of work that they enjoy, those that they find less satisfying and their longer-term aspirations. You will also know about the demands and possibilities of the work. In addition, you may have information or ideas about the emerging priorities for the organization as a whole and about the prospects and requirements that these may involve. These aspects are represented in the diagram.

Ideally the three discs would stack neatly on top of each other, meaning that the work being done fitted perfectly with the individual's aspirations and abilities and with the organization's priorities. Unfortunately the reality is more complex. The fit is rarely 100 per cent, and the discs keep shifting in relation to each other. For example, the work being done may lag behind the latest priorities, or the individual may have to do work that she or he does not feel capable of or want to do. Moreover, one disc can cause another to shift with it (as happens when an individual shifts the job to suit her or his abilities or when an organization changes its plans in the light of the possibilities revealed by a job). Alternatively, a disc can shift in the opposite direction to the others in reaction to developments (for example, when individuals try to set up a new project to ensure themselves greater opportunities).

So the discs keep moving, and your aim can only be to maintain a reasonable alignment among them by adjusting the job, by developing the individual or occasionally by seeking to adjust the organization's priorities (to take advantage, for example, of under-used skills).

From *Managing Voluntary and Non-profit Enterprises*, Book 6, *Choosing and Developing Staff and Volunteers*, Open University Business School.

Managers can play a significant role in helping people to develop. Their enthusiasm, their willingness to think about others' needs, their discipline in holding regular supervision sessions, their ability to give people work that provides development experiences and to help their staff learn from them are all-important ingredients. However, the extent to which individuals develop depends ultimately on their motivation and willingness to learn. Their attitudes are, in the end, the crucial determinant of their development.

## *Supervision*

The main vehicle that managers have for developing people is the regular one-to-one supervision session. This session provides the discipline to think about each individual in the team and her or his development needs. However, in many organizations the daily pressures of work conspire against finding time to develop people. The latest crisis always seems more important than the supervision session that inevitably has a long-term pay-back. Discipline in holding the meetings and commitment to preparing for them are needed to ensure that development takes place.

Supervision follows directly from delegation. When managers delegate work to individuals, they have a corresponding duty to review progress, help people overcome problems and give constructive feedback.

Supervision needs to be set in the context of individuals' objectives and the support that the organization has agreed to provide. It flows from the annual appraisal where objectives will have been agreed. Supervision needs to revisit these objectives, monitor progress in achieving them, review obstacles and agree new actions. Supervision should therefore aim to:

- review achievements against objectives
- ensure that delegated work is done to the agreed standard and within the agreed timescale
- check that people have received the resources required to achieve their objectives
- enable people to learn from their work experiences and develop their skills

- provide a channel for two-way feedback on any other work-related issues (including problems outside work that may affect people's performance).

The nature and frequency of supervision depends on both the work that has been delegated and the experience of the person being supervised. When the work is challenging, perhaps due to changes in the external environment or to the behaviour of clients being assisted, supervision needs to be more frequent and more supportive. Similarly, when the person being supervised is highly experienced and has been in the job for many years, supervision can be less frequent and more consultative in nature.

The nature of supervision varies enormously according to circumstances. A practice leader supervising therapists or counsellors has a very different task from that of the accountant supervising bookkeepers, the chief executive supervising divisional directors and the home manager supervising domestic staff.

In high-stress situations, such as providing counselling or therapy, social work and emergency aid, supervision focuses particularly on coping with the stress of the circumstance and is a more specialized skill (described in *Supervision in the Helping Professions*, P. Hawkins and R. Shahet, Oxford University Press, 1991).

The frequency of supervision is likely to vary from weekly (for a new, inexperienced person or someone working in a challenging environment) to quarterly (for an experienced person in a stable environment). For many people monthly or every other month will be an appropriate frequency.

Three elements, originally identified by A. Kadushin, writing about social-work supervision, provide a useful framework for thinking about supervision. He talks about the educative, supportive and managerial aspects of supervision. In the **educative** role, supervisors help to develop people's skills by helping them to reflect on their work, understand what they have achieved and how they might approach similar situations in the future.

In the **supportive** role, supervisors are attending to people's individual needs, a particularly important function for people working in challenging situations. In the **managerial** role, supervisors are concerned with clarifying objectives, reviewing outputs and controlling quality.

Supervision sessions can cover many issues. Most are either

concerned with the work people are doing or the development of people themselves. It is important, therefore, for the supervisor to clarify with people being supervised what they wish to achieve through a supervision session. Explicit clarification of the expectations of both parties can lead to much more productive supervision sessions.

---

## SOME OF THE ACTIVITIES OF EFFECTIVE SUPERVISORS

### Task-related activities

| | |
|---|---|
| *Shaping* | structuring the task |
| *Target-setting* | setting or agreeing specific goals and deadlines |
| *Explaining* | selling policies and plans |
| *Delegating* | devolving tasks and responsibilities |
| *Guiding* | giving advice, information, being a role model |
| *Limiting* | setting boundaries, reining people in |
| *Negotiating* | matching individual ideas with organizational policy |
| *Resourcing* | arranging back-up, funds, etc. |

### People-related activities

| | |
|---|---|
| *Coaching* | helping people to learn the work |
| *Encouraging* | being a sounding board, boosting morale |
| *Facilitating* | arranging introductions and putting people in touch |
| *Counselling* | giving assistance in exploring approaches to situations/dealing with anxieties |
| *Representing* | speaking on behalf of individuals |
| *Evaluating* | making judgements about achievements/ potential. |

From *Managing Voluntary and Non-profit Enterprises*, Book 6, *Choosing and Developing Staff and Volunteers*, Open University Business School.

## SUMMARY OF KEY POINTS

### Managing people is an art
- The challenge of instilling good people-management practices throughout an organization should not be underestimated.
- People-management skills are developed by practice.

### Managing your boss
- Managers need to manage their relationships with their boss.
- They need to understand his or her context, strengths and weaknesses and preferred working methods.
- Managers should use their boss's strengths and look elsewhere for the support that he or she is unable to provide.

### Getting performance from teams
- The size of the team needs to be related to the task.
- Team membership can be adjusted by including additional people for certain topics or creating sub-groups to address specific issues.
- Successful teams need clear objectives, to plan together, coaching from the leader and good administration.

### Delegating work
- There are many forces that work against delegation in value-led organizations.
- Delegation is the art of giving people responsibilities that are within their abilities.
- People management, policy-making, crisis management, matters involving confidential information and organization rituals should not be delegated.

### Supervising and developing people
- Supervision is concerned with managing people to perform their work tasks and providing opportunities to review progress and problems.

- Developing people is concerned with extending their skills.
- Regular one-to-one meetings are the best way of supervising and developing people.
- Managers should talk to supervisors about the types of supervisory support they require.

CHAPTER NINE

# Making a Success of Different Jobs

## 9.1 MANAGEMENT JOBS ARE DIFFERENT

Everyone recognizes that managers' jobs differ by function; the Director of Finance clearly has a very different job from that of the Director of Services. Equally important, however, is an understanding of how managers' jobs differ by level. Some people make the assumption that senior managers have greater responsibility but that their jobs are essentially similar to junior management posts. In practice nothing could be further from the truth. The roles of chief executives, divisional directors (a level that exists in larger organizations) and managers are fundamentally different.

Chief executives have particular responsibility for leadership of their organizations, for managing the crucial relationship between the board and the staff and for ensuring that the mission and strategy is clear.

Divisional directors have two different roles. As members of the senior management team they have to share responsibility with the chief executive for the overall management of the enterprise. Within their divisions they have to be able to manage managers; they have to support and coach their managers, set strategy and manage efficient services or campaigns.

Managers' jobs are different again. They are responsible for managing people to provide direct services, campaigns or internal services (such as finance and personnel). They have a 'small business' within the enterprise and have to develop strategy and deliver services and campaigns that achieve agreed objectives within a fixed budget.

Chief executives, divisional directors and managers all have to deploy the skills of managing their boss, getting teams to perform, delegating work and supervising people. But each has to deploy an additional range of skills:

- chief executives have to provide leadership
- divisional directors have to direct
- managers have to manage.

The skills that need to be deployed at each level are additional. Chief executives have to have mastered the art of divisional directorship (assuming they are managing a divisionalized organization) and the basic skills of management. Divisional directors need to use basic management skills as well as the skills of directing managers.

This chapter describes these different skills and how people acquire them.

## 9.2 SPECIAL CHARACTERISTICS OF THE CHIEF EXECUTIVE'S JOB

The role of chief executives of value-led organizations has changed dramatically in the last thirty years. The post used to be called General Secretary, and the role was seen as that of the administrative servant of the board. The post-holder was given comparatively little strategic authority, and the board could play a hands-on role because most organizations were small.

During the 1970s the title 'Director' started to creep on to organizations' letterheads, reflecting a change in the duties that the board expected the person to discharge. In the 1980s the language and role changed again. Organizations began to seek 'Chief Executives'. They wanted people with substantial management experience who could take charge of these increasingly large and complex organizations.

It is now widely accepted that having a talented chief executive is a critical ingredient of a successful organization. A chief executive is expected to be figurehead, politician and manager rolled into one. The job is undoubtedly demanding. To understand why requires some insight into why it is so different from all other posts.

**It is less structured.** Being responsible for everything means the chief executive can become involved in anything. This lack of boundaries differentiates the job from all other posts. As ex-ICI boss John Harvey-Jones says, 'It is only when you become aware of the range, scope and incredible responsibility of the job that you realize that there is an almost limitless opportunity to be ineffective unless you are totally clear about how you are going to set about it.'

**It is highly exposed.** The chief executive has nowhere to hide. He or she is expected to speak in public, to make press statements, to report to the board, to make presentations at gatherings of staff and to approve publicly available documents. Chief executives are on stage every day of their working lives.

**It requires the widest range of abilities.** Chief executives need to master an extraordinary range of skills. They need to understand the fundamentals of finance, marketing, service and human-resource management; they are expected to deploy strong inter-personal skills and at the same time master the policy issues of their field; they need consummate political skills to make things happen when there is no bottom line; they need to be tough when hard decisions have to be made and tender when compassion and sensitivity are required.

**It involves the widest range of constituencies.** Chief executives have to operate with many different groups including funders, service users, umbrella organizations as well as staff and board members. They have to adjust their style and approach to suit groups that often have different interests and different motives for contributing to the organization.

**It is a lonely position.** The chief executive often has no one inside the organization to seek advice from on sensitive issues because the very act of raising them can cause unnecessary anxiety, particularly if they are matters that are not subsequently pursued.

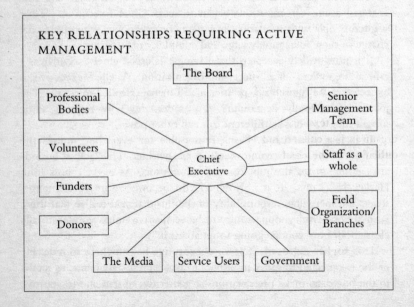

KEY RELATIONSHIPS REQUIRING ACTIVE MANAGEMENT

The Board

Professional Bodies

Senior Management Team

Volunteers

Chief Executive

Staff as a whole

Funders

Field Organization/ Branches

Donors

The Media    Service Users    Government

**It depends on maintaining a reservoir of goodwill.** Chief executives need the trust and active support of their board and their staff. They have to maintain the confidence of both groups in order to do the job.

**It is the critical link between the board and the staff.** The chief executive has to operate effectively both as head of the senior management team and as the servant of the board. These two groups frequently have different working styles and priorities. The chief executive has to work with both and manage the information flows between the two.

**It requires a longer-term perspective and short-term actions.** Chief executives have to think months or years ahead and simultaneously solve current problems that have not been resolved elsewhere in the organization.

Four further aspects of the role are common in managing value-led organizations.

**It is not well understood.** The special characteristics of the chief executive's job are often not well understood by the board, the staff and other people outside the organization. This results in conflicting expectations that will pull the chief executive in different directions until these people become clear about the role.

Chief executives have to **bridge many fundamentally different value systems**. Third-sector organizations all have a skill base such as medicine, education, social welfare and so on. Each skill base has associated with it a set of values that are predominant in that field. These values are seldom consistent with a managerial mind-set (see Appendix 2). The chief executive has to bridge the different values and help one group to see an issue from another's perspective.

Chief executives have to **challenge inappropriate values**. Modern management textbooks (including this one) stress the importance of the organization's culture and values. But values can also be a source of difficulty for the chief executive when they permeate all aspects of an organization's work in ways that are inappropriate.

Take, for example, the training organization whose commitment to training its own staff grows out of proportion to their need to perform their jobs; the trade union that is frightened to challenge the union its own staff belong to; the human-rights organization that uses the language of human rights to argue for equality of status for all staff; or the social-services agency that cannot bring itself to sack members of staff who are consistently not performing to the required standard. In these circumstances it falls to the chief executive to challenge the inappropriate application of value-led beliefs.

Finally, third-sector chief executives have to **deploy a combination of entrepreneurial and political skills**. They need the entrepreneurial abilities of taking risks and seizing opportunities that are usually associated with the private sector. They also need the ability to unite diverse political constituencies behind activities that everyone is willing to support – a skill that is more often associated with public-sector management.

## 9.3 STRUCTURING CHIEF EXECUTIVES' WORK

Because the chief executive's job entails endless variety, it is all the more important to structure the work. Without structure there is always the risk that chief executives become the servants of their in-trays – dealing with what appears to be most urgent rather than those things that are most important (and usually do not appear in the in-tray).

One way to structure chief executives' work is to think in terms of their responsibilities for the three Ps:

- the **purpose** of the organization
- the **processes** of managing it
- the **people** who work closely with the chief executive.

### *The purpose*

The paramount priority of the chief executive is to ensure that all parts of the organization have specific objectives that relate directly to its overall purpose.

Chief executives have a wide range of responsibilities relating to the purpose. Their first responsibility is to ensure that all parts of the organization are **focusing on achieving the purpose**. This is easier said than done. It is tempting for chief executives to allow the process of getting things done to become more important than the task itself. For many, managing by consensus is assumed to be the best way of working. It unites different constituencies behind a common purpose. But achievement of the task sometimes needs to take precedence over the process of gaining consensus. The balance is a delicate one. Chief executives who take too many initiatives to strengthen the purpose without seeking consensus will ultimately encounter opposition. On the other hand, chief executives who miss opportunities, or slow the pace of change because they always strive to gain consensus, risk being branded as weak and indecisive.

Chief executives need to concentrate on the **quality of the organization's services**. Ultimately the organization is about providing services to an agreed user group (or campaigns on agreed issues), to a specified standard and with agreed cost and time parameters. The chief executive needs to know whether this is happening, what the organization is doing to improve the quality of its services and what has been learned about the most effective ways of improving them.

Chief executives also need to ensure that all the **internal functions are providing high value-added services** to the rest of the organization. This includes finance, marketing, personnel, information technology, property maintenance and so on. It is remarkably easy for these functions to become engrossed in their own concerns and slip gradually away from the objective of meeting the needs of the organization's service providers. The absence of market mechanisms to keep them on their toes means that chief executives have to ensure that they are meeting their internal users' needs.

Chief executives are also responsible for ensuring that the organization has a **viable economic equation**. In the past chief executives believed their financial role was to ensure a balanced budget. As long as income was approximately the same as expenditure, chief executives had met their financial responsibilities. This, however, is insufficient, even in times of low inflation. Ambitious chief executives should ensure the organization makes a surplus to pay for future investments, innovation, experiments and working capital and to give them managerial flexibility.

In many third-sector organizations fundraising plays a role in balancing the economic equation. Although most have professional staff running fundraising, chief executives need to play **three critical roles in fundraising**. They have to:

1. ensure that the organization has an ambitious, realistic and achievable fundraising strategy. This is a challenging task. Fundraising is among the most difficult and subtle activities in third-sector management. It is surrounded by opportunities to make errors of judgement. Chief

executives of organizations dependent on fundraising have to challenge fundraising plans, ensure they are robust, provide imagination when they are dreary and give special support to the person who is responsible for their delivery.

2. give personal attention to key fundraising initiatives. Ultimately large donors and grant-makers expect chief executives to be involved personally in fundraising. They need to be assured that their grant or donation is being given special attention, and the best way to signify that is by the presence of the chief executive.

3. ensure that each type of fundraising activity is producing a financial return appropriate for that source of funds. Typical returns are £4–£5 per pound spent for 'warm' mailings, £80–£200 sales per square foot for shops, 5–7½ per cent profit margin for trading catalogues, £3–£4 for every £1 spent on local fundraisers' salaries and £20–£60 to attract a legacy inquiry and acquire a pledge.

Finally, chief executives have to **encourage** innovation. They have to ensure that the organization is continually moving forward and finding ways to campaign and deliver services that meet new circumstances. It means searching for new ideas, sometimes from other countries, sometimes from local branches and sometimes from organizations in other fields. It means putting staff time and money into new ideas and acknowledging that while many will fail, a few will become the engine for the organization's future development.

## The processes

More than anyone else in the organization, chief executives are responsible for managing the processes that are required to make things happen. This can be thought about at two levels. First, chief executives are responsible for ensuring that the necessary processes for good management described in Chapter 6 are established and continuously developed to meet changing circumstances. Second, chief executives have a day-to-day responsibility for guiding the processes used to take individual decisions. They have to define:

- the precise nature of each decision
- when the decision should be taken
- who needs to be involved
- the period of time over which the decision should be taken.

Chief executives have to decide how to structure the decisions to make it easy to proceed. Structuring decisions in ways that fit with staff and board perceptions makes decisions easier. For example, a decision concerned with improving the quality of a service could be cast as a decision about:

- the need for improved performance monitoring to pinpoint problem areas
- the need for a new service plan
- a pilot improvement programme to demonstrate a new approach to quality management
- an opportunity to raise new funds from a donor who wants the service to be successful
- firing the manager responsible.

More than anyone else, the chief executive has to decide which way to approach the problem to achieve the desired results.

The timing of initiatives often rests in chief executives' hands. It is tempting to concentrate on the substance of a decision and forget that the timing is equally important. Pushing for an urgently needed change (for example, the restructuring of a team) when no one favours the idea might lead to no change at all. A half-anticipated departure, however, might create circumstances in which the same change is agreed without resistance or difficulty.

Judgements about **whom to involve in a decision** are the next consideration. Sometimes omitting to consult a significant constituency can lead to a decision effectively being blocked. In other circumstances the consultation can lead to an impasse.

Finally, chief executives have to **pace decisions**. An attempt to rush key decisions through too quickly can lead to a build-up of opposition. But leaving issues to fester unresolved begins to immobilize organizations. Chief executives have to make frequent judgements about how fast to push people on critically important issues.

## The people

Chief executives have to work particularly closely with board members and the senior management team. They need to form relationships with, and maintain the confidence of, the majority of the individuals in both groups.

The starting point for developing relationships with individuals is to understand their motives. Members of the board and the senior management team each have their own motives for contributing to the organization, and they each have different aspirations – both for the organization and for themselves.

The effective chief executive needs to understand these motives and aspirations. They can be many and varied. Staff motives may include:

- commitment to the cause
- professional interest in the field
- autonomy in their job
- personal development and consequent career advancement
- material rewards
- job security.

Board members' motives are very different. They include:

- a desire to make a contribution to society and see the organization succeed
- the need for status or another role in life
- friendship and networking opportunities
- opportunities to advance a career in the third sector.

Value-led organizations offer abundant opportunities for people to meet their individual needs. To the extent that it is possible, the chief executive needs to see that these aspirations are being met by the organization. Otherwise good people will eventually move to other organizations that can better meet their needs. Board members, for example, need to be seen not just as decision-makers but as people who can engage with the organization in rich and diverse ways. They can represent the organization in other fora and join in the social life of the organization.

Managers can be encouraged to network with other similar organizations or to pursue an interest in a field that intrigues them personally. They can be encouraged to take on additional responsibilities or to take time out of work to study. Sometimes it may mean being particularly aware of people's personal circumstances and of stresses in their lives or difficulties they are facing. At other times they may need to be given extra support on an assignment. Chief executives cannot work miracles or offer one individual more opportunities than another. But they can hold on to good people if they do all they can to look after their individual needs.

AVOIDING BAD HABITS

Working with many chief executives has given me an opportunity to see some habits that need to be avoided. They include:

- talking too much in meetings
- allowing team members to talk too much
- consistently siding with one interest group within the organization while claiming independence
- blaming the board
- always seeing people's weaknesses rather than their strengths
- not delivering on tasks they committed themselves to
- not delegating explicitly
- criticizing team members behind their backs.

Everyone make mistakes. Successful chief executives strive to learn from their errors and find their own formula for working effectively as a leader.

## 9.4 CHIEF EXECUTIVES PROVIDE LEADERSHIP

Management is concerned with the efficient administration of the organization. It is about the establishment of processes that make the organization work, the creation of structures that link people together in an organized way, the development of plans, the control of budgets and the costing of services. Chief executives have to master all of these and more.

But truly effective chief executives have to rise beyond management and provide leadership. Leadership is required to clarify the mission, to motivate people, to seek new opportunities, to give the organization a sense of purpose and to focus people on the task.

The boundary between management and leadership is not crystal-clear. It is not that management is all boring administration and leadership is the fun activity. They sit on a continuum. But the distinction is important because organizations need an appropriate combination of management and leadership for their circumstances. Those that are over-led and under-managed may be exciting places to work, but they

## LEADERSHIP AND MANAGEMENT

Although a little stereotyped, the following helps to make the distinction.

| The Leadership Task | The Management Task |
|---|---|
| Create a long-term vision | Plan to meet current objectives |
| Set broad purpose and direction | Make best use of resources |
| Create a better future | Manage today's problems |
| Focus on the product | Focus on making processes work well |
| Inspire people to do more | Ensure people work to contract |
| Teach by example and praise | Seek improvements through training |
| Create more effective systems | Establish standard operating procedures |
| Focus on effectiveness | Focus on efficiency |
| Look to the future | Look at the present |

Adapted from *LEAD!*, Richard Lynch, Jossey-Barr, 1993.

may not have the practical capacity to deliver the work. Those that are under-led but over-managed may be capable of doing the work, but they are eventually overtaken by the imaginative organization that is run by a team of people who are motivated by leadership to produce the highest possible performance.

Organizations need leadership at the top. In value-led organizations that is seldom a role that chairs can provide unless they are dedicated virtually full-time to the cause. The chief executive has to lead both the board and the staff. This does not mean usurping the proper role of the board to control the organization. But experience shows that the most effective organizations almost always have chief executives who provide both the board and the staff with leadership.

Effective chief executives understand the difference between being a manager and being a leader. They strive to delegate managerial tasks to create the time to discharge their leadership responsibilities. They manage their time in such a way that they can turn their attention away from the daily deluge of seemingly urgent activities and towards the task of providing leadership.

They recognize that learning about leadership is a life-long process. It takes time and practice to learn what it means and how to behave as a leader. One way to start working on the development of leadership skills is to review your current behaviour against an inventory of leadership skills. The best list I have found comes from American not-for-profit consultant Richard Lynch. He suggests that there are ten elements to effective leadership, each of which points to actions to strengthen leadership skills.

The following is based on his ten points.

1. **Recognize people's efforts.** Effective leaders praise the work of their managers, the staff, the board and local branches. As monetary rewards are less significant in the third sector, personal recognition is all the more critical. Recognition is best when it is:

   - given frequently
   - varied
   - honest
   - about the person, not just the work
   - appropriate for the achievement
   - consistent
   - timely – given as soon after the event as possible
   - individualized to suit the recipient's needs.

2. **Develop a power base.** The chief executive's power depends primarily on maintaining the confidence of the board, the staff, and, in some cases, the broader membership as well. That implies both serving them well and, more important, gaining and maintaining their confidence. This requires chief executives to demonstrate that they are in command of the organization's affairs. Chief executives need to persuade the organization to face up to and resolve difficult issues and they have to stop the board or staff making decisions that would be difficult to defend. They also strengthen their power base by anticipating divisions of opinion between themselves, their boards and their staff. Each is a potential weakness that others can exploit if the chief executive is not in command of the resolution process.

## THE LESSONS OF EXPERIENCE

Douglas McGregor acted as teacher and consultant to many organizations. After being President of Antioch College in the United States, he had the honesty to admit that he had made some wrong assumptions about leadership:

'It took the direct experience of becoming a line executive, and meeting personally the problems involved, to teach me what no amount of observation of other people could have taught.

'I believed, for example, that a leader could operate successfully as a kind of adviser to his organization. I thought I could avoid being a "boss". Unconsciously, I suspect, I hoped to duck the unpleasant necessity of making difficult decisions, of taking the responsibility for one course of action among many uncertain alternatives, of making mistakes and taking the consequences. I thought that maybe I could operate so that everyone would like me – that good human relations would eliminate all discord and disagreement.

'I could not have been more wrong. It took a couple of years, but I finally began to realize that a leader cannot avoid the exercise of authority any more than he can avoid responsibility for what happens to his organization. In fact, it is a major function of the top executive to take on his own shoulders the responsibility for resolving the uncertainties that are always involved in important decisions. Moreover, since no important decision ever pleases everyone in the organization, he must also absorb the displeasure, and sometimes severe hostility, of those who would have taken a different course.

'A colleague recently summed up what my experience has taught me in these words: "A good leader must be tough enough to win a fight, but not tough enough to kick a man when he is down." This notion is not in the least inconsistent with humane, democratic leadership. Good human relations develop out of strength, not weakness.'

*Essays of Douglas McGregor*, MIT Press, 1966.

3. **Use authority effectively.** Chief executives, and in particular those employed by caring organizations, find it difficult to combine caring values with the need to be tough and decisive when circumstances demand a decision that will not please colleagues. The temptation is to give relationships a higher priority when in practice the long-term interest of the organization should be paramount. Authority used effectively increases people's respect for the leader.

4. **Use the power of the position.** People in positions of power, particularly those recently appointed, often shun the trappings of power. They stress that they are the same as everyone else and forgo the privileges relevant to the post. This is an understandable reaction, especially in organizations with a history of equality and consensus decision-making. It can nevertheless be shortsighted because, like it or not, the status attached to the post is one source of the chief executive's influence. Effective chief executives ensure that they retain an appropriate status for the post in the prevailing circumstances. They have an office that is appropriate for the job. They ensure they have appropriate administrative support. They sit at the head of the table at meetings.

5. **Build a reputation.** Managers respect chief executives who have a reputation in their field of endeavour. Chief executives who have the expertise to make press comments or give speeches strengthen their position within their organizations. They gain a reputation by networking with coordinating groups and by building a profile in their field through writing or hosting seminars.

6. **Develop skills and abilities.** Leaders constantly strive to increase their expertise both as managers and as people who understand the detail of their field of endeavour. When managers know that they can extend their abilities by working with their leader, their respect for the leader grows.

7. **Clarify personal objectives.** Leaders have a burning desire to achieve specific objectives. They are clear about what they want the organization to accomplish and how they are going to help the organization to realize it. When this is coupled with a passionate belief in what the organization can do, it rubs off on everyone else.

8. **Communicate with followers.** Leaders listen to others and the language they use. They put great emphasis on communicating a vision of the future in language that people can relate to. They take every opportunity to communicate verbally and in writing with as many constituencies as possible.

9. **Develop a positive self-image.** Effective leaders are confident of their abilities. They strive to increase confidence in themselves and in others. They are optimistic. They get into a virtuous circle in which their success feeds their self-image, which in turn leads to further success.

10. **Combine vision with attention to detail.** Leaders judge when to focus on the big picture and when detail has to be given attention. Focusing exclusively on either is a recipe for problems.

---

GOOD HABITS

Watching the chief executive of one of Britain's largest third-sector organizations, I noticed that:

- he went out of his way to praise staff for their achievements (both face to face and through personal notes)
- he demonstrated that he had listened to consultation by returning people's comments with his own views annotated in the margin
- he held a conference of all 120 senior managers once or twice a year to share the overall strategy and communicate his view of priorities
- he retained the authority of the position of chief executive by taking decisions when people could not agree
- he worked hard to retain the confidence of his board by keeping members well informed, anticipating difficult decisions and planning how they should be taken, often over a period of many months.

These are habits of chief executives who lead their organizations.

---

## WHAT FOLLOWERS EXPECT OF THEIR LEADERS

One of the characteristics of leadership is the ability to persuade others to follow. Research at Santa Clara University attempted to identify leadership characteristics that followers admire. It came up with some surprising results. It did not find that followers wanted chief executives to be the best strategic planners or the fastest decision-takers or to have the best 'people' skills. In a survey of 2,615 managers the researchers found the following four characteristics were most admired.

| Characteristic | % of managers selecting this |
| --- | --- |
| Honesty | 83 |
| Competence | 67 |
| Forward-looking attitude | 62 |
| Capacity to inspire | 58 |

This suggests that followers are not looking for someone with god-like characteristics. Rather, they want their leaders to be good at the basics:

**Honesty:** keeping agreements, telling the truth and behaving in a trustworthy way

**Competence:** having a good track record, being able to challenge, enable and encourage (but not necessarily having expertise in the core skill areas of the organization)

**Forward-looking attitude:** having a sense of direction, the ability to select a desirable destination for the organization

**Capacity to inspire:** being able to communicate a vision and to give people a greater sense of worth.

*The Leadership Challenge*, Kouzes and Posner, Jossey-Bass, 1987.

## 9.5 DIVISIONAL DIRECTORS DIRECT

Divisional directors are people who report to the chief executive and have managers reporting to them. This level of management exists in larger organizations where services are grouped together under a divisional director. I have called people working at this level divisional directors to emphasize the distinction between managers who are responsible for managing individual services and divisional directors whose main task is managing managers. The term 'director' is not being used to imply any legal responsibility that may be attached to being a director of, for example, an organization that is also a limited-liability company.

Directors have two equally important roles. They are responsible for managing their own department. They have to craft the people who report to them into a team. They need to establish clear objectives for the team, agree operating plans and work programmes for the department and procure the resources needed to deliver the plan.

They also share responsibility with the chief executive for the overall management of the organization. They have to support the chief executive in managing the overall strategy, shaping policies and plans and giving advice on major operational decisions. This second set of responsibilities requires directors to deploy a very different set of skills that will be described in this section.

In my experience, directors of effective organizations may spend between a third and a half of their time on their responsibilities as directors. To do this they have to delegate many of their managerial responsibilities, which necessitates building a strong team of managers. The nature of the delegation is different from that described earlier. When people are first appointed to a management post they have to learn to delegate work to create time to manage. When people are appointed directors they have to learn how to delegate management to create time to direct. This means that divisional directors have to help managers to set overall objectives, support them in developing the overall strategy for the service, guide them in building and managing a team and help them to delegate effectively.

### Skills of effective directors

People generally need to have had substantial management experience before accepting a director-level post. They need to have a functional expertise (for example, service delivery, finance or fundraising) and to have many years' experience using those skills. Ideally they should also have had management experience – perhaps running a unit of an organization, a geographical territory or an internal service. This will have given them experience of building a team, delegating work and getting performance from people. These skills will be invaluable when it comes to managing managers and coaching them to perform their tasks.

Once someone has been appointed a director, a new range of skills has to be developed. First, directors have to learn to see problems from an **organization-wide perspective**. Each director has to step into the shoes of the chief executive and contribute constructively to the overall management of the organization. This may mean shaping the development of the organization's policies, helping to establish organization-wide priorities or improving processes such as strategic planning, management information, budget-setting and performance review. It may involve chairing a task group or representing the organization in the media. Whatever the activity, directors need a clear overview of the organization and its work.

Second, directors have to learn to **think at a strategic level**. It requires the ability to stand back from practical details and take a longer-term and more conceptual view of the organization and its environment. This necessitates allocating significant time to reflecting, talking to other people about strategic issues and building the capacity to contribute constructively to the strategic thinking of the senior management team. This is not easy for managers who are used to being action-orientated, resolving today's crises and taking tomorrow as it comes.

To see the current situation in its correct context, directors need to learn about the organization's past. They need to develop a deep understanding of the organization's present situation and accurately anticipate key elements of the future. This requires an ability to stand back from the detail and summarize the current circumstances in a clear overview. It means talking to people to gain the 'helicopter' view of the organization. Directors need to make a contribution to the senior management team that moves beyond providing detail of their area of work. When they are equipped with this high-level context, directors can discharge their responsibilities for the strategic development of the organization.

Third, directors have to be much more aware of the changing **social, political and technical environment** around their organization. Changes in social policy, government policy and party policy are important issues for directors. Such developments require adroit changes in the way the organization thinks about its work. Directors therefore need to read widely and network extensively to keep their finger on these important external trends.

Fourth, directors need to learn how to **take responsibility** for work when they are often two or more levels removed from the detail. It means learning to appoint and develop people who have management skills and providing them with support without doing their job for them.

Finally, directors have to **judge when to intervene** in a situation and when to stand back. Although managerial experience will help here, it is more complex for directors. They have to judge both when to intervene in managers' work and when to delve one level further to have a hands-on involvement in front-line service delivery. Effective directors can use their experience to make a substantial difference at both levels, but they only have the time to get involved in those few decisions to which they can make a significant contribution. Examples of circumstances when directors are likely to have a hands-on involvement include capital investments, exploiting wholly new sources of funds or responding to significant changes in government policy. It is a mistake, however, to intervene too often. 'He never lets me do my job' is a common complaint and one that is often justified. Moreover, effective directors just do not have the time to become involved in the detail of all the services in their division.

## Learning directorship skills

Ensuring directors learn directorship skills is a responsibility that is shared by directors and their chief executives. Chief executives help, usually through supervision meetings, to identify development needs, to guide directors on changing their priorities and on actions to develop the required skills. As well as helping directors, this also sets an example to directors (and to other managers) who need to pay attention to the development needs of the people who report to them.

Directors also have to take personal responsibility for their own development. The chief executive may be able to help, but the good director is someone who knows their own strengths and weaknesses and takes action to develop the skills that require attention.

There are a variety of ways of encouraging learning:

- **Use a mentor**. Directors can use someone outside the line-management structure as a sounding board or mentor. A trustee with directorship experience, a director of another organization or a consultant can all be used to systematically review experiences and make learning a more systematic process.
- **Use your own team**. The people who report to you are an important source of learning. By regularly asking for feedback directors gain important information about their performance and how to improve it.
- **Review learning alone**. Directors can keep a personal record of learning points and routinely update it to build a body of experience and personal learning. They can also read and reflect to consolidate experiences and help to ensure they are applied in subsequent situations.

---

CREATING AN ACTION PLAN FOR PERSONAL DEVELOPMENT

Start by thinking back over an issue, a meeting or a decision. Consider what happened and select a part of it that was significant to you.

- Write a detailed account of what happened during that period of activity. Don't at this stage put any effort into deciding what you learned – just concentrate on describing what actually happened.
- Then list the conclusions you have reached as a result of the experience. These are, in effect, your learning points. Don't limit the number and don't worry about the practicality or quality of the points.
- Finally, decide which learning points you want to implement in the future and work out an action plan that covers:
  – what you are going to do
  – when you are going to do it.

Spell out your action plan as precisely as possible so that you are clear what you have to do and have confidence that it is realistic.

A. Mumford *et al.*, *Director's Development Guidebook*, Institute of Directors, 1990.

In some organizations directors are located in different parts of the country (and sometimes different parts of the world). For these people to work as directors and to be effective members of a senior management team special attention has to be given to communication and working together. Extra time has to be allowed for meetings because team communication has to be squashed into fewer occasions. Recently introduced technology for telephone conferencing can keep all team members in touch with each other between meetings.

In summary, the work of being a director is very different from that of being a manager. It requires a new layer of skills that can be learned and developed. The task of a director is to understand the differences and to use every means available to acquire the necessary skills. The rewards are potentially high. The divisional director who has mastered the skills and is making a substantial contribution to the overall management of the organization is well prepared to start applying for chief executive positions.

---

## THE EFFECTIVE DIVISIONAL DIRECTOR

Watching the divisional director of a national organization providing a wide range of services for people with a common disability, I noticed:

- she had reduced the number of managers reporting directly to her to give her time to discharge her director's duties
- she built her managers into a strong team and encouraged them to solve each other's problems
- she took the team out of the office three times a year to plan and monitor progress
- these actions gave her time to think about senior management team meetings, enabling her to have something useful to contribute to each item
- she worked hard to build a network of contacts outside the organization and used them for advice on organization-wide issues
- she volunteered to help on strategic problems in senior management team meetings
- she kept abreast of major developments in the disability field so she could see her organization in perspective.

These are the actions of an effective divisional director.

---

## 9.6 MANAGERS MUST MANAGE

In many third-sector organizations management was, until recently, not a valued skill. A legacy of this is that managers are expected to learn the skills they need by some mysterious process of osmosis. There is an assumption that management is all common sense – something any intelligent person has the innate skills to do. To make matters worse, managers are often managed by people who themselves have been promoted because of their specialist skills and have consequently had little management training. Most chief executives and divisional directors have not, unfortunately, been trained in the skills of coaching newly appointed managers.

Faced with a poor understanding of what being a manager means in practice and a culture that tends not to value management, many managers fall into the trap of doing rather than managing. It often appears easier to do a task yourself than to manage someone else to do it, particularly when you were promoted because you were good at doing that task. Managers feel comfortable when they are busy and they know that they can usually do the work more quickly than their staff and probably to a better quality. But doing the work is not the job of a manager.

The essential skills of a front-line manager are:

- setting objectives
- building teams
- developing individuals
- taking decisions
- monitoring performance
- resolving problems.

The problem in value-led organizations is, however, that their very nature makes seemingly straightforward tasks more complex in practice. This section explains some of the special characteristics that affect managers in value-led organizations and suggests ways of becoming a more effective manager in these circumstances.

Some of these points are relevant to chief executives and divisional directors as well as front-line managers. They are grouped together here because they impact most directly on the work of front-line managers.

The task of managing people in this sector has to be seen in the context of the types of people who work in it. The third sector attracts employees with different motives, particularly when compared with the private sector (P. Murvis writing in *Non-profit Management and Leadership*, Autumn 1992). This research has shown that they tend to have stronger ideals, they attach greater value to job satisfaction, pay is less important and job content is seen to be part of the compensation package. People who work in the third sector have been shown to be more caring in spirit, to be more trusting of others and less cynical in attitude.

The same research shows that people working in the third sector tend to have higher educational qualifications than people in equivalent jobs in the private and public sectors. In my experience, they also have greater difficulty in balancing their work lives and their private lives. This is hardly surprising; when people live for a cause the distinction between work and home becomes very blurred.

## Special challenges for managers

The first challenge managers have to face is the fact that value-led organizations have extraordinarily high ambitions. They all want to have a significant impact. Objectives such as saving endangered species, discovering a treatment for an incurable disease or alleviating poverty are both ambitious and without clear boundaries. For front-line managers this means there is always more they could do. Effective managers consequently have to learn to be realistic about what can be achieved and **ruthless in setting priorities**.

Consequently, an annual work plan is an essential management tool. It should set out what will be done by whom and it should leave space every month to deal with unforeseen problems. It also requires managers to check frequently in their own mind what their objectives are and whether some of their current workload can be avoided because it is not a top priority.

The second challenge is to **carve out an appropriate role for the circumstances**. The space that managers have to work in is often squeezed by different pressures. There is pressure from board committees, which expand their roles from their proper governance duties into the day-to-day problems of management. These interventions in management are often well intended and sometimes needed. But a board or committee that slips incrementally over the boundary of governance and into routine management reduces managers' authority and the scope of the managerial task.

Similarly, managers can face constraints if their boss does not give them sufficient freedom to get on with their job. The hands-on boss who wants to be involved in all the detail can be a significant impediment to a front-line manager.

Yet another pressure comes from professional groups (such as doctors, social workers and teachers) and articulate individuals who quite rightly guard against managerial incursions into what they perceive to be their professional domain. The boundaries are invariably grey. However, faced with a powerful board, an interventionist chief executive and strong professional interests, weak managers may find it increasingly difficult to define the contribution that they can make. They need to be quite clear about what they are doing and why they are doing it in order to have the freedom to discharge their managerial duties.

The third challenge is to overcome the common belief that third-sector organizations should be managed by consensus. People who are employed in these organizations understandably expect to be involved in decision-taking. But this expectation can shift subtly from the realistic desire to be consulted on some decisions to the unrealistic demand that all decisions should be made by consensus. As a result very little natural authority is given to managerial posts. Managers have to **earn their authority** by distinguishing between situations requiring consensus and circumstances in which they should take responsibility, make a decision and be held accountable. Managers consequently need to keep issues that are heading towards decisions under constant review and decide when to prolong discussion to achieve consensus and when to take command and make decisions.

The fourth challenge is that in some organizations the very notion of management sits uncomfortably alongside strongly held values about empowering disadvantaged people. From this perspective users have rights to define their needs and the way services should be provided. Many no longer want to be given charity. They want to determine what the organization should be doing for them and do not wish management to take decisions, often in a paternalistic and demeaning way. Managers of these organizations have to combine a strong commitment to **putting users' views first** with an ability to make things happen when decisions need to be implemented.

This may require extensive consultation with users. In some circumstances it may be appropriate to commission market research, and in other situations a user group may need to be established. This latter approach is particularly useful for services that are supplied within the organization, such as information technology, management accounts, personnel and property management.

The fifth challenge is to overcome unnecessarily strong pressure to keep administrative overheads to a minimum. While cost control is entirely appropriate, it can lead managers to penny-pinch at times when spending on overheads could lead to significant improvements in effectiveness. Managers are responsible for avoiding wastage of resources, but they also have to **argue for sufficient resources** to do their work efficiently.

This may require identifying specific savings that will result from the new investment or productivity improvements that could be achieved to release people's time for other activities. In other circumstances it may require managers to comb through areas of expenditure to identify cuts that should be made in order to fund a new investment or expansion of another area of work.

---

### MANAGERS' TASKS ARE EXTRAORDINARILY VARIED

Third-sector managers are expected to perform an extraordinarily wide range of tasks. The Leonard Cheshire Foundation has 130 homes and services in the UK and a further 200 homes in fifty countries around the world. Each home or service has a manager who has to deploy a wide range of skills. A recent survey identified the following skills that a home manager needs:

- day-to-day management of a home or service
- strategic planning
- marketing to purchasing authorities
- negotiating fees
- agreeing contracts
- building staff teams
- involving residents/clients in decision-taking
- preparing and monitoring accounts
- training staff
- disciplinary skills
- managing meetings
- dealing with the media
- delegation.

The sixth challenge is to ensure that you receive the necessary **induction, supervision and personal development**. When senior managers are overloaded (or unable to establish their priorities) supporting their staff is often the first activity to be squeezed out. This problem is particularly common in geographically spread organizations, where front-line staff are at separate locations. Because of physical separation these are often the very people who ought to get extra support. When managers are not receiving assistance, they have to push for the support they need to do the job effectively.

Finally, managers face particular difficulties when it comes to **changing people's roles**. People believe in their jobs. They have often worked tirelessly for the cause, so managers' suggestions for change are sometimes most unwelcome. An extreme example is the difficulty of moving people out of the organization altogether when their performance falls below expectations, when redundancies have to be made and when people have to be dismissed. Caring organizations are expected to care for their staff – so managers have to be particularly sensitive when they need to adjust the structure or change the membership of their team.

In summary, while the skills that front-line managers have to learn and use are those common to most managerial situations, the people whom the sector attracts and the nature of value-led organizations and of the jobs combine to create more demanding circumstances, which can be overcome only by better training, greater line-management support and hard-won experience.

## SUMMARY OF KEY POINTS

### Management jobs are different

- Chief executives have to provide leadership.
- Divisional directors have to direct.
- Managers have to manage.

### Special characteristics of the chief executive's job

- The chief executive's job is different from all other posts.
- It is less structured, highly exposed and lonely. It requires the widest range of abilities, involves the widest range of constituencies and depends on maintaining a reservoir of goodwill.

### Structuring chief executives' work

- Chief executives can avoid becoming servants of their in-trays by focusing on the three Ps:
  - the purpose of the organization
  - the processes of managing it
  - the people who work closely with them.

### Chief executives provide leadership

- Management is concerned with efficient administration, making processes work, creating structures, developing plans and controlling budgets.
- Leadership is concerned with clarifying the mission, motivating people and giving the organization a sense of purpose.
- Chief executives can systematically develop their leadership skills by recognizing people's efforts, developing a power base, using authority effectively, using the power of the position and building a personal reputation.
- They also need to develop their skills and abilities, clarify their own objectives, communicate with their followers, develop a positive self-image and combine vision with attention to detail.

### Divisional directors direct

- Divisional directors have both to manage their own department and contribute to the overall management of the organization.
- To become effective, divisional directors have to take an organization-wide perspective, think at a strategic level, follow trends in the external environment, take responsibility for work that is two levels removed from them and judge when to intervene and when to leave matters alone.

### Managers must manage

- The essential skills for front-line managers are setting objectives, building teams, developing individuals, taking decisions, monitoring performance and resolving problems.
- The special challenges of managing value-led organizations mean that managers have to carve out an appropriate role, be ruthless in setting priorities, earn their authority, put users' views first, argue for sufficient resources and push for personal support.

# CHAPTER TEN

# Managing Different Types of Organization

## 10.1 ORGANIZATION LIFE CYCLES

The third sector consists of an extraordinarily wide range of organizations. So far this book has concentrated on approaches to management that are common to many organizations. This chapter looks at the management of organizations at different stages of development and at the management of different types of organization. It concentrates on 'provider' organizations that are delivering services, offering mutual support and campaigning for change. The special case of 'funder' organizations, such as trusts, government agencies and companies, that are financing the sector is considered in Appendix 4.

The management of organizations at different stages of development is best understood by considering the notion of their life cycle. This idea was first introduced in Chapter 2 in relation to boards, but it can also be used to help understand the development of the whole organization.

The central proposition behind the life cycle is the idea that organizations develop in stages. It was put forward over twenty years ago in a *Harvard Business Review* article entitled 'Evolution and Revolution in Organizations'. It argued that periods of steady evolutionary growth and development are followed by periods of revolutionary development when everything seems to be changing at the same time. This behaviour pattern is very common in third-sector organizations.

The idea of a life cycle does not imply that all organizations will necessarily move through a pre-determined set of stages. That patently could not be true because organizations' futures are ultimately determined by governing boards and management decisions based on judgements made at a particular point in time. However, when one looks at many organizations and summarizes their behaviour a surprisingly large number have a similar evolutionary pattern.

The value of this life cycle idea is that it helps boards and managers to set the opportunities and issues they face into a broader context. It helps people to understand that their problems are not unique and

## ORGANIZATION LIFE CYCLE

**Size of Organization**

| | Birth | Youth | Adulthood | Maturity | Decline |
|---|---|---|---|---|---|
| | Dominated by founders | Many new staff | Strong leadership | Cause is well established | Needs change |
| | Run on adrenalin | New leadership | Strategically managed | Older staff | Membership and donations fall |
| | Few systems | Attempts to systemize | Board governs | Less entrepreneurial | Harder to attract quality staff |
| | Informal structure | Difficulty distinguishing good management and unnecessary bureaucracy | Managers manage | Highly experienced | Board members resign |
| | Consensus management style | Confusion between consensus and consultation | Systems established | Risk of being overtaken by other organizations | New purpose needed to allow rejuvination |
| | | Board/staff roles muddled | Professional people management | | |
| | | | Clear reporting and accountability | | |

**Time** →

▢ Periods of relative stability

▨ Periods of crisis

seemingly unresolvable. It enables people to explain behaviour in terms of a model that points to actions that need to be taken to help the organization move on to its next development stage.

There is, it should be stressed, no one correct set of characteristics in each stage. Every organization has its own characteristics and consequently needs to define its own life cycle. There are nevertheless some common patterns:

In the first stage organizations are often dominated by a founding figure. This person has the vision and energy to create an organization, to procure the necessary resources and to build a group of people into an organization. This stage can last from a few years to many tens of years. SENSE, for example, was a small mutual-support organization for over thirty years before, in the mid 1980s, it embarked on a period of explosive growth that took it through the next two stages in less than ten years.

Founders are critical in the first stage of the development of an organization. They have the foresight to recognize a social, educational or health problem or an artistic opportunity and the energy, commitment and charisma to create an organization to address the issue. They are entrepreneurial in approach and usually unwilling to be stopped by obstacles. Without these people organizations would never get off the ground.

However, they are also a common source of problems once the organization has become established:

- they find it very difficult to let go of the reins
- they often fail to train and coach their successors
- they are unable to adjust to the style and priorities of newcomers
- they see the growth of systems and procedures as unnecessary bureaucracy
- they sometimes plot to overthrow new management in order to put the organization back on to what they see as the right track
- they sometimes leave and establish another organization working in exactly the same field.

The departure of the founder is often a very difficult period for value-led organizations. Nevertheless, following a period of revolution, most organizations do move into the second stage. New management brings different approaches and fresh ideas, and the organization moves forward. There is still, however, much learning to be done in the second stage. Sometimes there is a clash of values between an old guard, which sees flexibility and opportunism as the very reason for the organization's success, and the new guard, which sees the need for improved planning, more formal decision-making processes, better information systems and more structured management. Often the roles of the board and the staff remain ill-defined for a period of years. Until these problems are resolved organizations stay in the youthful phase.

Eventually organizations grow into adulthood, often following a change of leadership. In its idealized form adult organizations separate governance and management, have a clear purpose and strategy, have effective management information and decision-making systems and develop people to achieve their greatest potential. In practice, few organizations attain this goal. Changes in board membership, staff and the external environment mean that it is a never-ending struggle to keep the organization in top management form. Some organizations may slip back into the youthful stage and have to work on their management to return to the adult stage.

Others move on to maturity. Once the cause is well established it becomes more difficult to remain 'fired-up' about the issues. These organizations probably have good connections with funders and policymakers. But they may not have the most motivated branches or attract the most ambitious staff and board members. They frequently become less entrepreneurial and risk being overtaken by other organizations.

Finally as needs change, funding, members and donations may start to fall. Unless organizations in this predicament can find a new purpose they will start to decline. Surprisingly, third-sector organizations seldom die. Some become smaller and less effective and slide into ever-increasing mediocrity. Others eventually merge with a larger or newer body that injects new life into the organization.

The value of the life cycle is that it helps to explain the behaviour of organizations when a number of problems surface simultaneously. This is often a time of great trauma when different management issues become entangled with each other. It is frequently a time when management consultants are brought in to help unbundle the problems and create an agenda of actions to move the organization on to its next stage of development.

Consideration of the stage of an organization's life cycle is the first aspect of managing different types of organization because the idea is applicable to all types of organization. The second aspect requires organizations to be separated into different types.

## 10.2 CLASSIFYING ORGANIZATIONS

Third-sector organizations are normally classified according to the activities they undertake: schools provide education, hospitals heal sick people, trade unions represent labour, disability organizations represent people with special needs and campaigning organizations argue for policy change. The International Classification of Non-profit Organizations

---

### CLASSIFICATION BY ACTIVITY

The International Classification of Non-profit Organizations groups organizations by activity:

**Group 1: Culture and Recreation**
Sports, arts, museums, zoos, recreation, social clubs

**Group 2: Education and Research**
School and higher education, vocational training
Medical research, science and technology, policy studies

**Group 3: Health**
Hospitals, rehabilitation, nursing homes, mental health
Public health, health education

**Group 4: Social Services**
Child welfare, youth services, services for families, elderly and disabled people
Emergency relief, income support, material assistance

**Group 5: Environment**
Conservation of natural resources, pollution control
Animal protection and welfare, wildlife and countryside preservation

**Group 6: Development and Housing**
Economic, social and community development
Housing
Employment and training

**Group 7: Law, Advocacy and Politics**
Advocacy organizations, minority groups, civic associations
Legal services, crime prevention, rehabilitation of offenders, victim support
Political parties

**Group 8: Philanthropic Intermediaries and Voluntarism Promotion**
Grant-making trusts, fundraising organizations
Intermediary organizations

**Group 9: International Activities**
Exchange programmes, development assistance, disaster relief
Human rights and peace organizations

**Group 10: Religion**
Religious organizations

**Group 11: Business, professional associations and unions**
Employers' organizations, trade unions, professional associations

**Group 12: Not elsewhere classified**

'A Comparative Study of the Non-profit Sector', L. Salamon and H. Anheier, in *Researching the Voluntary Sector*, Charities Aid Foundation, 1993.

(see box) is the best example I have seen. However, classifications that are more useful for managers subdivide organizations according to characteristics that cut across these traditional groupings. These classifications help to explain the types of strategic developments that are workable and those that lead to major problems.

This approach is the same as academic analyses of the private sector, in which organizations are divided into categories such as manufacturing and service businesses, capital-intensive and non-capital-intensive, vertically integrated and horizontally diversified. Such categorizations are valuable because they shed light on common behavioural patterns that cut across industries. The same process will lead us to a better understanding of third-sector organizations' behaviour.

These organizations can be categorized in many different ways – for example, by size, by geographical scope (international, national, regional or local), by their institutional structure (linear or federal) or by historical stage of development. These are interesting and significant distinctions, but for managerial purposes three types of classification are particularly useful. These are:

- the **broad purpose** of the organization
- the **main source of funds**
- the **composition of the board**.

This section describes these classifications and how different types of organization fit into each of the classifications. It then looks at the implications for managing the different types of organization.

## Classification by purpose

The first way of giving some coherence to this diverse sector is to classify organizations according to their primary purpose. This is a development of a typology that was put forward by Charles Handy in *Understanding Voluntary Organizations*. In this classification the primary purpose of third-sector organizations is one of the following:

- to **provide services**: examples include housing associations, colleges, schools, arts organizations and many voluntary organizations
- to **provide mutual support**: examples include trade unions, professional associations, employers' organizations and self-help groups
- to **campaign for change**: examples include campaigning organizations such as Greenpeace, Liberty and Amnesty International.

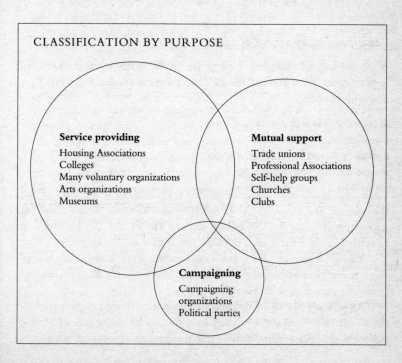

CLASSIFICATION BY PURPOSE

**Service providing**
Housing Associations
Colleges
Many voluntary organizations
Arts organizations
Museums

**Mutual support**
Trade unions
Professional Associations
Self-help groups
Churches
Clubs

**Campaigning**
Campaigning
organizations
Political parties

This simple division into three main purposes is complicated by the fact that some organizations fall into two categories and some into three. For example, one that began life as a mutual-support organization (say for parents of children with a disability) starts providing services. The services are successful, so they grow and develop. Before long the organization is a multi-million-pound service provider. However, it will probably have retained its mutual-support role, so consequently falls into both categories and faces the management issues of both types of organization.

Similarly, trade unions began as purely mutual-support or solidarity organizations representing the needs of their members. Today many sell a range of services (such as insurance) to members and non-members alike and also campaign for change.

As a slight aside, it is worth noting that the relative size of each group is not known. My experience is that service-providing organizations dominate the third sector, mutual-support organizations are smaller in number and size, and campaigning organizations represent a very small proportion of the sector, though they have a very high profile in proportion to their size.

## Classification by source of funds

A second way of imposing some order on the third sector is to classify organizations by source of funds. Organizations are funded from four different sources:

- sale of goods and services
- grants
- donations and fundraising activities
- membership fees.

In this classification I have included organizations at the core of the third sector and those at the periphery (which, some might argue, sit more appropriately in the public sector than in the third sector). It nevertheless gives the widest possible perspective on the sector.

Although some receive significant funding from more than one of these sources, most organizations receive the majority of their income from one or two of these sources.

The primary source of funding has a significant impact on organizations' strategic freedom. Organizations funded by donations sit at one end of a spectrum. They have great freedom to determine what they

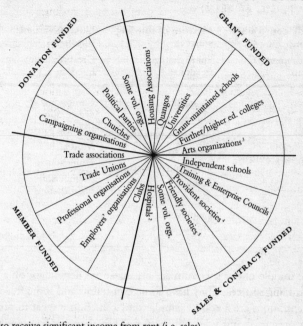

CLASSIFICATION BY PRIMARY SOURCE OF FUNDS

DONATION FUNDED

GRANT FUNDED

Housing Associations[1]
Some vol. orgs.
Political parties
Quangos
Churches
Universities
Grant-maintained schools
Campaigning organisations
Further/higher ed. colleges
Trade associations
Arts organizations[3]
Trade Unions
Independent schools
Professional organisations
Training & Enterprise Councils
Employers' organisations
Provident societies[4]
Clubs
Friendly societies[5]
Hospitals[2]
Some vol. orgs.

MEMBER FUNDED

SALES & CONTRACT FUNDED

[1] Also receive significant income from rent (i.e. sales).
[2] Located here since the purchaser–provider split was implemented.
[3] Also receive significant income from ticket sales.
[4] Examples include BUPA, Private Patients Plan and Western Provident Society.
[5] After February 1993 no new Friendly Societies could be registered.

will do and how they will do it. Their boards are comparatively unconstrained in how they choose to achieve their objectives. Aid agencies, for example, have extraordinary freedom to determine the activities they will pursue, the parts of the world they work in and their mechanisms for achieving change.

Organizations funded by contracts and, to a lesser extent, those funded by grants are more tightly constrained. Geographic coverage, type of service, qualifications and accreditation may all be fixed. Schools and further education colleges exist at this end of the spectrum. Their users are defined, the curriculum is constrained within fixed national boundaries, staff rewards often follow national schemes and success is measured by external examination.

IMPLICATION OF FUNDING SOURCES ON
STRATEGIC FREEDOM

| **Tightly constrained funding** | **Mixture of funding sources** | **Unconstrained funding** |
|---|---|---|
| Little strategic freedom | Some strategic freedom | Great strategic freedom |

→

| | | |
|---|---|---|
| Schools | Hospitals | Campaigning organizations |
| Further education colleges | Universities | Political parties |
| | Arts organizations | Most charities |
| Training and Enterprise Councils | Some charities | Foundations |
| | Housing Associations | Membership organizations |
| | Churches | |
| | Trade unions | |
| | Employers' organizations | |

In the middle of this spectrum are organizations dependent on a mixture of funding sources. They have some constraints and some freedoms. Arts organizations are a good example; they can choose what to present, when to present it and who will perform, but they are constrained by the requirements of funders and their local catchment area.

## Classification by composition of the board

The third way of classifying organizations is by the motives of the people who are appointed to its board. Organizations attract different types of people to join their boards. These people bring different skills and experiences. Although people do not necessarily fall exclusively into one category or another, three main types can be identified. They are:

- **experts**, who bring knowledge, experience and usually specific professional skills to a board
- **service users**, who have joined the organization to benefit from its work or services and who will usually have been elected to the board by the membership
- **concerned individuals**, who believe in a cause and wish to make their contribution by their voluntary effort as a board member.

Each group of people has different expectations of the role of the board and the way it should work. Experts bring a series of assumptions derived from their work and professional experience. These may often differ from each other when business beliefs and approaches do not sit comfortably beside public-sector approaches. They nevertheless all emanate from a professional perspective.

Service users bring different assumptions to the board. They have always had a direct personal interest in the organization. The services help them as well as other members, sometimes making it difficult to separate the best interests of the organization from personal preferences and prejudices. Service users will often bring expertise from a profession as well, but their fundamental motivation for joining the board is different from that of the expert.

Concerned individuals have another set of motives. They are distinguished by the fact that they feel so passionately about an issue that they are willing to give significant amounts of their time to the organization. They believe in the cause and are willing to work tirelessly to pursue social or political objectives.

Each of these three groups works in different ways. Even when a board consists of one type there will be differences of opinion within the group. However, these generally take much less time to resolve than the differences that arise from mixing experts, service users and concerned individuals on boards.

In summary, the majority of provider organizations can be categorized in three dimensions:

- by purpose
  - to provide services
  - to give mutual support
  - to campaign for change
- by source of funds
  - sales and contracts
  - grant funding
  - donations
  - members
- by composition of the board
  - experts
  - service users
  - concerned individuals.

## 10.3 PUTTING THE CLASSIFICATIONS TOGETHER

The purpose of dissecting the third sector into a series of classifications is, first, to reflect the extraordinarily diverse nature of the organizations and, second, to identify combinations of types that work well and those that are more problematic in managerial terms.

This approach builds on work done by David Billis (*The Roots of Voluntary Organizations: A Question of Choice*). He divides the voluntary sector into bureaucracies (systems of paid staff who are organized into hierarchical roles that are bound together by concepts such as account-ability) and voluntary associations (groups of people who come together to work on a particular problem). He argues that many organizations are a mixture of a bureaucracy and a voluntary association. He calls these bodies agencies, which he then divides into three types depending on whether they are funded by the state, by selling their services or by membership and donations.

In a similar way, the three classifications that I have described above can be used to identify combinations that work particularly well and combinations that present greater managerial challenges. The com-binations with a straightforward fit are:

| Purpose | Main sources of funding | Composition of the board |
|---------|------------------------|--------------------------|
| Service | Sales, contracts and grants | Experts |
| Mutual support | Members | Service users |
| Campaign | Members and donations | Concerned individuals |

Although the boundaries between these types are not clear-cut, the central logic that drives each of these combinations is straightforward. These organizations are easier and less stressful to manage. Less time is spent resolving conflict and less experienced managers and board mem-bers are required.

However, in some circumstances it is entirely appropriate to mix types of organization. When an organization has matured and has the management capacity to cope with running two logics simultaneously, the benefits can be considerable. The direct experience of service users can greatly enhance service-delivery standards or the concerned individuals can bring fresh new perspectives to a service-delivery organization. In my experience, problems of moving across boundaries usually arise when organizations drift unintentionally into another category.

A common example is the mutual-support organization that believes it should help people outside its membership and starts to offer services. At first sight this is an obvious and sensible decision. The consequences are nevertheless significant. A pure mutual-support organization has a straightforward logic: members pay fees and the organization provides them with services. When it moves into service provision for non-members it needs a different logic, concerned with defining user needs, marketing services and seeking funds to pay for them. Furthermore members' needs are no longer the organization's sole priority. The situation becomes more complicated when, as often happens, the service activities become much larger than the original mutual-support activities. An organization with an institutional structure suitable for offering mutual support can become a multi-million-pound service provider, which may need very different structures and management processes.

Another example comes from the service-providing organization that starts campaigning. Campaigning has yet another logic concerned with defining policy objectives and devising strategies to achieve them. Campaigning needs new sources of funds (e.g., from donors) and new structures to manage the work (e.g., policy committees, press officers, lobbying skills).

Additional management challenges arise when organizations have funding sources that do not fit with their primary purpose. Combinations that cause problems include:

| Purpose | Primary funding source | Potential problems |
| --- | --- | --- |
| Service | Donors | Service dependent on continuing support from donors |
| Mutual support | Grants | Grants are often time-limited, which leads to instability in the organization |
| Campaign | Grants | Funders can (often unintentionally) have disproportionate influence on campaign priorities |

The basic message is that an expansion from one purpose to two is a major strategic decision with wide-ranging consequences. It may require new funding sources, a different management logic and different skills on the board. It is a decision that should be taken with great care.

Having given this overview, the next three sections take the classification by purpose and look at the management of each type in turn.

## 10.4 MANAGING SERVICE-PROVIDING ORGANIZATIONS

Service-providing organizations dominate the third sector. Examples from the core of the sector include many voluntary organizations, arts organizations and housing associations. Examples at the periphery of the sector include schools, colleges, hospitals and universities.

These organizations were often founded by an individual or a group of social entrepreneurs. Examples from many years ago include the founding fathers of Oxford University and St Bartholomew's Hospital. Examples of organizations in the voluntary sector that have taken their founders' names include Barnardos, The Leonard Cheshire Foundation and the Sue Ryder Foundation.

Service-providing organizations exist for service users. This contrasts with mutual-support organizations that consist of people who themselves benefit from their organization. The key characteristic of service-providing organizations is that they offer a range of services to specific groups of service users who are not necessarily members of the organization. This section therefore describes propositions that are particular to service-providing organizations.

### Strategic questions

The first strategic question that many service-providing organizations need to answer is: **why are they providing the service**? This is not as straightforward a question as it may appear at first sight. It could be any one or a combination of:

- meeting users' needs
- demonstrating the value of the service
- testing a new approach

- providing experience to support campaign work
- making a surplus to invest in other services
- meeting volunteers' needs.

Answers to this question shed light on the primary objective of the organization's services. If, for example, the purpose is to test a new approach (e.g., to experiment with the French 'foyer' approach to helping single homeless people in the UK), then the primary objective might be to monitor how it works. Alternatively, if the purpose is to support campaign work, the organization will have to gear itself up to fit the service into its campaign strategy and manage the service, not just for the benefits the service provides but also to demonstrate the results that were achieved.

This leads to the second strategic question: **how will the organization be financed** in the long run? Value-led organizations are tremendously innovative when it comes to putting together a range of different sources of funds to finance a service. However, there are also many organizations that do not monitor the extent to which their services are being funded by grants or contracts, subsidized by donors or paid for by service users. In some cases services that should be fully funded by the state are being unintentionally subsidized by donors. Managers of service-giving organizations need to be clear about who is funding the service, whether it should be funded in this way and whether the funding is sustainable in the longer term.

The third question is **whether the organization wishes to provide the service itself in the long term**. In the past many organizations established services to demonstrate to the state how a particular objective could be achieved. Other organizations have established services with the intention of hiving them off as separate organizations. The National Council of Voluntary Organizations has been particularly successful at that, founding Age Concern, the Charities Aid Foundation, Citizens Advice Bureaux and many other less well-known organizations.

The fourth question is **whether the service should be provided by one organization alone** or as a partnership between different organizations. Partnerships between third-sector organizations and businesses are increasingly common. RNIB publishes its electronic newspaper in conjunction with the *Guardian*, housing associations undertake joint ventures financed partly by City institutions and Oxfam imports products from small businesses in non-industrialized countries to sell via its mail-order catalogue.

## *Meeting users' needs*

Having established the primary purpose of the service, the central logic that needs to pervade these organizations is that of understanding users' needs and providing services to meet them. This sounds simple in theory. However, there are many dimensions to user needs. They include the exact nature of the service, its quality, the way it is delivered, where it is provided, when it is available and so on.

In the private sector these different aspects of the service are bundled together and a price is attached to delivery of the service. When the business is not meeting that bundle of needs, sales tend to fall and managers know that action must be taken to pinpoint the problem and make improvements.

Many value-led organizations do not have such a sensitive feedback mechanism because users seldom pay the full cost of the service. As a result there are only muted signals about service quality. In some organizations there is virtually no connection between funder and user. Consequently other issues, such as the needs of staff, board politics and policy debates, can creep incrementally up the agenda. There is an ever-present danger that meeting the needs of service users will not be given the attention it requires.

The logic of managing service-providing organizations is therefore dependent on developing and maintaining a deep understanding of user needs. This may require research, data-gathering from user groups, group discussions, feedback forms and so on to replace the market mechanism and ensure that managers develop a clear view of user needs. Much has been written about marketing for service-giving organizations (see Further Reading) so the concepts are not repeated here.

Having understood user needs, the service-delivery system needs to focus on meeting them. Objectives should focus on user needs and clarify what the organization aims to do to meet those needs. The strategy should focus on how the organization will meet those needs. The performance-monitoring system should gather information on the extent to which users are satisfied with the service. The people-management process, including induction, supervision and appraisal, should incorporate sections on meeting user needs. Finally the system for monitoring overall performance of the organization should provide information on the number of users assisted, the extent of the assistance and its quality.

The effect of not having a direct market mechanism to keep service-giving organizations on their toes cannot be overestimated. Third-sector service providers have to compensate for this by taking every opportunity to ensure that all parts of the organization are geared up to seek out, listen and respond to users' needs.

## Demand management

In many service-providing organizations, demand for the service far exceeds the funds available to pay for it. Economic theory tells us that as prices for a service fall, demand increases. In many of these organizations prices are zero – so demand could potentially be infinite.

Organizations therefore have to adopt techniques to manage demand that depend on factors other than money. Some organizations allow waiting lists to grow. As they get longer, more and more people will seek the service from elsewhere or solve their problem in another way. Educational organizations have entry qualifications to manage demand. Housing associations measure the extent of people's housing need, so only people with the greatest need are eligible. Some organizations consciously avoid marketing or promoting their service to avoid being swamped by demand.

Using different mechanisms to control demand is an important task for many service-giving organizations. It may require a balance of:

- qualifying criteria (e.g., degree of disability)
- means testing (e.g., income, savings)
- price (e.g., rents, ticket prices, user charges).

There is often an element of conflict between the need to market services, to ensure that their availability is known to those most in need, and the need to manage demand in order to avoid being swamped with people wanting the service. Managers may feel that they are being pulled in two directions simultaneously. It is sometimes necessary to do both in order to concentrate resources on people with the greatest need. Marketing initiatives may need to be focused on particular groups, such as ethnic minorities, to ensure they have access to the service, while simultaneously opening hours may need to be restricted as a way of controlling availability of the service.

## Responding to the contract economy

One of the most significant changes in the management of many service-providing organizations has been the recent switch from grant to contract funding. For many years the proportion of funding that these organizations received from central and local government grew steadily. But the money came mainly in the form of grants, giving organizations considerable freedom in how the money was actually spent.

The change to funding by contract has many implications for third-sector organizations. It means:

- some organizations that had previously cooperated now find themselves competing with each other
- historically stable sources of funds can no longer be relied upon
- entrepreneurial newcomers are taking work from well-established organizations
- funding may increase, but it will be focused on the services that funders are obliged by law to provide and not on the education, advocacy and research that value-led organizations have always seen as important
- the traditional focus on quality of service will be replaced by value-for-money considerations.

This change has two important implications for management. First, it requires organizations to revisit their fundamental purpose to determine whether to participate in the contract economy in the first place. Organizations that have been highly dependent on grants to fund their services may have little choice. Those that are funded by donations or the sale of services to users have greater choice in the matter.

The decision is not as straightforward as it may appear at first sight, particularly for organizations that have not previously received significant government funding. The new money may appear attractive but:

- having to compete for contracts can be a restraint on organizations that mount campaigns against the policies or actions of government. They worry that their campaign activity may tip the decision about awarding the contract towards their competitors
- many organizations were established as independent bodies aiming to bring about change, not to become a surrogate supplier of government services.

Having determined that seeking contracts is within the spirit and mission of the organization, management has to develop a new range of skills, some of which are described elsewhere in this book. They include:

- **understanding potential purchasers:** managers have to identify the often limited number of purchasers of services. They have to understand the purchaser's organization, their personnel and their decision-making processes and to ensure that potential buyers know of the supplier's ability to deliver the services
- **costing services:** managers need to know how to build up the costs of a service to ensure their decisions about pricing contracts are based on the full cost of providing the service
- **tendering for contracts:** managers need to learn the art of submitting tenders that sell the services that they can provide effectively, set competitive prices and convince purchasers to buy the service
- **negotiating:** before and after contract tenders are won there is often a period of negotiation. Managers need to learn how to negotiate to ensure that the organization concludes a fair deal with its purchaser
- **financial management:** most organizations' financial-management systems are not designed to capture information by contract. Income and expenditure accounts by contract are essential to enable managers responsible for contracts to manage expenditure within contract income and for the organization to ensure that it is not unintentionally subsidizing contract work
- **performance monitoring:** contracts usually require organizations to monitor services more closely than they had to under grant-funding regimes. Suppliers need to be able to inform purchasers how many people were assisted, what level of assistance was provided, what outcomes were achieved and so on. Most organizations have to sharpen up their monitoring procedures to capture and evaluate this information
- **manage purchaser–provider relationships:** special skills are required to manage these relationships. They are concerned with keeping purchasers informed of progress and finding open and constructive ways of working together. These skills need development, particularly in organizations that are used to donor income and are consequently less experienced in reporting to funders.

To summarize, governors and managers of third-sector service-delivery organizations have to ask some fundamental strategic questions about why they are providing the service; they have to orient all their organization's systems around meeting users' needs; they often have to market the service and manage demand simultaneously; and they now need to develop new skills to survive in the contract economy.

## 10.5 MANAGING MUTUAL-SUPPORT ORGANIZATIONS

Mutual-support organizations include trade unions, professional associations, employers' organizations, trade associations and many voluntary
organizations established and run by members.

The fundamental difference between service-providing and mutual-
support organizations is that members both benefit from mutual-support
organizations and control their management. The special dimensions to
the management of these organizations all emanate from this critically
important relationship.

### Values and management are inseparable

Mutual-support organizations are distinguished more than anything else
by the values and beliefs of their members. These organizations usually
consist of people who are dedicated to the cause that the organization
stands for – committed trade unionists, enthusiastic members of their
profession or dedicated members of a voluntary organization.

In the case of voluntary organizations, many board members may
have had a significant life experience that motivated them to join the
organization. Common examples include the birth of a child with
disabilities and the death of a relative as a result of a terminal illness or
an accident. Whatever the motive, members of these organizations have
something in common. Consequently, **the culture is deeply influenced by members' experiences** and the cause that they champion.

The impact starts at the top with the board. It is elected by the members to represent their interests and views. Board members are therefore
particularly aware of their constituency. They are not only thinking
about the best interests of the organization, its staff and its lobbying
actions. They also have to keep their minds fixed clearly on members'
views of the decisions and actions they take.

The values and beliefs of members also have a less obvious but nevertheless significant impact on the way their organization works. **The
very nature of the cause spills over into management.** Take, for
example, mutual-support organizations where there is hope, perhaps, for
special training for the children with disabilities. In these circumstances
members' ambitions and enthusiasm for the cause lead to positive
attitudes about achieving the goals. At the other end of the spectrum,

organizations for people with terminal diseases can have a very different atmosphere. Unless values are fully acknowledged, as happens successfully in many hospices, anger, despair and resentment can spill over into the management of the organization. Members can become angry with staff and sometimes with each other as well. Debates and decisions become highly politicized and increasingly separated from the facts.

The point is that values are central in mutual-support organizations, both explicitly and implicitly. Management's task is to make things happen within the framework of the organization's values. Management may sometimes have to challenge the values (for example, to persuade members of the need to modernize their approach to services), but they will achieve significant change only if they carry the members with them.

## Tensions between members and staff

Mutual-support organizations are created when people come together around a common cause. In the beginning, and sometimes for many years, they have no staff. Members do the work until it becomes too much for volunteers and the organization appoints its first member of staff. This is often followed by a period of tension. Some members may begrudge paying staff to do work they used to do voluntarily. They continue to involve themselves in the detail of the organization only to find that staff resent their interference in what they believe is their work. Time may need to be set aside to clarify roles and understand each other's perspectives if their problems are to be overcome.

Even when this is done, **tension between members and staff is seldom far below the surface**. There are good reasons why this is the case, and it is worth acknowledging them explicitly. Members believe, quite rightly, that they own the organization. They set it up, they pay their membership fees and they control the governing board. However, their involvement is very much part-time and, as the organization grows, they just cannot keep on top of the detail of the organization's work. They have to delegate to staff who inevitably begin to feel they are responsible for the future of the organization.

This problem becomes more acute when the organization has hired good staff and has paid less attention to the quality of the organization's governance. Staff come to feel they know what is best for the organization.

These tensions should not be allowed to fester because they demotivate members and staff alike. The respective roles of the staff and, in particular the board and its committees, needs to be discussed, clarified and documented.

There is a further complication that affects management. **Tensions are common between members themselves.** Some may have high ambitions for the organization, some may vigorously argue a particular policy position and some may have different ideas about the future direction of the organization. These differences need to be acknowledged. They are all part of the pull and push of a group of diverse people who share one common cause. They need to be talked through, because people often have many common views and a few differences of opinion. In difficult cases an independent third party may help to resolve the problem. Where differences cannot be resolved and are incapacitating the organization, one side or the other should leave. The organization needs to go one way or the other and not remain in suspended animation, unable to proceed in any direction.

Employees often include people who are also members of the organization. Indeed, many organizations go out of their way to recruit people who have had, or are having, direct experience of the needs and the services that the organization provides. It means user needs are built into day-to-day management. This, however, is not without its difficulties. **Employees who are personally affected can cause problems.** They do not always have a broad perspective on members' needs. They may hold strong views, which can bring them into conflict with staff who are not personally affected by the problem. It requires adroit management to have a user on the staff and not let the organization become dominated by their viewpoint.

Organizations for people with terminal diseases provide a particularly difficult example of this issue. Members with the disease inevitably hold very strong views about priorities. Staff feel they have to be responsive to those views. It is difficult to challenge people when they have all the authority provided by their circumstance. Yet it has to be done when they hold a minority viewpoint. Management has to be seen to be sensitive and simultaneously move the organization forward for the benefit of the majority.

## The special case of intermediary organizations

One particular type of membership organization is the intermediary body. These are organizations whose members are other organizations.

They exist in most fields to provide an umbrella that enables a number of organizations to work together and speak with a common voice. The National Federation of Housing Associations, the National Council for Voluntary Organizations, the National Association of Health Authorities and Trusts and the Trades Union Congress are typical examples.

These present a special set of issues. Many of the people who sit on their boards do so as part of their job rather than entirely voluntarily. Their commitment is consequently very different from that of voluntary board members. Their primary loyalty is to the organization they represent and not the intermediary body. This makes the jobs of chief executives of these organizations significantly more difficult. They have to be adroit politicians as well as effective managers. They have to be able to judge which issue or proposals will command the support of the majority of member organizations and which will not.

Like other membership bodies, these organizations become more complex to manage when they start to offer services to non-members. The core skills required to manage effective services are very different from those required to represent members. So when the representative machinery starts to involve itself in the management of the services, problems often ensue.

One way around these problems is to keep the two types of activity in separate compartments. The services can be run as a subsidiary, perhaps with its own committee, or as a department with clear boundaries between it and the rest of the organization. Then the head of services can be given a clear brief and the freedom to manage the services within the agreed strategic and financial boundaries.

Another common problem is that intermediary organizations which start to offer services can find themselves competing with some of their members. This calls for even clearer separation of the representative processes from the service-management processes. Otherwise commercially sensitive information may be unwittingly passed to a competitor.

## 10.6 MANAGING CAMPAIGNING ORGANIZATIONS

Campaigning organizations are only a tiny proportion of the third sector, but they have a disproportionately large impact despite their number and size.

Pure campaigning organizations include Greenpeace, Amnesty International and organizations fighting for minority rights and women's rights and against poverty and prejudice. However, many service-giving and membership organizations also run campaigns, so parts of this section are relevant to them too.

In my experience campaigning organizations are particularly difficult to manage. They are often staffed by idealistic and highly articulate people. Many will have had little experience of managing people, working in a team or being a manager when they find themselves with significant management responsibilities.

The first ingredient of successful campaigning is **leadership**. Successful campaigns depend on individuals who passionately believe in the cause and can argue the case for change, both within the organization and externally to the press and media. Campaigning organizations need people who can present a cogent case and can simultaneously champion the cause and sound eminently reasonable.

Campaigning also depends on people with **creative skills** to mount campaigns that capture the public imagination. It needs the skills that are found in advertising and public relations agencies. These people have to have the ability to think in images and to create new ways of communicating complex messages to the public. Only when the messages are clear can the organization build a strong constituency of people who support the cause both politically and financially.

This activity also depends on having the **political acumen** to identify campaigns that can be fought and won. Campaigning organizations need managers who can make judgements about changes that are achievable and who can then galvanize people into action around that change. Campaigns with unrealistic goals soon lose steam. Greenpeace has short-term objectives and calls them 'small wins' – the essential steps in the political process that lead to desired long-term changes.

These organizations also require **management**. Fired up by the day-to-day tensions of running campaigns, people often put insufficient energy into looking after the organizations themselves. They do not run on idealism alone. Responsibilities need to be divided and individuals made accountable. Teams need to work both in and across the line-management structure. People need to be managed. Campaign managers must work within budgets and have the information they need to control costs. Fundraisers need to be able to compare the cost-effectiveness of different fundraising methods. In short, tight management practices are needed to enable people to do the all-important campaigning work.

Boards of campaigning organizations play an important role in achieving the right balance of campaign flair and sound management. Although board members will also be passionately dedicated to the cause, they need to be able to stand back from the details of individual campaigns and play a more strategic role.

The board's role in securing effective management of the organization is equally important. It needs to insist that staff pay sufficient attention to looking after the organization itself. Otherwise working for the organization can become so frustrating that even the motivation of the cause itself is insufficient to retain good campaigners. Since staff are the critical resource, the board needs to ensure that time and money are invested in good administrative systems.

Strategic planning in campaigning organizations has to separate out the strategies of each campaign from building the capacity of the institution. Campaign strategy is concerned with the objectives of the campaign, the strategies that are chosen to achieve the objectives and the resulting action plans. These are often given close attention. But equally important are the strategies for building a donor base, supporting local groups and creating an organization that can respond quickly and effectively to campaign opportunities.

A major strategic issue for campaigning organizations is the choice of campaign priorities. There are always more issues requiring attention than resources available. Difficult choices have to be made by the board about competing claims for staff time and money. A logical approach is to tailor-make a set of criteria against which alternative demands can be assessed. Such criteria are likely to include:

- the importance of the issue
- the potential for making progress
- the unique role of the organization on the issue
- the resources required
- the need to work with other organizations.

Management and board members can then give each campaign that is competing for resources a rating, say on a 1–5 scale, to make the process of choosing priorities more rigorous. Such an approach does not obviate the need for the board to use its wisdom to make good judgements. It does help to provide a framework within which these judgements can be made.

## SUMMARY OF KEY POINTS

### Organization life cycles

- Organizations develop in stages: periods of stability are followed by revolutionary change.
- Life cycles for individual organizations differ in detail. The power of the concept is that it helps boards and staff to see their problems in a broader context.

### Classifying organizations

- The most useful ways to classify organizations to gain insights into their management is by:
  - the broad purpose of the organization
  - the main source of funds
  - the composition of the board.
- The purpose of classifying organizations is to determine combinations of purpose, funding source and board membership that fit together well and to identify combinations that cause problems.

### Putting the classifications together

- Combinations that are comparatively straightforward to manage include:
  - service organizations funded by sales, contracts or grants and governed by experts
  - mutual-support organizations funded by members and governed by service users
  - campaign organizations funded by donations and governed by concerned individuals.
- Organizations that have other combinations are more managerially challenging.

### Managing different types of organization

- Keys to the successful management of service-delivery organizations include:
  - clarifying the fundamental purpose
  - orienting systems around meeting users' needs
  - marketing the service and simultaneously managing demand
  - developing the skills needed to survive in the contract economy.

- Managers of mutual-support organizations have to work with the values associated with the cause. Tensions between members and staff are common and need to be addressed openly.
- Successful campaigning organizations require strong leadership, creative skills and political acumen. They need to avoid the pitfall of giving insufficient attention to the practicalities of management.

# CHAPTER ELEVEN

# A Glimpse into the Future

Until comparatively recently the third sector was in decline. Ideas and services that emanated from the third sector were gradually being taken over by the state. Provision of housing, schools and health care was increasingly seen as a government responsibility. Many services that had historically been provided or supported by charitable institutions were slowly being incorporated into the public sector.

For a period, particularly from the Second World War to the early 1970s, the charities that remained in the core of the third sector were seen as playing only a minor role and one that was secondary to that of the new public services.

Fifteen years ago the situation began to change. It started when charitable organizations began to reassert their influence, often driven by idealistic people who were determined to take action to address the pressing social, health, environmental and educational problems that society faced. A combination of imaginative new ideas and increased funding from donors and the state led to the beginning of a period of explosive growth. For a period the top 200 charities were growing ten times faster than the economy as a whole.

In the last five years there has been a more fundamental change, which has the potential to transform the sector even more dramatically. The assumption that the best way to provide public services is by means of large public-sector organizations, funded and managed by the state, has been challenged.

It has led to the conclusion that services can sometimes be provided more efficiently when the state decides what it wants to purchase and makes providers compete against each other to deliver the services. Although the whole notion of making people and organizations that are deeply committed to public service compete against each other is an anathema to many, it is almost certainly here to stay.

The implications for the third sector are huge. Governmental organizations that needed public-sector approaches to management will start to depend on the skills and approaches used by the third sector. They will increasingly see themselves as independent suppliers of public services whose success will depend on their ability to innovate, to provide what purchasers want and to have highly effective management. This final chapter therefore takes a glimpse at this exciting and challenging future for the third sector. It is a personal view derived from my experience of working in the sector. It contains a mixture of some predictions and some aspirations for a sector of the economy that I believe will become a much more dominant force in years to come.

My main points are that:

- the sector will grow dramatically as more public-sector institutions exploit the huge opportunities that result from their greater independence and return to the fold
- organizations will have to become much more nimble in their strategic development
- organizations with first-class management skills will thrive – the less well-managed ones will decline and usually end up being taken over.

The chapter ends with a summary of the characteristics that the successful organizations will need to exhibit.

## The sector will flourish

Third-sector organizations thrive when board members and staff have a strong commitment to their cause and work tirelessly to achieve it. They also produce their best performance when they have to compete for funds, irrespective of whether the money comes from donations, sales or contracts. Competition forces them to clarify what they are doing and to communicate this to their funders.

The commitment of government to separate the functions of purchasing and providing public services provides the foundation upon which the third sector will grow. The process has already begun. Some grant-maintained schools see that their growing independence opens up many new opportunities. Staff can relate more closely to the mission of the school than to the bureaucracy of the education authority; new opportunities can be pursued and, as a result, new sources of finance can be tapped. In short, these schools are starting to behave like many other third-sector organizations, using entrepreneurialism and commitment to survive in a competitive environment.

Education colleges are moving in a similar direction. They have already been released from the managerial control of local authorities and have to compete for students and funds. However, in many cases years of control by the state has dulled their sense of mission. In the new environment they are discovering that the entrepreneurial behaviour and dedication to achieving the mission that exemplifies the best of the third sector will serve them well. They too will benefit from the independence that comes from moving into the third sector.

NHS hospital trusts will also move closer to the third sector, but this will happen more slowly. Public and professional commitment to the idea of one National Health Service is very strong. But it has created a bureaucracy and a culture that can be resistant to change. The more pluralistic approach to health care will lead the more forward-looking trusts to see themselves as semi-independent organizations dedicated to providing health for people living in their areas.

One of the last groups to move towards the third sector will be the universities. The pressures for greater accountability and value for money have yet to make a significant impact on these organizations. They are still comparatively insulated from the need to be highly entrepreneurial, but I suspect that new methods of funding and user demand for efficiency and flexibility will eventually persuade them to change. The managerial practices of the best American not-for-profit universities will provide models that will be increasingly useful in the UK.

These trends will combine to create a stronger, more vibrant and more effective third sector. Whereas the charity sector now accounts for less than 5 per cent of GDP in the UK, the new third sector could account for 10 per cent if NHS trusts, universities and colleges become so independent that they are no longer considered to be part of the public sector.

This much enlarged sector will have two distinct parts. One part will consist primarily of contract-funded service-delivery organizations. It will include schools, colleges and hospitals. Their priority will be the delivery of the highest possible quality of services within available funding. The other part will be donor- and member-funded organizations that exist primarily to champion causes and create a better world.

There will be no clear dividing line between these two broad categories. Many organizations (e.g., MENCAP, RNIB, MIND) will continue to provide services and champion their cause simultaneously. They benefit from being able to run campaigns based on their own experience. They allow the public to donate money to support services and campaigns, so artificial separation into different legal categories, suggested by some policy thinkers, could be unhelpful and destructive.

## Strategic developments

The growth and arrival of new entrants into the sector will require organizations to become more strategically nimble.

First, competition for contracts, donors and sales will force organizations to specialize in those services where they have most expertise and to back out of services where they have fewer skills. Niche providers will grow faster than generalist organizations that diversify into many services and inevitably develop cumbersome management overheads. The movement of whole services, including the funding and the staff, between organizations will increase as boards and management strive to create a better match between organizations' core skills and the objectives and strategies that they are pursuing.

Second, organizations will need to find ways to streamline the services that remain in their portfolio. The prevalent assumption that reducing costs automatically leads to a reduction in quality will be challenged as innovative organizations discover imaginative ways of achieving the desired outcomes with fewer material and human inputs. Although effectiveness is not a concept that social, educational and health-care organizations are necessarily comfortable with, it will become a measure of success as organizations compete against each other for funds.

Third, partnerships between organizations will be needed to bring together different combinations of skills to address social and environmental problems. These partnerships will increasingly cross the boundaries of the third, private and public sectors as organizations see the advantages of joint ventures.

## Improved management

As well as becoming strategically more nimble, third-sector organizations will need to become much better at integrating their mission with their management. The very essence of the best third-sector organizations is their ability to combine dedication to the cause with pragmatic managerial skills. Organizations therefore will have to bring mission and management together to be successful. Some large voluntary organizations have acquired the necessary skills. They provide excellent models that can be followed by those organizations (often from the public sector) in which professionals and managers are at loggerheads with each other. These voluntary organizations have adopted and adapted the concepts of strategy, individual accountability and cost-effectiveness, but they also succeed in promoting the mission as the ultimate purpose of the organization.

Management will have to pay more attention to outcomes. Objectives, strategies and plans will have to be based on achieving positive outcomes for services and campaigns. Organizations will need to pay greater attention to monitoring outcomes and reporting performance in terms of outcomes. It will require significant investment in systems that allow organizations to follow people up months, and sometimes years, after the service was provided to pinpoint the difference that the service made. Boards and managers will then be able to adjust their services and prioritize approaches that have been demonstrated as having the greatest impact.

Financial-management information systems will also have to improve significantly. Managers will need accurate, up-to-date accounts of their income and expenditure shortly after the end of each month. The best businesses achieve this at the end of each week. Third-sector organizations will have to learn to produce the information that managers need to maintain tight control on costs and exploit every opportunity to achieve the same outcome with fewer resources.

By combining improved outcome information with better financial data, organizations will be better able to compare the cost-effectiveness of different activities and adjust their portfolio of services accordingly.

Internally, organizations with cumbersome boards and committees will need to streamline their structures to increase their effectiveness. The notion that committees automatically add value will be challenged: sometimes they are a positive impediment to progress. In future they will need to focus on the critical issues of purpose and performance to justify their existence.

All this will require greatly increased effort to be put into management development. Training courses, mentoring, shadowing and coaching will all play greater roles in the daily lives of managers. Skill acquisition will become a major objective of ambitious managers. Organizations will have to respond by making time and resources available for learning and development.

## Characteristics of successful organizations

To meet these challenges organizations will need to exhibit many characteristics. They will require:

- a clear vision of what they want to achieve
- a sense of mission that pervades all parts of the organization
- concise objectives and clear strategies for achieving each objective
- imagination and the entrepreneurial skills needed in a competitive era
- a strong board that governs the organization and lets management manage
- a charismatic chief executive who is able to provide leadership to the organization
- a group of senior managers who work as a team and are skilled at directing the organization
- management processes that knit all parts of the organization together
- flexible management structures that change quickly to respond to new circumstances
- managers who strive to develop the people who work for them
- income sources that are suitable for the types of activities the organization pursues
- two-way communication between the field and the headquarters.

An ambitious list, you may say. But most third-sector organizations want to make a significant impact on the world we live in. To achieve that ambition will require excellence in all aspects of management.

# Economists' Theories About Not-for-profit Organizations

The third sector has always presented economists with problems. It does not fit the theories of the behaviour of firms or of consumers. Equally it does not fit theories about taxation and the provision of public services that describe the public sector. This appendix summarizes some of their theories about not-for-profit organizations. I have used their term not-for-profit in this appendix, since the definition of the third sector in this book is wider than that used by economists.

Attempts to explain not-for-profit organizations have led economists to put forward three theories. The **public goods** theory says that not-for-profit organizations exist because some people want public services beyond those that governments can afford to provide with income from tax-payers. In economists' language, governments are limited to providing services that the average or, to be more precise, 'median' voter is willing to support through paying his or her taxes. Those people who want to pay for additional public services do so voluntarily by making donations.

A good example of this theory is medical research charities. Some people want more work to be done to find cures for diseases. They are willing to pay more for this public service by making donations to not-for-profit organizations.

This theory leads to the conclusion that, from an economist's perspective, the special characteristic of not-for-profit organizations is the additional contribution they make to a particular field or endeavour.

The second theory starts from the idea of **contract failure**. It suggests that third-sector organizations exist because funders and, in particular, donors have no way of knowing whether their money is being well spent, so they have to trust an organization that cannot itself profit from their donations.

According to this theory, the normal contract that exists in the private sector (people pay for goods and services and check their quality) breaks down, so people need a third party whom they can trust to give them confidence that the service will be supplied efficiently and to a high quality.

International aid agencies provide a good example. Donors have few ways of knowing that their money has been well spent but trust that the board and the staff of an organization will strive to spend the money as efficiently as possible.

Similarly, some services that are paid for by government or foundations can never be evaluated fully by purchasers. They trust that the values and beliefs of third-sector organizations will motivate them to provide quality services rather than cut corners and give each other unnecessary perks.

The third explanation for not-for-profit organizations is known as the **consumer control** theory. According to this theory, consumers both want a service or campaign from an organization and want to control the organization itself. Membership organizations such as trade unions, campaigning organizations, professional associations, employers' associations and trade associations fit this theory well. Members need an organization's services but also want to have control over the policies the organization pursues and the actions it takes.

These three theories go some way to explaining why third-sector organizations exist. Economists have one other theory, which relates to the tax status accorded to many third-sector organizations. This theory suggests that some organizations choose not-for-profit status to gain tax exemptions. This is an increasingly sensitive point as third-sector organizations now compete regularly with private suppliers for contracts to run state-funded services. The private suppliers argue that tax breaks give third-sector organizations an unfair competitive advantage.

Some interesting evidence on this point comes from another part of the third sector. In the insurance business mutual societies have competed with businesses for many years. To date there has been little convincing evidence that either makes a greater surplus or provides a better service than the other as a direct result of their 'for-profit' or 'not-for-profit' status. Other factors – for example, quality of management – may therefore be more significant than choice of tax status.

In short, despite the importance of not-for-profit organizations, economists have given the sector remarkably little attention. Readers wishing to study this topic further should see an American text: B. Weisbrod, *The Non-profit Economy*, Harvard University Press, 1988.

# Understanding Organization Culture

The idea of culture provides useful insights into the behaviour of organizations and has been referred to in a number of places in the main text. This appendix introduces the ideas of organization culture and explains how managers can influence it. Understanding an organization's culture helps managers to make things happen because it is easier to build on the prevailing culture than work against it. Managers who pursue strategies and actions that inadvertently confront strongly held cultural beliefs usually come to grief.

Organization culture has been defined in many ways. The easiest definitions are:

- 'the way we do things round here' (M. Bower, *The Will to Manage*, McGraw Hill, 1966)
- 'the way we think about things round here' (C. Geertz, *The Interpretation of Cultures*, Basic Books, 1973).

A more useful definition is:

- 'the commonly held and relatively stable beliefs, attitudes and values that exist within an organization' (N. Margulies and A. Raia, *Conceptual Foundations of Organizational Development*, McGraw Hill, 1978).

## Three levels of organization culture

Culture is best understood by considering the three different levels at which it is expressed. At the most superficial level there are the artifacts of an organization's culture – its buildings, the routine procedures of meetings, the management structure and the language that people use. These are visible manifestations of culture. Visit a well-established housing association with its offices in the business park and one cannot help noticing the smart photographs of its properties on the wall, the tidy reception area and the magazines laid out neatly for visitors to read.

This gives a very different impression from a campaigning organization with its offices in a dilapidated property in a run-down area of town, newspapers piled high waiting to be clipped, desks cramped together, walls piled to the ceiling with T-shirts, pamphlets and posters and phones ringing incessantly. Two extremes, perhaps, but they illustrate the different physical manifestations of culture.

The second level of culture is related to the organization's justification for itself. This is concerned with what people say – the conscious thought processes that justify decisions and actions. The mission statement and the strategic plan are good examples of this level of culture. They are justifications that people have agreed to, although, it should be noted, they may not reflect everyone's underlying beliefs about the organization.

The third, and most important, level is the underlying beliefs. These are assumptions that are taken for granted. They are the unconscious values that inform people's behaviour. For example, some organizations have implicit assumptions about consensus decision-making. Other organizations expect leaders to take decisions and people are surprised if they are consulted. Underlying beliefs are often strong in organizations with a preponderance of people from one profession. Welfare organizations involving people with a social-work background have a very different culture from medical organizations, where the rational scientific model is an important underlying belief. These can be contrasted again with campaigning organizations, which have their beliefs rooted in a political model of the way things work.

## Characteristics of culture

To understand the concept of organization culture more thoroughly it is worth looking briefly at its characteristics.

1. **It is learned.** It results both from people's experiences before they joined the organization and from the influences of the organization itself.
2. **It is determined by the organization's history.** It is defined by decisions people have taken in the past, particularly those taken by significant individuals such as the founder.
3. **It is partly subconscious.** Over time assumptions develop and become implicit influences on people's behaviour. Such beliefs and assumptions affect the way people think about things.

4. **It is heterogeneous.** Different parts of an organization have different cultures. A common difference is that between staff in the headquarters of an organization, concerned with public profile, fundraising, lobbying and the inevitable politics of large organizations, and people in the local branches who are more concerned with service delivery and valuing volunteers.

Culture is particularly important in third-sector organizations because people usually believe in the cause for which they work. Housing homeless people, campaigning for human rights, championing the rights of people with disabilities and educating people with special needs are all activities that people easily take to their hearts.

Consistency between the values and beliefs held by key members of an organization is an essential prerequisite for action. This explains why small groups of highly motivated people can achieve so much. When there are implicit agreements between people about the primary purpose of an organization, everyone's effort can be devoted to the actions needed to 'make things happen'. When these agreements are not in place, an extraordinary amount of time has to be allocated to discussion and debate in order to achieve greater consistency of beliefs and understanding.

Successful strategic management depends on people sharing beliefs and understanding. Any organization can go through the motions of preparing a strategic plan and achieve agreement on its contents. But if significant individuals or groups do not hold common beliefs about both the substance and the methods of implementation, it is hardly worth the paper it was written on.

Effective strategic management needs to be rooted in an understanding of the different beliefs held by people in different parts of the organization. When people hold values that are sufficiently different that they begin to affect the performance of the organization, managers need to identify them. Rather than just pushing harder and marshalling more and more arguments to defend one position, managers need to understand the beliefs that are leading people to disagree. Then they need to find means to address those obstacles in ways that meet the concerns of people who are raising resistance.

For example, the faculty of a college department was unable to agree on priorities. Half the staff wanted to be entrepreneurial and seek new contracts with businesses and the other half wanted to persuade the college to provide better funding. Progress was made only when each explored the underlying beliefs of the other side; one half assumed that unless the department was seen to be more entrepreneurial it would be wound up, and the other half believed that the college had failed to recognize the value of its work and needed to be convinced of the case for increased funding.

Another example comes from the different beliefs of managers and people providing services. Managers have beliefs about the importance of procuring the necessary resources, marketing the organization and its services and the allocation of resources to different activities. These are very different from the beliefs of service providers (for example, teachers, doctors, social workers), whose thinking starts from concerns about service users and the needs of their fellow professionals. All too frequently arguments between managers and those professionals concerned with the delivery of services are rooted in deeply held cultural assumptions that both managers and providers find difficult to explain to each other.

However, having said that successful strategic management depends on people having similar values, organizations also need to be able to see their strategic situation from different perspectives. A common pitfall is that organizations of very like-minded people fail to see the need to change their strategy. The world around an organization may have changed (for example, through contract funding replacing grant funding) but no one anticipated the change (and prepared contract bids before grant funding was finally withdrawn). The 'way the organization thought about things' did not change until it was too late.

Those organizations that adapt their culture to new circumstances continue to thrive. Those that do not adapt, and those that adapt in inappropriate ways, start to decline.

## Influencing organization culture

So how do managers influence an organization's culture? E. Schein, Professor of Management at the Massachusetts Institute of Technology, identifies five types of action (E. Schein, *Organizational Culture and Leadership*, Jossey-Bass, 1992). First, culture is influenced by **what leaders pay attention to**. The issues that leaders systematically work on give signals to the rest of the organization about what is considered to be important. The leader who consistently pays attention to financial management encourages a culture in which tight financial control rises up the agenda. The entrepreneurial leader who welcomes new ventures encourages a culture that values innovation and development.

Second, the implicit **criteria used to allocate money** to different activities influence people's view of the culture. They sends out signals about the types of activity that are perceived to be valued. For example, if the board consistently approves projects for people from ethnic minorities, the importance of minority groups will climb up everyone's agenda.

Third, the implicit **criteria used in the recruitment and promotion of people** are indicators of beliefs. The organization that champions the rights of people with disabilities, and takes positive action to recruit people with disabilities to its own staff, gives important signals about its underlying beliefs.

Fourth, **the way people react in a crisis** is an influence on culture. Crises are important because people watch each other's actions more closely and because they often lead to learning that is remembered clearly. For example, an organization that handles redundancies badly leads people to believe that it doesn't accord high value to caring for its staff.

Finally, deliberate **role modelling and coaching** influence the culture. Managers implicitly teach their staff through their actions. Reviewing people's plans, commenting on achievements and guiding people on how to improve their work all help to change beliefs and values.

The notion of culture sheds light on people and their behaviour. It helps managers to analyse, in a dispassionate way, problems that are rooted in different values and beliefs. One of the most enduring features of third-sector organizations is that they are value-led. Indeed, a factor that differentiates these organizations is people's willingness to recognize and acknowledge different values. Effective managers encourage people with different values to see each other's perspectives. This helps them to maintain diverse values but continue to work together to achieve a common goal.

# The Contribution Approach to Financial Management

## Hold service managers accountable for financial contribution

This is not a book about financial management. However, one financial concept can help board members and managers to get a better grasp of their organization's strategic situation. This is a fundamental principle of management accounts that is particularly applicable to service-delivery organizations funded by statutory authorities and service users. The principle is used widely in commercial organizations but seldom in third-sector bodies. As contract funding, in particular, grows it will become increasingly useful.

The principle is that managers should be held accountable only for income and expenditure that they are responsible for controlling. They should not be held accountable for costs that may be attributable to their service but that they cannot control in practice (for example, a proportion of the cost of the headquarters).

In summary a service manager's account should have the following lines:

| | £ |
|---|---|
| **Income from providing the service** <br> (grants, sales) | a |
| **Direct costs of the service** <br> (costs incurred exclusively in providing the service) | b |
| **Contribution to overheads** <br> (or subsidy required to finance direct costs) | a – b |
| **Overhead costs** <br> (i.e., proportion of fixed overhead charges to the service) | c |
| **Surplus or deficit from the service** | a – b – c |

Service managers are responsible for managing the contribution line. They usually have control over the income, which can be increased by raising prices (for example, to purchasing authorities) or by seeking additional grant-funding. They also control expenditure, and they should be in a position to reduce expenditure if income falls and to increase it if demand for the service and income rise. They should not, however, be held accountable for the bottom line (surplus or deficit) because they do not take the decisions that affect overhead costs.

Service managers do have a need to know what the bottom line is because this information will influence the setting of prices. Furthermore, they should be informed of the overhead costs that are being allocated to their service, so everyone can make judgements about whether overhead expenditure is providing value for money.

Once accounts have been set out on a contribution basis, the contribution budget of each service can then be built up into a contribution account for the organization as a whole.

The contribution approach neatly illustrates one of the perverse aspects of managing third-sector organizations. In business, when a service is successful, growth in the number of customers leads to a larger financial contribution. The line a − b grows and, provided overheads do not grow, the business makes a larger profit. Many third-sector organizations have inverse economic equations. Because direct costs are often higher than service income, every increase in the number of users leads to a larger deficit. So the more successful the service is at meeting users' needs, the greater the financial loss. As any experienced manager knows, this is a fact of life in the third sector. The advantage of the contribution approach is that it makes the economic equation of the organization entirely explicit. When each service has its own economic equation, it becomes much easier for the board and senior management to understand the financial consequences of decisions to expand or contract different services.

In the Care Homes example, opening a third home on the same economic equation as that of the current homes would lead to a further call on funds from the successful headquarters fundraising programme. Expanding the Care in the Community service would not require further fundraising as it makes a positive contribution to overhead costs.

## CONTRIBUTION BUDGET FOR CARE HOMES

| £'000 | Homes | Care in the Community | Head-quarters | TOTAL |
|---|---|---|---|---|
| **INCOME** | | | | |
| Grants | 30 | 50 | 50 | 130 |
| Fees | 950 | 160 | 0 | 1110 |
| Donations | 20 | 0 | 320 | 340 |
| TOTAL | 1000 | 210 | 370 | 1580 |
| | | | | |
| **EXPENDITURE** | | | | |
| Staff | 800 | 150 | 180 | 1130 |
| Materials | 250 | 50 | 90 | 390 |
| TOTAL | 1050 | 200 | 270 | 1520 |
| | | | | |
| CONTRIBUTION[1] | (50) | 10 | 100 | 60 |
| | | | | |
| OVERHEAD COSTS | 30(a) | 10 (b) | (40)[2] | 0 |
| | | | | |
| SURPLUS/DEFICIT | (80) | 0 | 190 | 60 |

[1] Service managers are responsible for managing income and expenditure to meet this target.

[2] Costs recharged to services (i.e. (a) and (b)) for pricing purposes.

# Increasing Funders' Effectiveness

## A4.1 CATEGORIZING FUNDERS

One of the distinguishing facets of third-sector organizations is their ability to raise finance and resources from an extraordinarily wide range of sources. Members, donors, shops, investments, grants, contracts and the sale of services are all part of their entrepreneurial approach to funding.

The majority of funding comes from institutions such as national and local government, health authorities, foundations and businesses. This appendix focuses on the management of funding programmes run by these institutions and how they can help to increase the effectiveness of the organizations they finance.

### Historical context

For many years government departments and local authorities gave organizations core grants to cover general administrative costs. Foundations saw their role as giving gifts, and businesses often saw themselves as donors and had little further involvement once they had received publicity for their donation.

Nowadays the situation is different. Government funders want to see value for money and are rapidly switching from grant-funding to contracts let by tender. Foundations continue to receive many applications and are having to become more rigorous in selecting whom they fund. Many companies no longer see funding as the distribution of largesse. They want to make a contribution that is related more directly to the success of their business.

Funding institutions have different but often overlapping reasons for putting resources into third-sector organizations. Central and local government provide funds because third-sector organizations:

- can be less expensive and more efficient than public- or private-sector suppliers
- are creative and good at trying out new ideas
- can engage with user groups that are sometimes beyond the reach of statutory agencies
- are good at gaining political and financial support from a diverse range of sources
- use voluntary labour (which, some people argue, is exploited by government)
- are at arm's length and can provide a useful input to policy development
- are a means for government to take action on a policy issue (and avoid blame if things go wrong!).

Foundations, on the other hand, fund organizations because they:

- are a source of social innovation
- are good at championing the causes of minority groups
- are quick to respond when new problems emerge (for example, HIV/AIDS)
- speak with authority
- need capital and are seldom able to borrow investment money.

Businesses have an additional reason for providing funds. They want to engage with organizations that will promote their companies. They want to be seen as enlightened, caring and playing an active role in the communities they serve. As well as being genuinely philanthropic, they also want to link up with causes that are directly related to their business objectives.

These funders can be categorized according to their relationship to the sector.

1. Central government, local authorities, health authorities and businesses are entirely outside the sector. They have other objectives, and funding the third sector is part of their strategy for achieving these wider aims.
2. Semi-independent government agencies that fund housing, the arts, sports, museums and, increasingly, education and health sit on the boundary of the sector. They are often not considered to be part of the sector, though their management fits third-sector theory better than any other.

3. Foundations are part of the third sector itself. They have managerial needs similar to those of the providers they are financing, and much of this book is relevant to them.

4. Finally, there are some organizations that are both providers and funders, including many aid agencies, some social-welfare organizations and some research bodies. They have to apply the methods of providers to manage their services and the methods of funders to manage their grant-giving programmes.

Together these organizations distribute a huge sum of money. Central government gives grants worth over £600 million per annum to the voluntary sector alone. The semi-independent government agencies are dominated by the Housing Corporation and its equivalents in Scotland, Wales and Northern Ireland. They give funding worth almost £2 billion per annum to housing associations. The top 500 foundations make grants worth £800 million per annum and the top 200 businesses give over £200 million per annum in cash and kind.

These funding institutions are an increasingly important determinant of the success of third-sector organizations. On the positive side, funders' ability to design and manage appropriate funding programmes, to distribute funds to the most effective providers and to monitor the outcomes of their funding helps to focus providers on achieving their objectives. On the negative side, funders can seduce bodies into accepting money that distracts the organization from its primary purpose. They sometimes allow organizations to become too dependent on their money. They can weigh organizations down with cumbersome bureaucracy and interfere unnecessarily in their management. At their worst, poor funders can be a positive hindrance to an organization's effectiveness.

This appendix describes how funders can strengthen key elements of their funding processes. It demonstrates how funders can provide maximum benefit to providers by:

- focusing sharply on their own objectives
- selecting different strategies for achieving different objectives
- adopting administrative practices that assist providers
- monitoring the performance of providers and of their funding programmes as a whole
- creating value-added relationships with providers.

## FUND ALLOCATION PROCESSES

For larger funders and those offering contracts the process of managing a funding programme has eight distinct stages:

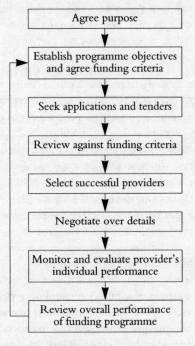

Agree purpose

Establish programme objectives and agree funding criteria

Seek applications and tenders

Review against funding criteria

Select successful providers

Negotiate over details

Monitor and evaluate provider's individual performance

Review overall performance of funding programme

Smaller foundations are more responsive in nature. Their funding process often takes the following form:

Receive requests

Identify ones that meet funding criteria

Decide at trustee meeting

Make grants and (sometimes) request progress reports

It is aimed primarily at large funders. However, much of it is applicable to those smaller foundations that pride themselves in their low administration costs but, in my experience, sometimes give away significant sums of money to ill-considered projects and often do not monitor whether their money has achieved the desired objectives.


## A4.2  CLARIFYING PURPOSE AND OBJECTIVES

Funding institutions are in a privileged position. They have access to financial and human resources and the power to decide how both are allocated to providers. They determine who receives the resources, how much they receive, the types of work that are funded and the duration of their support. This privileged position carries with it some specific responsibilities that funders need to discharge. The starting point for doing this is to be clear about the overall purpose of the fund or funding programme and the specific objectives that the funder wishes to achieve. This section looks at purpose and objectives in turn.

### *Focus on purpose*

The notion of the purpose of a funder or funding programme is analogous to the notion of the mission (see section 2.3) of a service-providing organization. Indeed, mission is an entirely transferable concept for foundations since they exist to achieve change by providing resources. The idea of a mission in this context is less appropriate for government and business organizations because funding the third sector is one small part of their work.

The purpose statement of a funder or funding programme should explain its *raison d'être*. It should answer the question 'What, overall, does this fund aim to achieve over the next three to five years?' It should be precise and focused, avoiding the trap of a set of words that could be applied to any funder in any circumstances. It should, however, stand above statements of specific objectives of each programme of work within the funding organization.

There are three reasons why it is important to clarify purpose. First, funders are accountable to their 'owners' or 'paymasters' for how they spend their money. Government departments are accountable to

Ministers and Parliament; local authorities are accountable to councillors and voters; foundations are accountable to trustees and donors; and businesses are ultimately accountable to shareholders. Each requires a basis for that accountability. Clear statements of purpose enable funders to review what their funding programmes have achieved and account to their paymasters for their performance.

Second, funders need to concentrate their efforts on the limited number of areas where they can have greatest impact. Entrepreneurial third-sector organizations quite rightly use every means at their disposal to winkle money out of funders. Good applications, lobbying and personal contacts are all part of their tool kit. However, funders can have expertise only in a limited number of fields. That expertise is needed to ensure that resources are targeted precisely at areas of greatest need and at organizations that will use them effectively.

Third, clear statements of purpose discourage third-sector organizations from wasting their time on speculative applications. These take great effort to prepare, and processing them devours funders' resources.

## Sharp thinking on objectives

Objectives describe what the funder wishes to achieve in each area of work. They take the thinking one level further and articulate a series of specific aims that the funder wishes to pursue.

Funders' objectives fall into four broad categories.

First, they can be concerned with **groups of people**. These may be demographic groups such as children, young people, families, women or elderly people. They can be groups with special needs, such as people with addictions, mental health problems or disabilities, or they might be minorities.

Second, objectives can focus on **types of service**. These include, for example, social-welfare services, health services, housing, education or the arts.

Third, objectives can be concerned with **specific issues**. Typical examples include the environment, minority rights and free-market economics.

Finally, objectives can aim to achieve **specific developments** – for example, to encourage innovation in a particular field by promoting new approaches. Alternatively, objectives may aim to improve quality – for example in a particular art form or approach to teaching.

## THE ALLIED DUNBAR DOMESTIC-VIOLENCE PROGRAMME

The Allied Dunbar Charitable Trust focuses its grant-giving on a limited number of issues. It aims to make a substantial impact on the issues it chooses to fund.

In 1994 it began to fund a programme aimed at victims of domestic violence. Trustees agreed to spend £2 million over a four-year period. The key objectives of the programme were:

- to increase the number of secure places for women and children escaping violence in the home by giving priority to the development of new refuges
- to give priority to women and children isolated in rural areas or in black and other ethnic minority communities.

## A FUNDING PROGRAMME WITH INNOVATION AS THE PRIMARY OBJECTIVE

The New York State Department of Social Services had for many years funded organizations working to reduce teenage pregnancies. The Department believed that more innovative approaches to the problem were required. It therefore established a fund of $50,000, called the 'Local Innovations Initiative', that had the specific objective of encouraging innovative applications that identified new ways to tackle the growing problem of teenage pregnancies.

In particular, the fund assumed that successful projects are most often explained by individual leaders, or 'spark plugs', whose energies, talent, focus and optimism galvanize action. The assumption was similar to that of venture-capital firms, which believe that it is the entrepreneur, not the plan or the budget, that is the key to successful business start-ups.

The fund was overwhelmingly successful, receiving almost ten times the number of applications per dollar available compared with the main programme and achieving the desired objective of encouraging innovation.

## The process of sharpening focus

Clarifying purpose and objectives is seldom an easy task for funders. It is just as difficult for funders to specify objectives as it is for third-sector organizations themselves. The problems of capturing aims when the purposes are social, artistic, spiritual or educational are rarely straight-forward.

Nevertheless, people responsible for funding organizations and programmes need to take time out to work on them. The process is invariably iterative, as each person involved helps to move the thinking forward. It usually involves dedicating time at away-days to work on it.

Once agreed, the purpose and the objectives need to be reviewed regularly. Social circumstances change, the abilities of providers grow and new needs emerge. Indeed, as funders gain a better grasp of their purpose and the changing context they are working in, they can become more proactive in anticipating needs and focusing their resources on emerging needs and new ways of addressing problems. So, while the purpose may remain relatively unchanged for a consider-able period of time, the objectives can be adjusted to suit changing circumstances.

## A4.3 FUNDING STRATEGIES

Funders need strategies for achieving their objectives. They need to satisfy themselves that they are deploying their resources in ways that are most likely to achieve their objectives. Funders face a range of strategic alternatives for achieving their objectives.

The first strategic choice funders have to make is whether to achieve the objective by taking action within the funding organization or by funding another organization to do the work. With the exception of government, the majority of funders' activities are usually concerned with funding other organizations and individuals. Some foundations are exceptions and have their own programmes of work.

Having resolved whether the work is to be done internally or extern-ally (or by a mixture of both), funders have a range of strategic options for achieving the objectives of each funding programme. These options are based on a typology suggested by Diana Leat (*Grant-giving: A Guide to Policy Making*, Joseph Rowntree Foundation, 1992). The options exist on a continuum ranging from low funder involvement with providers at one end to high involvement at the other end.

The greater the funder involvement, usually the higher the costs of establishing and managing the funding programme.

Each strategy is appropriate in different circumstances.

The first is based on **responding to needs** expressed by providers. They apply for money or non-financial assistance, and funders respond because they see the value of the project or the organization and wish to support it. Funding may not be considered against rigorously adhered-to criteria. It is likely to result in the awarding of a grant. There may not be many conditions attached to the funding, and payment may well be made in advance of the work being done. Many foundations have historically pursued this strategy for much of their work. Similarly, government departments and local authorities that give core grants in response to requests from providers are using this strategy. Businesses in the past also tended to respond to appeals for funds.

This strategy has the advantage of meeting very directly the needs expressed by providers. It incurs very low costs and is appropriate where the funder does not understand the field well and wishes to be responsive to the needs expressed by front-line providing organizations. It is also appropriate when funders wish to learn about a field with the

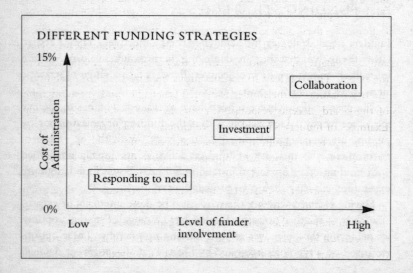

DIFFERENT FUNDING STRATEGIES

intention of pursuing other strategies in the future. Its disadvantages are that:

- when demand exceeds the funds available it is difficult to be systematic in choosing which applications to fund
- funders may be able to get better value for money from a more rigorous approach
- funders may end up with disparate sets of projects and no coherence to their overall programme
- funders may not be able or willing to sustain a long-term commitment to the project or organization.

**Investment strategies** are used by funders who know what they want to achieve. They may ask organizations to tender competitively for funding, and they may search for organizations that have the ability to achieve the investors' objectives.

Pursuing investment strategies requires funders to have more expertise in the fields they are funding than if they are using gift-giving strategies. They may consider alternative ways of achieving their objectives. When choosing between applicants they evaluate bids or proposals against agreed criteria.

Funders who pursue investment strategies are likely to take great interest in the achievements of the providers. Monitoring progress is important to determine the success of the investments. Reviewing service outputs and outcomes is therefore a central part of their work. Periodically they may commission evaluations to obtain independent views on the results of their investments. Sometimes they ask to receive copies of board papers, and sometimes they insist upon having a seat on the board. This can lead to complications because the accountability of the organization to the funder is diluted when the funder, as a member of the board, accepts responsibility for the work of the organization. Examples of funders who relate more closely to the needs of the organization than to the duties of the funder are common.

Investment strategies are appropriate when the funder knows the field it is working in and wishes to achieve specific goals and when there are a number of potential providers. Funders pursuing investment strategies take more of a leadership role. If providers are not meeting their requirements, they invest in other organizations.

Pursuit of an investment strategy provides a basis for monitoring the overall performances of the fund or funding organization. It enables the funder to compare intended and actual achievements. By gathering together the results of each investment, the funder can begin to gain a view of the achievements of the funding programme as a whole.

Investment strategies are less appropriate when funders do not know the field well or when there are few current providers. In these circumstances the collaboration strategy is more appropriate.

In **collaborative strategies** funders identify issues that they believe require attention and choose one or more partners to work with to achieve the desired objectives. The funder knows broadly what it wants to achieve and actively seeks partners with whom it can work to achieve it. This approach is effective when there are few or no organizations ready to do the work. It may require the establishment of entirely new projects or even organizations. Funders work with their partners to agree objectives, plans and costings, then fund the work alone or with other funders.

Since the appropriate strategy depends on the circumstances, funders need to use different strategies to achieve different objectives. For example, a foundation that has funded the provision of family centres for many years and has expertise in this area can invest by seeking bids from competing suppliers. If that foundation wanted to explore provision of family support for ethnic minorities in inner-city areas, it might need to collaborate initially with a provider already in this field.

However, funders need to recognize that expertise in how to pursue each type of strategy is also required. Funders who have historically pursued 'respond to need' strategies have to learn the skills of pursuing other strategies. They will need staff with appropriate abilities and the willingness of board members or decision-makers to work in different ways, with different application procedures and different monitoring arrangements.

## A4.4 MONITORING PERFORMANCE AND SELECTING PAYMENT METHODS

Having chosen an appropriate strategy, funders face choices over alternative methods for monitoring the performance of projects and paying organizations for their efforts. Although the two are closely related, they need to be considered separately because the monitoring method does not automatically point to a reward method.

## Monitoring performance

Until recently many funders did little to monitor systematically the performance of providers. Government often gave core grants but did not expect more than a cursory report of progress. Foundations and companies may have asked for an annual report or for nothing at all. There was a sense that, since people who work in third-sector organizations do not benefit personally from extra money, they should be trusted to do a good job.

With the advent of contracts, funders have become more demanding about the information they require. Some now require **output** information, which measures the volume of activity undertaken – for example, the volume and quality of services provided. A few are starting to require **outcome** information, which measures the results of the service for users. This looks at what was actually achieved as a result of the service – for example, the number of trainees successfully obtaining jobs or the desired policy changes achieved.

Providers should gather this type of data and summarize it for funders. They should be expected to demonstrate as precisely as possible what has been achieved with the funding they received. Funders ideally ought to be able to set achievements of grants alongside their value and so get a sense of value for money.

However, funders need to take care to use the data in context. Removed from the complexities of front-line service provision, it is easy to over-emphasize simple facts and figures and undervalue more nebulous but equally important achievements. Common problems that numerically driven monitoring systems fail to take account of are:

- **the complexity of the problems presented by users.** Quantitative measures encourage organizations to take on the easier cases in order to achieve their targets rather than focusing on people with the most difficult and often most pressing problems.
- **variables outside the organization's control.** Outcome measures in particular are affected by external factors entirely outside the organization's control. For example, successfully getting people into jobs depends on the state of the local job market.
- **the importance of quality.** Monitoring systems tend to focus on things that can be measured whereas quality is often critically important.

Generally these difficulties can be overcome. For example, funders can specify the complexity of the cases as part of the monitoring system; providers can take account of local circumstances when agreeing to annual targets; and quality can often be specified. Each party should see the figures in context and use them, in conjunction with qualitative assessments of the organization, to measure performance. Funders should stress that performance measures are only an indication of success.

## Payment methods

In addition to choices about the strategic approach and the monitoring system, funders have choices to make about the method of paying the provider. The appropriate method depends on the circumstances.

Payments can be **project-based**. Here the organization is funded for carrying out the work, irrespective of the work that is done or the outcomes. This method is suitable when it is difficult or inappropriate to pay according to the amount of a service supplied. Research projects, capital projects and policy work are typical examples in this category. The majority of grant-funding arrangements and some so-called 'service-level' contracts are funded this way. The organization does what it said it would do in the proposal and is funded, sometimes in advance, for doing the work.

When the volume of work to be done can be measured and quality specified, rewards can be **volume-based**. Many central-government schemes and local-authority contracts are funded in this way. The advantage of this method for the funder is that organizations are paid only for the work they do. However, the disadvantages are that organizations may be tempted to:

- reduce quality in order to meet targets
- supply services to people who are not a priority group because the payment method encourages maximizing the volume supplied.

More recently government has begun to pay organizations on a **performance or outcome basis**. With this method providers receive all or part of their funding when they achieve the desired outcome of the work. For example, part of the funding may depend on demonstrating that the target number of people with alcohol or drug dependency have overcome their problem.

Theoretically, this method should encourage organizations to focus their work on achieving desired outcomes. In practice the method needs to be applied with great caution. In addition to the problems identified under the volume-based method:

- it is often difficult to measure whether the outcome was successful
- the service may have been successful in the short term but the improvements may not last, casting doubt on the value of the service
- success, or failure, may be attributable to factors outside the organization's control
- there is pressure to provide services only to users who are likely to achieve successful outcomes and a disincentive to work with people whose need for the service may be greater.

## A4.5 STRENGTHENING FUNDER–PROVIDER RELATIONSHIPS

Both funders and providers can take practical steps to create strong and effective working relationships. These relationships should be seen as partnerships in which both parties are working together to offer maximum benefit to service users. Both can take actions to make this happen.

### *Good funder practices*

Funders can make a significant contribution to the effectiveness of third-sector organizations through their own funding practices. Unfortunately, most providers can recount tales of poor funding practices. They include funding agreed part-way through the period it relates to, payments made months or even years in arrears and review criteria considered only when the review is about to be undertaken. There are many examples of cumbersome application and tendering documents and processes, sudden policy changes leading to termination of funding with inadequate warning and funding given to organizations when the funders really did not understand their field of work.

Good practices in funding third-sector organizations include:

- **clear guidance on funders' objectives.** Funders who have clear and concise views about their objectives, the types of activities they do and do not fund and the criteria that applications or tenders have to meet help to avoid providers making unnecessary applications.
- **long-term commitments.** Funders who urge providers to have long-term strategies and plans often commit themselves only to year-on-year funding. This discourages organizations and their staff from developing longer-term strategies and plans. Some funders are wary of giving longer-term commitments because they do not necessarily know what their own financial situation will be. However, many can give a firm commitment to fund an organization over a period with a break clause in case of financial problems or poor performance by the provider. They can even review a multi-year grant annually to keep providers on their toes. These actions are much more valuable than annual funding, which is extended on a year-by-year basis and leaves the provider in a continuously insecure position.
- **equal opportunities.** Funders can help providers by requiring them to implement equal-opportunities policies. These should relate to equal opportunities in the provision of the service (e.g., access for people with disabilities, promotional materials in different languages for ethnic minority groups). They should also be concerned with the recruitment and selection of staff.
- **agreement on review criteria and timescale.** Funders help providers by agreeing at the time of funding the criteria they will use to review achievements and the timescale of the review. The criteria may change as work proceeds, but there is less room for misunderstanding if both parties agree what is being changed. The timescale needs to allow the review to be completed and decisions on future funding to be taken well before the end of the funding period.
- **contributions to overhead and training costs.** The traditional system by which some funders pay project costs and others pay core costs encourages inefficiency. Core costs invariably creep upwards without necessarily having a close connection with project needs. Funders can encourage providers to include apportioned overhead costs in project applications so all parties can see where costs are being incurred. Funders also need to recognize that training is an essential element of providing quality of service and encourage providers to cost this into proposals and tenders.

- **timing of payments.** Third-sector organizations seldom have significant working capital. Smaller organizations often have almost none. Ensuring that payments are made as work proceeds or, when appropriate, in advance avoids unnecessary cash-flow crises.

These practices set providers a good example. They help to establish the clear and constructive relationships that enable providers to gain maximum benefit from the funding.

## Good provider practices

Funders know well that there are good and bad providers of services. Many funders, particularly foundations, are inundated with applications that fall far below required standards. Funders receive many applications that are mass-mailed to organizations whose names appear in directories of funders. Their mail includes requests for money that are quite remote from their purpose or objectives. Indeed, one businessman recently commented that his morning mail includes more begging letters than business post.

Even when they have been funded, some providers are not good at reporting on progress, and others are poor at giving the funder appropriate credit.

Providers can take actions to create strong relationships with funders. They should:

- **deliver the service as specified.** Above all else, funders want providers to deliver the service to the highest possible standard and with maximum effectiveness.
- **report on progress.** Funders need succinct reports on progress, summarizing achievements, problem areas and planned actions. When funders have key facts about the service provided, the quality and the benefits to service users, it is easier for them to commit themselves to continued funding.
- **raise problems.** Although providers are often reluctant to be totally honest with funders, most funders say that they prefer to deal with providers who raise problems at an early stage than with those that give funders merely a public relations treatment.
- **help the funder to learn.** Funders learn from providers' experience. Providers can help by briefing them on what they have learned from delivering the service and identifying things that work well, ways of

improving efficiency, methods of quality control and how to target services at specific people. This is all useful learning for funders, particularly those funding a number of providers in the same field.

- **promote the funder.** Many funders need publicity. Government and businesses, in particular, need to demonstrate that their money is enabling projects to happen. Promoting funders' names in publicity material, annual reports and media releases helps to strengthen funder–provider relationships.
- **look after the funder.** Funders are not just mechanical cash-dispensers. They are people who appreciate being looked after. Inviting them to annual meetings, to inspect the organization's work and to social functions helps to create stronger relationships and, sometimes, opportunities for further funding applications!

In summary, funder–provider relationships work best when both parties see themselves as partners each of whom has different needs that can be satisfied by the other party.

# Further Reading

There are relatively few books focusing on the overall management of third-sector organizations. This further-reading section therefore draws on relevant literature from both the public and private sectors. It also relies quite heavily on books from the USA, since much more has been published about managing not-for-profit organizations in the USA. Books that draw primarily on American experience are marked USA.

I have purposely been selective in writing this section, believing this will be more useful to busy practising managers than a lengthy bibliography citing every book, report and article I read to produce this book.

Selection criteria included:

- significant works on 'not-for-profit' management
- major private- or public-sector works that are transferable to the third sector
- practical and useful publications for busy managers.

## SETTING THE CONTEXT

James, E., *The Non-Profit Sector in International Perspective*, Oxford University Press, 1989

An international group of scholars present fifteen articles about the contributions that governments make to non-profit organizations and the problems that subsidies create.

Leat, D., *Managing Across Sectors: Similarities and Differences Between For-profit and Voluntary Non-profit Organizations*, VOLPROF (City University Business School), 1993

An insightful report comparing business and third-sector organizations.

SOME USEFUL NUMBERS FOR OBTAINING THESE
PUBLICATIONS

| | |
|---|---|
| Association of Charitable Foundations | 0171-404-1338 |
| Centre for Voluntary Organizations, London School of Economics | 0171-405-7686 |
| Charities Aid Foundation | 01732-771333 |
| Directory of Social Change | 0171-435-8171 |
| Industrial Society Press | 0121-454-6769 |
| Institute of Chartered Secretaries and Administrators | 0171-580-4741 |
| Joseph Rowntree Foundation | 01904-629241 |
| Jossey-Bass, UK Distributor, IBD/Prentice-Hall | 01442-881900 |
| London Voluntary Service Council | 0171-388-0241 |
| National Council for Voluntary Organizations | 0171-713-6161 |
| Open University | 01908-654723 |
| Third Sector Magazine | 0171-247-0066 |
| VOLPROF, City University Business School | 0171-477-8667 |

McCarthy, K., and associates, *The Non-profit Sector in the Global Community*, Jossey-Bass, 1992
   Twenty-eight articles on the role and significance of the non-profit sector in industrialized countries, Eastern Europe, the old Soviet Union and developing countries.

Powell, W. W., *The Non-profit Sector Research Handbook*, Yale University Press, 1987 (USA)
   The Bible for researchers, containing twenty-four articles about theory of non-profits, relations with other sectors, functions of non-profit organizations, management and funding.

Prochaska, F., *The Voluntary Impulse*, Faber and Faber, 1988
   A fascinating book placing philanthropy in Britain in historical context.

Saxon-Harold, S., Kendall, J., and others, *Researching the Voluntary Sector*, Charities Aid Foundation, 1993 (first volume), 1994 (second volume)
    Thirty articles in two volumes covering local, national and international research into all aspects of the voluntary sector.

## GOVERNING BODIES

Carver, J., *Boards that Make a Difference*, Jossey-Bass, 1990 (USA)
    An interesting and radical view of governance based on the view that the board's role should be strictly limited to a few key policy issues.

Chait, R., *et al.*, *The Effective Board of Trustees*, American Council on Education, 1993 (USA)
    Board-effectiveness guru on the different roles of the board, based on particularly thorough research at the University of Maryland.

Harris, M., *Do We Need Governing Bodies?*, Centre for Voluntary Organizations, London School of Economics, 1994
    Article analysing the functions of governing bodies and the gap between intentions and practices.

Houle, C. O., *Governing Boards*, Jossey-Bass, 1989 (USA)
    Fifty years of experience with boards brought together in a wise book with an American perspective.

Ingram, R., and associates, *Governing Independent Colleges and Universities*, Jossey-Bass, 1993 (USA)
    Twenty articles to guide trustees and chief executives responsible for managing colleges and universities. Much pertinent material as UK colleges and universities become more financially independent from government.

Kirkland, K., *The Good Trustee Guide*, NCVO, 1994
    The UK guide to the role, responsibilities and workings of effective governing bodies. Packed with valuable advice for trustees and board members.

National Center for Non-profit Boards, Non-profit Governance Series, NCNB (USA)
    A series of sixteen booklets on key aspects of governance. American in orientation but increasingly relevant to the UK. Available from NCVO.

NCVO, *On Trust: Increasing the Effectiveness of Charity Trustees and Management Committees*, National Council for Voluntary Organizations, 1993

>Report of the NCVO–Charity Commission Working Party that identified the scale of the problem and actions required to improve the effectiveness of management committees.

Palmer, P., and Harrow, J., *Re-thinking Charity Trusteeship*, Institute of Chartered Secretaries and Administrators, 1994

>A review of the role and purpose of charity trustees.


## MANAGING THIRD-SECTOR ORGANIZATIONS

Adirondack, S. M., *Just About Managing*, London Voluntary Service Council, 1993

>A very practical introduction to managing smaller voluntary organizations.

Batsleer, J., *et al.*, *Issues in Voluntary and Non-profit Management*, Addison Wesley, 1991

>The reader for the Open University 'Managing Voluntary and Non-Profit Enterprise' course. Sixteen articles covering a wide range of issues.

Billis, D., *A Theory of the Voluntary Sector*, Working Paper 5, London School of Economics, 1989

>An excellent analysis of how the voluntary sector sits between the public, private and personal sectors and why this leads to ambiguity in their management.

Billis, D., *The Roots of Voluntary Agencies: A Question of Choice*, Centre for Voluntary Organizations, London School of Economics, undated

>Insightful article analysing the factors underlying management problems in voluntary organizations.

Drucker, P., *Managing the Non-profit Organization*, Butterworth-Heinemann, 1990 (USA)

>Classic Drucker; punchy, relevant and practical book incorporating nine edited interviews with practitioners.

McLaughlin C. P., *The Management of Non-profit Organizations*, John Wiley, 1986 (USA)
> A wide-ranging academic book covering the theory of non-profits, strategic decision-making and management-control systems.

Paton, R., and many others, *Managing Voluntary and Non-profit Enterprises*, Open University, 1993
> Twelve excellent books for the Open University course with the same title. Expensive for non-course participants.

Young, D., *et al.*, *Governing, Leading and Managing Non-profit Organizations*, Jossey-Bass, 1993 (USA)
> Fourteen articles on governance, human and financial resources, management strategies and public policy issues, written mainly by academic researchers.

## STRATEGIC MANAGEMENT

Barnard, H., and Walker, P., *Strategies for Success*, NCVO Publications, 1994

Bryson, J,. *Strategic Planning for Public and Non-profit Organizations*, Jossey-Bass, 1988 (USA)
> Bestselling introduction to strategic planning.

Campbell, A., *A Sense of Mission*, Hutchinson Business Books, 1990
> Although this is a business book, the early chapters, which unpack the idea of mission, are equally relevant to third-sector organizations.

Johnson, G., and Scholes, K., *Exploring Corporate Strategy*, Prentice-Hall, 1993
> The popular basic text on all aspects of corporate strategy. Aimed primarily at business, it has a few public- and third-sector examples.

Martin, N., and Smith, C., *Planning for the Future*, NCVO Publications, 1993
> A practical introduction to business planning in voluntary organizations.

Mintzberg, H., *The Rise and Fall of Strategic Planning*, Prentice-Hall, 1994
> A critical reassessment of strategic planning, focusing on the private sector, but the conclusions are transferable.

Mintzberg, H., and Quinn, B., *The Strategy Process*, Prentice-Hall, 1992 (USA)
> Succinct summaries of forty-eight of the best articles on strategy, organization and the contexts in which strategy is used. A business-oriented book, some of which is relevant to the third sector.

Nutt, P., and Bachoff, R., *Strategic Management of Public and Third Sector Organizations*, Jossey-Bass, 1992 (USA)
> A helpful overview and some useful techniques for strategic planners.

Schein, E., *Organizational Culture and Leadership*, Jossey-Bass, 1992 (USA)
> A tightly defined introduction to managing organization culture, written by one of the culture gurus.

Williams, A., *et al.*, *Changing Culture: New Organizational Approaches*, Institute of Personnel Management, 1993
> A very accessible introduction to culture, illustrated with ten corporate and two public-sector examples.

## MANAGEMENT PROCESSES

Bruce, I., *Meeting Need: Successful Charity Marketing*, Institute of Chartered Secretaries and Administrators, 1994
> A practical and thorough book on marketing in voluntary organizations. Written by the Director General of the Royal National Institute for the Blind and consequently very applicable to UK organizations.

Kotler, P., and Andreasen, A., *Strategic Marketing for Non-profit Organizations*, Prentice Hall, 1991 (USA)
> A wide-ranging and comprehensive book about marketing, now in its fourth edition.

Lawrie, A., *Quality of Service: Measuring Performance for Voluntary Organizations*, NCVO/Directory of Social Change, undated
> A practical introduction to measuring performance in voluntary organizations.

Lockett, J., *Effective Performance Management*, Kogan Page, 1992
> A strategic guide to getting the best from people that integrates people-management processes into a performance cycle. Business-oriented but transferable.

Manley, K., *Financial Management for Charities and Voluntary Organizations*, Institute of Chartered Secretaries and Administrators, 1994
An introduction to the whole process of planning, budgeting, controlling and reporting on financial matters, aimed particularly at service-giving charities.

## MANAGEMENT STRUCTURES

Billis, D., *Welfare Bureaucracies*, Heinemann Educational Books, 1984
Theories about the design of social-welfare organizations.

Butler, R., and Wilson, D., *Managing Voluntary and Non-profit Organizations,* Routledge, 1990
Reports of research into the structure of four different organizations and the relationship between structure and strategy.

Mintzberg, H., *Structure in Fives*, Prentice-Hall International, 1983
One of the best-known textbooks on designing effective organizations.

## MANAGING PEOPLE

Blanchard, K., and Johnson, S., *The One-minute Manager*, Fontana, 1983
The famous guide to setting goals, praising and reprimanding people. Packed with insightful advice that needs regular re-reading.

Bruce, I., and Raymer, A., *Managing and Staffing Britain's Largest Charities*, VOLPROF, Centre for Voluntary Sector and Not-for-profit Management, 1992
Report of survey investigating the structure, desirable management attributes and recruitment of top managers in voluntary organizations.

Grummitt, J., *Team Briefing*, The Industrial Society, 1993
Guide to implementing team briefing with advice on overcoming objections.

Handy, C., *Understanding Organizations* (rev. ed.), Penguin, 1994
The bestselling book on how to get people working together in different types of organization.

Handy, C., *Understanding Voluntary Organizations*, Penguin, 1988
*Understanding Organizations*, revised to shed light on people management in voluntary organizations.

Hunt, J., *Managing People at Work*, Pan, 1981
Another bestselling book on managing people at work. Written by a London Business School professor, but very transferable to third-sector organizations.

Jenks, J., and Kelly, J., *Don't Do: Delegate!*, Kogan Page, 1986
A very readable book on delegation. Examples are private-sector but the messages are equally applicable to third-sector organizations.

Sheal, P., *The Staff Development Handbook*, Kogan Page, 1992
Practical advice on training, monitoring and coaching staff, including a chapter on conducting performance reviews.

## LEADERSHIP

Adair, J., *Not Bosses but Leaders*, Kogan Page, 1990
Adair introduces a new manager to leadership concepts. A quick and easy read.

Adair, J., *Effective Leadership: A Self-development Manual*, Gower, 1983
One of the classic texts on leadership, packed with advice and exercises.

Bryson, J., and Crosby, B., *Leadership for the Common Good*, Jossey-Bass, 1992
Leadership of public and non-profit organizations in a world where pluralism means 'no-one-is-in-charge' of the big public-policy issues.

Green, M., *Leadership for a New Era: Strategies for Higher Education*, American Council on Education, 1988 (USA)
Twelve articles on leading and managing higher-education institutions.

Herman, R., and Heimovics, R., *Executive Leadership in Non-profit Organizations,* Jossey-Bass, 1991 (USA)
> Insights into leadership, focusing particularly on the leadership role of the board, and on chief executive–board relationships and how to make them more effective.

Kouzes, J., and Posner, B., *The Leadership Challenge*, Jossey-Bass, 1987 (USA)
> Ten commandments for effective leadership, based on research in the USA. Makes compelling reading.

Lynch, R., *LEAD!*, Jossey-Bass, 1993 (USA)
> The best book on leadership of public and non-profit organizations. Explains how managers bring out the best in themselves and their organizations.

## MANAGEMENT OF FUNDING PROGRAMMES

Gutch, R., *Contracting Lessons from the US,* National Council for Voluntary Organizations, 1992
> Summary findings of a US tour with implications for the way things are moving in the UK.

Hazell, R., and Whybrew, T., *Resourcing the Voluntary Sector: The Funder's Perspective*, Association of Charitable Foundations, 1993
> Summary of seminars covering resourcing by government, trusts and companies.

Hedley, R., and Rochester, C., *Good Grant Making: A Practical Guide*, Association of Charitable Foundations, 1993
> Advice on the practicalities of managing a grant-making programme.

Leat, D., *Trusts in Transition: The Policy and Practice of Grant-giving Trusts*, Joseph Rowntree Foundation, 1992
> Well-researched report on the changing policy and practices of grant-making trusts.

Leat, D., *Grant-giving: A Guide to Policy Making*, Joseph Rowntree Foundation, 1992
> Practical guide for grant-making trusts linked to *Trusts in Transition* report.

Williams, H., and Webb, A., *Outcome Funding*, The Rensselaer Institute, 1992

A book promoting the idea that organizations should be funded according to the achievement of agreed performance targets. Another American idea that is gaining ground in the UK, despite people's qualms. Available from NCVO.

## PERIODICALS

### *Academic Journals*

*Non-profit Management and Leadership*, published by Jossey-Bass
The most useful journal for practising managers who want to keep in touch with academic research into the management of not-for-profit organizations.

*Non-profit and Voluntary Sector Quarterly*, published by Jossey-Bass
This journal focuses on policy issues. It is sponsored by a research group that specializes in voluntary action.

*Voluntas: International Journal of Voluntary and Non-profit Organizations*, published by Manchester University Press
This journal takes an international perspective. It covers policy issues and has less on management than the other journals.

### *News Magazines*

*Third Sector*, published by Arts Publishing International Ltd
A recently launched bi-monthly news magazine focusing mainly on the voluntary sector.

*Charity*, published by the Charities Aid Foundation
The well-established news magazine aimed at charities.

# Index